Building
WEALTH

Also by Lester C. Thurow

Poverty and Discrimination (1969)
Investment in Human Capital (1970)
The Impact of Taxes on the American Economy (1971)
Generating Inequality: Mechanisms of Distribution in the U.S. Economy (1975)
The Zero-Sum Society (1980)
Dangerous Currents: The State of Economics (1983)
The Management Challenge: Japanese Views (1983)
The Zero-Sum Solution (1985)
Head to Head: The Coming Economic Battle Among Japan, Europe and America (1992)
The Future of Capitalism: How Today's Economic Forces Shape Tomorrow's World (1996)

Building
WEALTH

The New Rules for Individuals, Companies, and
Nations in a Knowledge-Based Economy

Lester C. Thurow

HarperBusiness
An Imprint of HarperCollins*Publishers*

First HarperBusiness edition published 2000.

Designed by William Ruoto

The Library of Congress has catalogued the hardcover edition as follows:

Thurow, Lester C.
    Building wealth : the new rules for individuals, companies, and nations in a
    knowledge-based economy / Lester C. Thurow. — 1st ed.
      p. cm.
    Includes index.
    ISBN 0-88730-951-8
    1. Saving and investment—United States. 2. Knowledge management—United
States. 3. Ability—United States. 4. Wealth—United States I. Title : knowledge-
based economy.
HC110.S3T47 1999
332—dc21   99-20595

ISBN 0-88730-952-6 (pbk.)

00 01 02 03 04 ❖/RRD 10 9 8 7 6 5 4 3 2 1

Anni:
To a fabulous adventure together—
looking back, now, and looking forward

Acknowledgments

I would like to thank Pitiporn Phanaphat for being a very dedicated research assistant who always found what needed to be found. I would also like to thank all of those who were subjected to earlier versions of this book. Although they did not know that their feedback was being fed into this book, they provided an invaluable sounding board.

Contents

Prologue

On the back of the dollar bill there is an unfinished pyramid with a brilliant glowing eye at the top. It comes from what had been the ignored back of the Great Seal of the United States, and it was placed on the dollar bill by President Roosevelt in 1935, in the middle of the Great Depression, when America's wealth was in sharp decline. The pyramid was meant to represent economic strength and durability. It is unfinished to symbolize the possibilities of ever-increasing American wealth. Americans needed hope, that an imploding economy would be replaced by an economy that would last forever, that America's best days were ahead—not behind it. One Latin inscription (*Annuit Coeptis*) tells Americans that God favors their undertakings. The other (*Novos Ordo Seclorum*) prophesies a new American order of wealth. Thus in their darkest economic days, Americans were both invoking man's oldest symbols of durable success and praying to the gods for help. Behind the glittering eye, a symbol of divine guidance, is the unfinished top of the pyramid, which has yet to be built. Americans could see what had to be done to achieve success. They just had to muster the resolve to be builders.[1]

Today Asians see a world very much like that seen by Americans in the 1930s. A boom has gone bust. Individual, corporate, and social wealth is rapidly disappearing. The Indonesian stock market is down more than 80 percent.[2] What just a short time ago was seen as an unstoppable economic juggernaut that would dominate the twenty-first century now looks like a permanent derailment. The economic progress that seemed rock-solid now seems more like a melting snowbank.

The Asian model of export-led economic growth, which gave most of the rest of the third world hope that they could rapidly close the economic gap with the developed world, lies in tatters. The successful have fallen. Asia's financial meltdown threatens the foundations of success in every third world country, such as Brazil. The capital and technology that used to pour in from the first world are leaving, and forecasters are systematically downgrading future economic prospects. With old routes blocked, what is the right route to accumulating wealth?

Continental Europeans see a world where their preferred model, the social market economy, where welfare payments are high and state interventions to disperse economic wealth widely are large, isn't working. While there are cyclical short-run ups and downs, the long-run trend for European unemployment is relentlessly up. Double-digit unemployment rates that haven't been seen since the 1930s are now accepted as a permanent state of affairs. A continent that thought it could guarantee jobs for its citizens finds that it cannot. Politicians promise to do something, but everyone knows that nothing will be done.

In the new man-made brainpower industries of the twenty-first century, all of Europe is an also-ran. Nowhere is it an industrial leader. Its last indigenous computer maker was sold to the Taiwanese in 1998. It talks about catching up but knows that the technological gap between it and the United States grows larger every day. The continent that invented culture now imports its culture from America. The equivalent of "Intel Inside" could be printed on almost everything new in Europe. The restructuring, downsizing, and shifting to offshore manufacturing that used to be seen as to-be-avoided American-style capitalism have arrived.

In Europe, Asia, and the rest of the third world, economic anxieties are high. All would like the strength and durability of the pyramid symbolized on the U.S. dollar bill.

The only seeming exception to this pattern of high anxiety is America itself. America is back! In the 1990s it will be the best performer in the industrial world. The economic gap between it and the rest of the world is once again growing. The $2 trillion that will be added to its gross domestic product during the decade of the 1990s is larger than the GDPs of all but one other country—Japan.[3] Far from slowing or sinking in the wake of the Asian meltdown, America's 1998 economic performance was a robust 4.3 percent growth rate. Unemployment is at historic lows, and inflation simply does not exist.

The world's wealthiest man is once again an American. The wealthy oil sheiks have been eclipsed. American billionaires number in the hundreds.

American firms are back on top. While there were only two American firms among the world's ten largest in 1990, nine of those firms were American in 1998.[4] Similarly, where none of the top fifteen banks were American at the beginning of the decade, nine were American by the end of 1998.[5] Below the very top the dominance is just as great. Twenty of the twenty-five largest firms in the world are now American. When it comes to playing in a knowledge-based economy, no one is better. Americans invented the game.

The American locomotive once again pulls the world. Without exports to a growing American market, a worldwide recession would be under way in 1999. American's economic power has been re-created and reunited with its military hegemony.

It is the best of times in America.

Yet even in America there are undercurrents of anxiety. In an up economy, a powerful down escalator seems to exist for many. Most Americans believe that their children will have a lower standard of living than they have had—not surprising given that for two-thirds of the workforce, real wages are below where they were in 1973. What they believe will happen to their children is already happening to them.

The middle class is shrinking. Some are moving up, but a larger number are moving down—not surprising given what's happening to wages for midrange skills, but still disturbing. The financial pages report daily on a stock market boom, but the median household's wealth is falling, not rising, and it has less than $10,000 in financial assets. The bottom 20 percent of the population owe more than they own.

In the midst of an economic boom, 500,000 to 700,000 workers are downsized from profitable corporations every year—680,000 in 1998.[6] Those downsized at over fifty-five years of age will not find reemployment at good jobs. Those under fifty-five will take substantial wage cuts to be reemployed. Plotting a good lifetime career has become a major mystery—even for college graduates. How does one become a durable winner? Where is economic security to be found? High-wire acts are fun to watch, but it isn't fun to actually be on the high wire. As in the Great Depression, it is far better to be at the top of a durable wealth pyramid that will last forever.

Most disturbingly, productivity growth is down by a factor of three since the 1960s. For in the end, it is productivity growth (the ability to produce more output using fewer inputs) that ultimately drives *real* wealth creation. Temporary stock market bubbles can produce great market wealth in the short run, but without vigorous productivity growth there are no long-run treasures of wealth to be found.

On the dollar bill, the glittering eye at the top of the pyramid diverts attention from the base of the pyramid. So too the glitter of great wealth at the top of the wealth distribution—the new billionaires—obscures the base of the pyramid, upon which all wealth rests. But even if the excitement lies in being at the top, real pyramids are built from the base up, not from the top down.

At the end of the twentieth and beginning of the twenty-first century, six new technologies—microelectronics, computers, telecommunications, new man-made materials, robotics, and biotechnology—are interacting to create a new and very different economic world. Advances in the basic sciences underlying these six areas have created breakthrough technologies that have allowed the emergence of a whole set of big new industries: computers, semiconductors, lasers. These same technologies provide opportunities to reinvent old industries: Internet retailing supplants conventional retailing; cellular telephones are everywhere. New things can be done: genetically engineered plants and animals appear; a global economy becomes possible for the first time in human history. Descriptively it is an era of man-made brainpower industries.

The old foundations of success are gone. For all of human history, the source of success has been the control of natural resources—land, gold, oil. Suddenly the answer is "knowledge." The world's wealthiest man, Bill Gates, owns nothing tangible— no land, no gold or oil, no factories, no industrial processes, no armies. For the first time in human history the world's wealthiest man owns only knowledge.

Knowledge is the new basis for wealth. This has never before been true. In the past when capitalists talked about their wealth they were talking about their ownership of plant and equipment and natural resources. In the future when capitalists talk about their wealth they will be talking about their control of knowledge. Even the language of wealth generation changes. One can talk about "owning" capital equipment or natural resources. The concept of "owning" is clear. But one cannot talk in the same ways about "owning" knowledge. Owning knowledge is a slippery concept. The human beings who possess knowledge cannot be made into slaves. Exactly how one controls (owns?) knowledge is in fact a central issue in a knowledge-based economy.

The current transformation is often misleadingly described as the information revolution or the information society. It is far more. Speedier or cheaper information by itself isn't of much value. Information is only one of many new inputs used to build a different economy populated with very different products and services. More information is no more important than the new materials, new biological entities, or new robots in building this new knowledge-based economy.

How do societies have to be reorganized to generate a wealth-enhancing knowledge environment? What causes the entrepreneurs necessary to effect changes and create wealth to sprout? How does knowledge-based wealth arise? What skills are needed? Where do natural and environmental resources fit into this new knowledge economy? What is the role of tool-building in a knowledge-based capitalistic economy where physical tools (capital) no longer lie at the heart of the system? What is the process whereby private marketable wealth emerges? Fundamentally, how does one use "knowledge" to build a new wealth pyramid for an individual, for a company, and for a society? These are the questions to be answered if success is to be found in a knowledge-based economy.

What is important about any pyramid is not found by climbing to the top, but by locating the tunnels that lead to the hidden treasures within. How does one take advantage of new technologies to revolutionize the production of old products and create revolutionary new ones? What are the new construction techniques that will allow even greater stones (higher productivity) to be lifted into place? How can we use these new technologies to build higher and wider wealth pyramids in the future?

Building a durable wealth pyramid requires that we first explore the new economic landscape that is being created. Somewhere within this landscape there is a new wealth pyramid. Once found, the pyramid's archaeology must be clearly understood. How was it constructed? Where are the entrances? Without this information, treasure hunters cannot find the economic riches buried within.

And only after being explorers, archaeologists, and treasure hunters can humans turn to the real task—learning how to build for ourselves, our companies, and our societies a great new, durable wealth pyramid.

Part One
Exploring a
Knowledge-Based
Economy

1.   The Economic Landscape

Two hundred years ago, at the end of the eighteenth and the beginning of the nineteenth century, the industrial revolution brought eight thousand years of agricultural wealth creation to an end. Agricultural activities, which had been the sole economic activity for 98 percent of the population in the eighteenth century, were the sole source of income for less than 2 percent of the American population by the end of the twentieth century. By providing a source of energy much bigger than either animals or humans could provide, the steam engine opened up opportunities to do things previously impossible. Leonardo da Vinci could imagine all kinds of brilliant mechanical devices, but all of them remained on paper, unbuilt, because he could not imagine an engine to power them. With the advent of the steam engine, much of what he could only imagine quickly became reality.

A hundred years later, at the end of the nineteenth and the beginning of the twentieth century, electrification and the invention of systematic industrial research and development created what economic historians know as the second industrial revolution. Night literally became day. New industries emerged—the telephone, movies, aluminum—and old industries were transformed (steam railroads went underground to become subways).

Not left to chance, technological frontiers moved outward much more rapidly than they had in the past. Local economies died and new national economies emerged.

It took Americans and the rest of the world the first half of the twentieth century to learn how to make these national economies work. Antitrust laws had to be invented to control the monopolistic tendencies of the new national corporations. Companies only too quickly learned that there was more money to be made from combining into monopolies and restricting output than from expanding output. Standard Oil was broken up in 1911. For the first time a national currency was needed. The Federal Reserve Board was established in 1913. A central bank had not been necessary in the first three centuries of the American experience.

It took the searing experiences of the Great Depression to teach Americans that unfettered financial markets can implode and bring whole economies down with them. In response, government regulations were imposed to eliminate the weaknesses (insider trading, phony bookkeeping) that had been revealed in the structure of finance. The Securities and Exchange Commission (SEC) came into existence. The Great Depression proved that banks could not be allowed to default on their depositors if prosperity was to be assured. Depositor's insurance was invented.

World War II taught America that big technological breakthroughs were possible (radar, the atomic bomb) if governments financed basic advances in science. Industrial R&D could be made much more productive. New products could roll out the door faster than Americans ever thought possible.

After World War II Americans assumed that capitalism would spontaneously combust in Europe and Japan. It did not happen. Three years after the war was over, Americans woke up in 1948 to find that Europe and Japan were not recovering. There was a real danger that Europe and Japan might abandon capitalism for communism. It took massive aid, the Marshall Plan, to get capitalism going again. Americans had no choice but to pay attention to the economic health of the rest of the world if they wished to be healthy themselves.

Today a third industrial revolution is under way. Microelectronics, computers, telecommunications, designer materials, robotics, and biotechnology are transforming all facets of life—what we do and how we do it. Biotechnology is changing the characteristics of life itself. Genetic diseases do not have to be accepted. New plants and animals with different characteristics are being built.

What comes first, the Internet that permits the faster and cheaper flow of information or the new materials such as fiber optics that permit the Internet to exist? What really changes is not the information that we have about what we might wish to buy, but the way we buy the everyday necessities of life—and what we buy. Physical stores go out of business; electronic stores come into business. In both we buy clothes sewn from Lycra and Kevlar rather than cotton.

Microelectronics make possible the lasers that power the trunk lines of the telecommunications industry, but those same lasers allow eye surgery that will make glasses an unneeded remnant of a past age. In medicine, microsurgery is a revolution all by itself. Larger robots are revolutionizing production of almost everything else. Computers on a chip are changing how our car engines and suspensions work. The laser in the CD player in the trunk of the car is changing the nature and quality of the music to which we listen.

In this third industrial revolution, technologies are changing so rapidly that no one knows where future profits will be made. The CEO of the old AT&T decided to split off its research laboratories (Bell Labs) and its hardware manufacturing arm (Western Electric) into a new company called Lucent. As the CEO of the old AT&T he could have made himself CEO of the new AT&T or the new Lucent. He got it wrong. He made himself CEO of the new AT&T. The new Lucent quickly became more profitable and acquired a market capitalization one-third bigger than that of the new AT&T. The CEO of the old AT&T couldn't even plan his own career—and he's not dumb. The same confusion and chaos about where success is to be found exist almost everywhere in our economy. Great profits are being made, but where they are to be made is changing very rapidly.

Addendum: Under a new CEO, the stock value of the new AT&T surged in early 1999 and suddenly caught up with the value of Lucent's stock, following (1) the sale of a major division, (2) an acquisition more than three times as large as the previous sale, (3) a 14 percent downsizing, (4) a repricing of cellular phone charges, (5) a big voluntary early-retirement plan (15,300 managers gone), (6) another acquisition three times as big as the first, (7) a merger of international operations with those of British Telecom, (8) the institution of minimum monthly charges for long distance service, and (9) the purchase of IBM's global communications system while outsourcing the AT&T computer system to IBM.[7] But with the current degree of stock market volatility, who knows? Maybe it will plunge again. In the knowledge-based economy, stable values (profits) are hard to find.

Like the ancient Archimedes with his newfound knowledge of levers, the modern CEO might say, "Give me a place to stand and I will move the earth." But there were no stable mechanical points for the ancient Archimedes, nor are there any stable economic points for the modern CEO. Everyone has to operate without a solid fixed point of stability upon which to base their plans.

In the first and second industrial revolutions, workers were leaving agriculture (a low-wage sector) and entering manufacturing and mining (high-wage sectors). In the third industrial revolution, workers are leaving manufacturing and mining (high-wage sectors) and entering services (a generally low-wage sector with a wide dispersion of wages). Revolutions that led to higher and more equal distributions of earnings have been superseded by a revolution leading to lower median and more unequal distributions of earnings. Like CEOs, modern workers need that missing fixed point upon which to base their plans for economic prosperity. But where is it?

Just as the second industrial revolution moved us from local to national economies, so the third industrial revolution is moving us from national economies to a global economy. For the first time in human history businesses can buy from wherever on the globe costs are lowest and sell wherever on the globe prices are highest. That most American of American companies, Coca-Cola, now has 80 percent of its sales outside the United States. That most American of American products, the automobile, contains parts from all over the world.

The history of the move from local to national economies teaches us that in the best of circumstances, learning how to make this new global economy work will take a substantial amount of time, with lots of surprises and mistakes along the way. But the transition from national to global is going to be far more turbulent than the transition from local to national. When the world was moving from local to national economies, it already had national governments ready to learn how to manage the process. In contrast, there is no global government to learn how the new global economy should be managed.

The existing international institutions—the International Monetary Fund, the World Bank, the United Nations, the World Trade Organization—were not meant to deal with a global economy. The IMF was designed to deal with temporary balance-of-payments problems between wealthy industrial countries. The World Bank was designed to finance basic infrastructure projects in developing countries. The UN was designed to stop world wars. And the WTO was designed to ensure free trade among nations. All were designed to be creatures of existing national governments. None can tell national governments what they must do. Quite the reverse, national governments tell these organizations what they must do.

What exists are imposing facades with no structure behind

them. The Americans bring a WTO case to force the Europeans to open their markets to Central American bananas rather than giving preference to former French and British colonies in Africa and the Caribbean. The WTO finds Europe guilty, but consistent with its charter it proposes no explicit remedies. The Europeans ignore the results. The Americans threaten countervailing sanctions on European products. The Europeans threaten to counterretaliate. Quickly the world is back to negotiations between national governments, with an irrelevant international agency standing in the background.

The logical answer to this management problem would be global institutions that could give orders directly, without needing the permission of governments to act or having to work through existing governments when they decide to act. It isn't going to happen. Nothing is more disliked in the U.S. Congress than the word *supernational*. Congress won't even vote to pay America's bills to international agencies such as the IMF and the UN, which are constrained by American veto powers from doing anything Americans don't want done. Real management of the global economy would mean that at least occasionally the global manager would force the American government and the American people to do things Americans did not want to do. A global economic manager would not just be giving orders to Mexico or Malaysia.

In short, no one is going to set up a global government in the foreseeable future—regardless of whether it is or is not needed. As a result, the world is going to have a global economy without a global government. This means a global economy with no enforceable, agreed-upon set of rules and regulations, no sheriff to enforce codes of acceptable behavior, and no judges and juries to appeal to if one feels that justice is not being done.

Continental Europeans often refer to what is now happening as "cowboy capitalism." The global economy is like the Old West, where economic disputes (cattle rustling) were settled with gunfights at Tombstone's OK Corral. As in the Old West, the strong push the weak out of the fertile economic areas, away from the gold deposits, and force them to settle on reservations in the deserts and badlands. Everyone is on the globe, but in the coming era everyone will not be a player in the new global economy.

Wealth will have to be built in a global economy that will not be working smoothly and that will from time to time produce completely unexpected economic storms. Such a storm hit Asia in 1997. What began in countries that represent less than 1 percent of the global gross domestic product (GDP) had by mid–1999 spread to affect almost everyone. Major banks (Bankers Trust, Bank of America) announced billion-dollar losses when Russia was sucked into the Asian economic hurricane. Supposedly more conservative Swiss banks did even worse. Brazil needed massive global assistance (more than $45 billion) to avoid being blown over, and even with this massive assistance it was still tottering in the financial winds. In the United States, a trillion-dollar hedge fund, Long Term Capital Management (legally a company incorporated in the Grand Cayman Islands but with headquarters in Connecticut and offices all around the world), threatened to melt down and pull the world's biggest capital market down with it. The U.S. government had to organize a private rescue mission. The Fed lowered interest rates three times in the fall of 1998, once on an emergency basis. Things quieted down and the stock market recovered. But for how long?

In 1999 the world stands anxiously watching the Japanese government to see what it will do. Most of its great companies (NEC, NTT, Hatachi, Fijitsu, Nissan, Toshiba) are losing money. Herbert Hoover–like do-nothing policies have already created something that may well come to be called the Great Stagnation—eight years of minimal growth with negative growth in 1998 and expected again in 1999. Will Japan act? Or will it remain mired in an expanding recession that will eventually engulf the rest of the world?

In the twentieth century as local economies were replaced by national economies, national governments gained power. They needed to be given the powers necessary to control national economic systems. A global economy reverses this process. National governments lose their powers to control the economic system. Global financial markets are the most vivid illustration, but it is happening in other areas as well. National governments are losing control. No one finds it possible to stop illegal immigration. Millions move when they feel like moving, and in the process, what it means to be a country fades. A country that cannot control its own borders is in some fundamental sense not a real country. Pornography is produced electronically somewhere in the world where it is not illegal, and national governments can do nothing to enforce their own citizens' standards of decency.

Countries themselves are being put into play. Fifteen countries emerge where the old U.S.S.R. used to be. Czechoslovakia divides in two. Yugoslavia becomes at least five and perhaps as many as seven different countries. The English give quasi-independence to Scotland. The Basques and Catalans want independence from Spain. The northern Italians want to kick the southern Italians out of Italy. Canada endlessly debates independence for Quebec.

Indonesia is unlikely ever again to be one country. It was thousands of independent islands when it was conquered by the Dutch, forcibly made into their East Indies colony, and then ruled by two military dictators. An economic meltdown leads to a political meltdown. There is no there there to glue it back together again.

Borders are going to be moving everywhere in Africa.[8] Ten thousand different ethnic groups aren't going to live forever in a handful of countries defined by the accidental meetings of British and French armies in the nineteenth century.[9]

The British unified India, the central planning of socialism held it together after the British left, but what is to hold it together now? Why should the prosperous parts be impeded by the backward parts? Economic principalities will probably emerge looking much like the political principalities conquered by the British a few centuries earlier.

At the same time, historic countries are slowly disappearing in Europe. Eleven have become one. Countries without their own currencies aren't fully independent. The remaining four members of the European Economic Union will join—sooner rather than later. Others in Eastern Europe are knocking on the door. Future steps, such as the tax harmonization now being discussed, will make members even less like real countries. The United States of Europe may well be a reality before the end of the next century.

As the scope, reach, and powers of national governments shrink, the role of global companies expands. Increasingly they can play countries off against each other. Big global companies locate plants in countries that will give them the best deal in terms of cash payments, cost subsidies, and tax reductions (e.g., Israel buys an Intel semiconductor plant).

But companies, like countries, are also in play. Mergers activity ($2.4 trillion in 1998) is five times as great as it was in 1990 and 50 percent greater than it was in the previous record-high year (1997), with cross-border and European mergers growing at an even faster pace.[10] Nine of the ten largest deals ever made were made in 1998.[11] The other one was made in 1997. Mercedes buys Chrysler; Deutsche Bank buys Bankers Trust. Are these new companies German companies, American companies, or global companies? The answer, of course, is global. The emerging global companies are larger than any national companies ever seen. The market value of the world's largest company in 1990 (a national company, Nippon Telephone, in Japan) would not be close to large enough to allow it to make the 1998 list of the ten largest companies in the world.[12]

At the same time, slice and dice is the name of the game. Companies like Siemans, which even a decade ago would never have sold off divisions, sell off their noncore activities to concentrate on their core activities. Royal Dutch Shell puts 40 percent of its chemical operations up for sale; Deutsche Bank spins off $28 billion in industrial holdings.[13] Workers go to bed working for one company and wake up working for another. They are not slaves, since they can quit working for their new employer, but like slaves they have been sold without anyone asking their permission.

Those who like the risks of exploring a new and unknown environment have always been few in number. With both countries and companies in flux, how does the individual play the economic game with some degree of both success and security? Whose team am I on? My nation and my employer are rapidly losing both the ability and the willingness to help me. How do I play the game by myself?

2. The Glittering Eye at the Top of the Wealth Pyramid

Croesus! The world's first wealthiest man, who became the measure of great wealth for all who would later follow. He is to wealth what infinity is to numbers. To be the world's richest man is to be "richer than Croesus."

Midas! The legendary king who got his wish that everything he touched would turn to gold.

Alchemy! The never-found chemistry of turning base metals into gold.

El Dorado! The fabled city of gold that lured the Spanish to conquer South, Central, and much of North America.

The forty-niners! The discovery of gold drove tens of thousands of Americans west to California.

Rockefeller, Carnegie, Morgan! The billionaires created during the second industrial revolution at the end of the nineteenth century.

Bill Gates! The world's wealthiest man (net worth in excess of $83 billion at the end of 1998—a sum equal to the wealth held by the least wealthy 110 million Americans). The symbol of the great wealth being created by the third industrial revolution at the end of the twentieth century. In absolute terms Gates is twice as wealthy as Rockefeller, but relative to the size of the economy in their times, Rockefeller was thirteen times as wealthy as Gates.

Everyone would like to be wealthy. Those who are wealthy—no matter how wealthy—without exception want to be wealthier. To comfort themselves, those without wealth manufacture myths about the unhappiness wealth brings: Midas turned his beloved daughter into gold and could not eat because his food turned to gold as he touched it. But what everyone instinctively knows to be true—the wealthy are not unhappy—is confirmed by modern social science surveys: the greater one's wealth, the happier one becomes.[14]

Wealth conveys the ability to buy more consumer goods, but much more important, the power to do what one wants. Great wealth allows one to hire, fire, promote, and demote other humans and to open, shut, and move businesses from one location to another. The game of Monopoly becomes a real game. Companies can be bought and sold. Those with great wealth can control the physical and human environment around them. Those without wealth have to adjust to their environment.

Great wealth allows individuals to place their footprints in the sands of time. Everyone knows the billionaires of the last half of the nineteenth century—Rockefeller, Morgan, Carnegie, Mellon. Few remember the U.S. presidents of that era. Those with great wealth are the stuff of history books. They are the modern immortals. Universities and art museums are named after them (Carnegie-Mellon University, the Getty Museum). If they wish, they can become famous in their own time—that's what buying athletic teams is all about. Who would know the name of George Steinbrenner if he didn't own the New York Yankees?

Political influence can be quietly bought. Campaign contributions effectively give the wealthy more than one vote.

Direct political power can be noisily acquired. Without asking anyone's permission or serving the normal political apprenticeships, those with great wealth can become serious candidates for the presidency (Steve Forbes, Ross Perot) and win lesser offices. Over half the members of the U.S. Senate have wealth that puts them in the top 1 percent of the population, and many prominent senators and governors (e.g., Kennedy, Rockefeller) have great wealth.[15] In an era when the necessities of campaign finance effectively corrupt every politician without great personal wealth, the wealthy are the only honest ones—they don't have to sell their souls to finance their campaigns.

Wealth ultimately is the way the score is kept in capitalism. The current grand champion, Bill Gates, is on the cover of every magazine. His thoughts and movements are recorded and traced as if he were the president. He is treated like a movie star. Paparazzi follow him around. Jack Welch, the blue ribbon winner in the creation of corporate wealth at General Electric, is not far behind. Warren Buffett, the second wealthiest American, has played on the world stage for decades.

Those with great wealth are important, to be courted. They are deserving of respect and demand deference. They are the winners.

Wealth has always been important in the personal pecking order, but it has become increasingly the only dimension by which personal worth is measured. It is the only game to play if you want to prove your mettle. It is the big leagues. If you do not play there, by definition you are second rate.

As other sources of fame, prestige, and power disappear, the economic game rises in importance. Without big wars, generals cannot become heroes. With globalization, governments lose much of their ability to regulate and control economies to help people, and politicians become less important. With the new electronic media relentlessly probing into their personal lives, none can maintain their dignity, and the aura of high political office vanishes. Working in groups, modern inventors, unlike Thomas Edison or Alexander Graham Bell, are unknown even in their own times. Few ever knew, and even fewer remember, who invented the TV, the VCR, the semiconductor chip, or the computer. The names of those who first flew into space or first stepped on the moon are not household words. They were not Columbus opening new worlds for later conquest.

Other avenues of human advancement have to make do with lesser human talent. In these other areas, achievements are measured more and more often by how much wealth they generate. In some sports (tennis, golf), players are officially ranked based on how much money they make, but everywhere they are unofficially so ranked. Michael Jordan rates the cover of *Fortune* magazine and is talked about because of the money he makes—most of it off the basketball floor.

Since the acquisition of wealth has completely overshadowed other forms of human achievement, talented young people with ambition focus more and more of their personal drive on that goal. Measured any way you like—by intellectual ability, drive, creativity, willingness to take risks—the students getting M.B.A.s today are vastly superior in both numbers and quality to those of the 1960s. And unlike those who went to business school in the 1950s, these students don't want to become organization men and women. They want to get rich!

To have great wealth is to have it all. It is not surprising that get-rich-quick books sell, even though the buyers know the books will convey nothing helpful. They are the modern equivalent of alchemy. Neither exists, but it would be so nice if they did that many are willing to suspend their critical faculties and believe in the unbelievable. Fairy tales both sell and give comfort—even when they are known to be fairy tales.

The Best of Times

Humankind is living through its greatest technological decade ever. Wherever one looks, wondrous things can be seen. Virtual reality and cyberspace are here. The Internet and laptops with the speed of yesterday's mainframes make electronic shopping a reality. Fewer stores are needed, travel patterns alter, and the geographic patterns of our cities change. Global position devices guide our planes and ships—and are about to guide our automobiles. The better, smarter, taller, more beautiful, partially man-made human being is on the horizon—better things built with microbiology. The spectacular follows the spectacular. A land of great new economic opportunities has been discovered.

These technological opportunities are creating fortunes faster than they have ever been created. The United States in the last fifteen years has created more billionaires than ever in its history—even correcting for inflation and changes in average per capita gross domestic product. The 13 billionaires in 1982 had been joined by 176 others by 1998. Together these 189 people owned assets worth $738 billion. Another 29 would have been on the list if the measurements had been taken in July and not October, and with the recovery in the stock market, they were probably back on the list by the end of the year.[16] To be among the fifty wealthiest Americans required a minimum of $2.9 billion in 1998.

The richest Americans don't hide their wealth. They actively seek to get their names on lists of the wealthiest, bringing in their financial records to back them up. They want to be seen as economic winners.

If the slightly less wealthy cannot make the lists, they can show their wealth in other ways. Conspicuous consumption is up. While general consumption is up 29 percent, adventure travel is up 46 percent, gourmet chocolates 51 percent, pearls 73 percent, luxury cars 74 percent, and yachts 143 percent.[17] Bill Gates can spend $100 million on his house and still have only the second most expensive house under construction in the United States.[18]

It is the best of times for Americans.

But this isn't true to the same extent elsewhere. Relative to their population, Americans are five time more likely than Europeans to be billionaires and nine times more likely than the Japanese. Why the huge differences?

Furthermore, this wealth explosion isn't usual in America. In the 1950s, 1960s, and 1970s, what is happening today was not happening. The economy was growing much faster (it grew twice as fast from 1950 to 1970 as it did from 1970 to 1998), average wealth was going up, but great wealth was not suddenly erupting. Americans in the 1950s, 1960s, and 1970s were no less talented, no less inventive, and no less ambitious. The political and economic systems (democracy and capitalism) did not change. The opportunities to get wealthy simply weren't there.

What is being seen in America today was last seen in the 1890s. Then the second industrial revolution was under way, and two inventions changed the nature of economic advancement and opened up opportunities for creating great wealth.

In creating their chemical industry, Germany developed the concept of systematic industrial research and development. As a result, technical advances no longer happened randomly but could be systematically planned. Using science, new products could flow in a never-ending stream from the industrial laboratories of companies such as I. G. Farben. The corporate research laboratory was born.

Previously the economy had advanced on the brilliance of what we might call great entrepreneurial tinkerers (Watt, Bessemer, Arkwright). Technological advances were not closely coupled to scientific advances. Bessemer, for example, never knew the chemistry of what made his blast furnace work. He just fiddled around until it worked.

In the twentieth century, economic leadership would become a matter of systematic investment in R&D to deliberately invent new technologies. To capitalize on this new ability educational systems had to change to generate large numbers of scientists, engineers, technicians, trained managers, and ultimately skilled workers—not just a trained religious or political elite as before. Cultures had to be rebuilt to accept rapid technical change.

The old leader, Great Britain, could not make the necessary social changes and fell behind. The superficial reasons are well known. In the first quarter of the twentieth century, as economic leadership was passing to Germany and the United States, U.S.

R&D spending was twelve times as high as that of Great Britain. The United States had eight times as many university students, three times as many civil engineers, and was proportionally investing 70 percent more in plant and equipment. The net result was a productivity growth rate four times as high.[19]

But at a more profound level, what were the cultural reasons that prevented Great Britain from adapting to this new environment and making the necessary organizational changes? Why couldn't it build an educational system that would generate the necessary skills to allow systematic research and development? Whatever these deeper reasons, Britain never mastered the new realities of the second industrial revolution. Britain's position of economic leadership slowly flowed away and was lost.

One hundred years later in 1998, the British were still writing reports to themselves about these issues. Why are they 50 percent less skilled than the Germans?[20] Why are they sixteenth out of the nineteen OECD (Organization for Economic Cooperation and Development) countries in R&D spending—spending half as much as the French? Why are they bad at transferring academic research into industrial expertise? Why do they register less than 4 percent of the patents registered by Americans?[21] Why is labor productivity in their automotive sector only half that of Japan?[22]

Having invented systematic research and development, Germany maintained its scientific and technological lead for the first half of the twentieth century. But no one was faster at shifting from elite classics-based education (Latin, Greek) to mass technological education than the Americans. Using this mass educational base, America replaced Britain as the world's wealthiest country early in the twentieth century, even though it was not the world's technological leader. The famous British entrepreneurs of the early nineteenth century were replaced by the equally famous American entrepreneurs of the late nineteenth century. The place to become rich at the beginning of the nineteenth century, Britain, was not the place to become rich at the end of the century, the United States.

Interestingly, many of America's new wealthy saw the educational base upon which their individual success rested and wanted to enhance it for others. Carnegie built libraries across the United States so that those who had not had a chance to become educated in school could do so on their own. Rockefeller, Carnegie, Eastman, and Mellon all endowed new universities.

The United States would not displace Germany as the world's technological leader until after World War II. In the first half of the century, those who wanted a leading-edge scientific education went to Germany. During World War II, Germany was the only adversary to deploy ballistic missile technologies; it had prototype jet engines; and much of the urgency behind America's Manhattan Project was the fear that Germany would be the first to invent atomic weapons. In the end it was not the physical destruction of losing a war but its racial policies that cost Germany its scientific and engineering leadership. The physical damage could be repaired. The human damage could not. America had gained the Einsteins, the Fermis, and their intellectual descendants. It seized global scientific and technological leadership.

The second invention that changed the nature of economic advancement in the 1890s was electricity. Electrification allowed a whole new set of industries to emerge (telephones, movies) and radically altered the productive processes of every old industry. In the steam era, a giant engine powered a central rotating shaft with machine tools running off pulleys in long linear factories. In the new electric model of production, small motors could be attached to each machine tool, and very different, more productive configurations of machinery could be arranged on the factory floor. It was an earlier industrial version of what today is known as distributive processing in the computer industry.

With the electric lightbulb, night literally became day. The price-performance curve of the lightbulb looked like today's price-performance curve for the computer. To get the lighting that can be bought for 33¢ in a 100-watt bulb at Home Depot today would have cost $1,445 in 1880 (adjusted for lumens of light, length of bulb life, inflation, and changes in per capita income). The same percentage price declines would turn a $13 million computer into a $3,000 computer—not far from what has actually happened since the 1960s. The first lightbulb was used as a fire prevention device on the steamship *Columbia*. It was too valuable to be used simply for light. Lamp oil was much cheaper.

Having something to do after dark changed basic habits. People slept much less. What had been an average of nine hours of sleep fell to slightly over seven hours.[23] With electricity came transportation systems (underground and street railways, elevators) that allowed the emergence of big cities. Electricity powered the telephone communication system that allowed small local markets to become big national markets.

The second industrial revolution created a sharp discontinuity in economic affairs. What had been was obsolete. What was to follow would be very different. These discontinuities created opportunities to do things that had never been done before and to do old things in new ways. The smart and/or the lucky did not have to be in highly competitive businesses producing commodities at bond market equilibrium rates of return. In the jargon of economists, high disequilibrium returns replaced low equilibrium returns.

Entrepreneurs could create new businesses with few or no national competitors and produce new high-value-added products with financial returns and growth rates far above those in the economy as a whole. Entrepreneurs could use these new technologies to transform old industries, dramatically cut their costs, and make profits far above those made by firms using the old technologies. With limited competition in both the new industries and the old industries using new technologies, costs fell faster than prices and profits soared. Financial markets capitalized these streams of higher current and future profits at high price/earnings (P/E) multiples (just as they do today). Those who created and owned the new national companies became fabulously wealthy. A generation of great wealth suddenly emerged.

RULE ONE: No one has ever become very rich by saving their money. The rich see opportunities to work and invest in situations where large disequilibriums exist. This was as true for John D. Rockefeller as it is for Bill Gates. In both cases their lifetime savings constitute a small fraction of their total wealth. Carefully saving one's money and investing in normal equilibrium situations can make one comfortable in one's old age but never really wealthy.

Eventually disequilibrium conditions always disappear. New industries with high returns and high growth rates become old industries with much lower equilibrium returns and normal growth rates. As technologies mature, profits get squeezed as competitors arise to drive down selling prices faster than technology is driving down costs. Penetration rates for the new products reach saturation levels. Growth markets become replacement markets. But *eventually* often means several decades. It takes time to attract enough capital and people into these new industries so that they expand and become normal competitive industries. In the meantime there are great fortunes to be made.

3. Finding (and Losing) the Treasures of the Wealth Pyramid

Just as economic historians now speak about the second industrial revolution at the end of the nineteenth century, a century from now economic historians will undoubtedly talk about the third industrial revolution at the end of the twentieth century. As in the second industrial revolution, firms that are positioned to take advantage of the third industrial revolution can achieve high returns and high growth rates even though the economy's growth rate is slower than in the previous three decades. New big firms, and with them new big fortunes, can grow almost overnight. Eight of America's twenty-five biggest firms in 1998 did not exist or were very small in 1960. Three of those that did not exist in 1960 were among the world's ten biggest in 1998.[24]

Disequilibrium means great threats as well as great opportunities. Only four of the twenty-five biggest firms in 1960 were on the list in 1998. Most had merged with other companies, but two of the twenty-five had gone completely out of business. Technological breakthroughs occur, the economic environment changes, but they could not successfully adjust. In the 1950s and 1960s, neither the opportunities nor the threats were there. Billionaires weren't sprouting like mushrooms. But millions of workers weren't being permanently downsized either.

Big old firms understand, and often even invent, the new technologies that transform the world, but they have a structural problem that is almost impossible to solve. When new breakthrough technologies come along, old firms must destroy themselves to save themselves. They must cannibalize themselves, but they cannot. Four of the five makers of vacuum tubes, for example, never successfully made transistors or semiconductor chips when transistors emerged to replace the vacuum tube—and the fifth is today not a player. When the microprocessor allowed the personal computer to replace the mainframe as the dominant growth market in the computer industry, the old industrial leader (IBM) fell off a cliff and new leaders (Intel, Microsoft) emerged. IBM understood the new technologies and wanted to compete but could not destroy the old mainframe business to build the new.

New firms have the great advantage of not having to destroy themselves to save themselves.

Eleven of the twelve largest American companies at the beginning of the twentieth century will not be around to see the beginning of the twenty-first. Survival is not impossible. General Electric was one of the twelve largest firms at the end of the nineteenth century, and it will be near the top at the end of the twentieth century (currently it is number two)—but it is the great exception, and it confirms the rule that destroying oneself to save oneself is very difficult. General Electric independently discovered the transistor shortly after its invention at AT&T's Bell Labs, but it was the dominant maker of vacuum tubes. To save its economic position it would have had to destroy its vacuum tube division. It just could not do it. It has never been a player in the transistor or semiconductor business.

The same need to cannibalize and reinvent oneself occurs at the national level. As we have seen, Britain could not shift to the German model in the second industrial revolution. The final results of the third industrial revolution are not yet in, but Japan is a good illustration of the cannibalization problem. Japan became a master at the second industrial revolution's economic game after World War II, but in the 1990s it has demonstrated enormous weaknesses in playing the game in an era of man-made brainpower industries. A country that wants and needs creativity to start new industries using the new technologies cannot have as one of its most frequently invoked aphorisms "The nail that stands up gets hammered down." Standing up and doing something different are what the third industrial revolution is all about.

Japan has to create a new industrial system, and thus far it has been unwilling to do so. This along with its financial meltdown explains why its growth rate in the 1990s (0.4 percent per year) is far below that of the 1980s (4 percent per year). It is too early to say that Japan won't make the necessary transition, but it is not too early to say that Japan is struggling.

The biggest changes of the third industrial revolution may well occur in retailing. Just as the first industrial revolution ended eight thousand years of human reliance on agriculture, the third industrial revolution may end five thousand years of going to the local store to buy the necessities of life. Internet sales have been increasing by a factor of ten every five years.[25] If the issue is buying good things cheap, electronic shopping will always be cheaper than conventional shopping, since it does not require expensive locations, fancy buildings, large inventories, or as many people to service the customers.

This new technology makes it possible for very small companies to compete with Wal-Mart—America's largest retailer. As a conventional retailer in the old game, Wal-Mart is unbeatable. But it has too much invested in the old technology (land, stores, and people) to lead the transition to the new game. Wal-Mart's own current customers would be the first to move to Wal-Mart's new, cheaper electronic store. Worst of all, Wal-Mart's customers might decide to visit its old physical stores to pick out what they want (leaving it with its old cost structure) but buy what they have chosen in Wal-Mart's new, cheaper electronic store (forcing it to add extra costs). Wal-Mart would have to close thousands of stores. Billions of dollars in closing costs would have to be absorbed. Managerial profit-linked bonuses would vanish for a decade or more. If Wal-Mart jumped into the new technology aggressively, it would take its own customers away from itself much faster than any outside electronic retailer could. In the short and medium term, it makes more money by sticking with the old technology.

In accordance with this structure of incentives, Wal-Mart recently set up an electronic store, but it carefully kept the prices slightly higher than those in its physical stores. Yet the whole advantage of electronic retailing is the fact that costs are intrinsically less and prices can be significantly lower.

Recently I received a consulting report predicting that half of the retail stores in America would close by the year 2010. That seems a bit too fast to me, but the report is certainly right about the direction of change. Which stores will close and how fast will depend more on sociology than on technology. Humans are herd animals and like to do things in crowds. "Entertainment" shopping will be able to compete with electronic shopping for some products, but no one knows which products. Which customers will be willing to pay more if they buy in an entertaining environment and which ones just want to buy at the cheapest possible price? Those who figure it out first will become rich.

Electronic shopping is just one of the profound changes being caused by the revolution in electronic communications. Globalization will lead to more business travel, but video conferencing will lead to less business travel. Which effect will dominate? Does the world need more or less hotels, airports, airlines, and taxis? As an investor, how would you choose?

With electronic reporting to one's boss, the necessary levels of management, the location of one's boss, and the need for traditional corporate headquarters all change. White-collar workers will be able to work from their home computers, but how much will this reduce the need for traditional office space, lower rents, and reduce the wealth of those owning office buildings? Here again, sociology, not technology, will make the determination.

To say that work can be done at home alone is not to say that anyone wants to work at home. Working at home alone is lonely—"extremely isolating," in the words of those doing it, who no longer get to talk to anyone around the water cooler or the printer. Humans aren't hermits. They like to work together. That's where their friends are. Going to work builds commitments that telecommuting doesn't, increasing organizational loyalty. Suspicious that telecommuters may not be working, employers lock onto them with electronic surveillance not all that different from the electronic surveilance systems used to watch criminals out on bail or under house arrest. Big brother is watching. Studies show that productivity falls sharply if workers telecommute for more than a day or two per week, but companies save most of their money by not having offices for the telecommuters.[26]

Oil is a good example of the impact of the third industrial revolution on an old industry. What used to be an industry of luck and brawn (see the James Dean movie *Giant*) is now an industry dependent upon brainpower. Supercomputers permit three- and now four-dimensional acoustical soundings. Hit rates for finding new oil fields are up by a factor of ten; extraction rates have doubled. Drilling in water two miles deep, Norway has become the world's second largest exporter of oil rather than being out of oil, as was predicted two decades ago. On the offshore oil rigs, the well-paid illiterate roustabouts of yesterday have been replaced by well-paid knowledge workers. The industry still produces oil, but in ways so different that it might be considered one of the new knowledge industries. Because of these new technologies, reachable oil supplies have expanded much faster than demand, and real prices have fallen to the lowest levels in human history.

Or consider a very different business—flowers. With today's electronic technology, the cut-flower business is in the hands of neither those who grow flowers nor those who sell them. It is in the hands of the Dutch, who have built a global logistics system for growing flowers at the point of least cost on the globe and selling them at the point of highest price. Many can grow flowers. Many can sell flowers. But only the Dutch can deliver an Easter lily grown in Colombia to a purchaser in Maine and guarantee that it will bloom on Easter. Because of this ability, the Dutch make most of the money in the flower business.

Similarly, a seller of outdoor clothing located in rural Maine, L. L. Bean, can sell hundreds of millions of dollars worth of clothing in Japan without having stores in Japan. Internet, fax, telephone, and catalog sales allow them to jump the hurdles (laws prohibiting large stores, the impossibility of renting good retail locations) that have made it impossible for conventional foreign retailers to break into the Japanese market in the past.

Just as the movement from local to national economies allowed the emergence of a new set of big national firms, so today's movement from a national to a global economy allows the emergence of an even bigger set of new global firms. "Intel Inside" is found all around the world. Most big U.S. firms have at least half of their sales outside the United States. Global sourcing, global production, and global selling are all combined in a seamless global supply chain. Where firms aren't global, mergers are making them global. Mercedes combines with Chrysler; Ford takes over Mazda and Jaguar; BMW gets Rover and Rolls Royce; Volkswagen gets Bentley; General Motors buys Saab.

The Mercedes takeover of Chrysler is a good example of both the opportunities and the problems. If the two can be put together right, their announced merger will create a brand-new company neither German nor American. It will be a global company, with both sides having much to learn from the other.

One makes cars for the mass market; the other makes cars for the luxury market. One is good in small trucks; the other is good in big trucks. One has a fast development cycle; the other has a slow development cycle. One is noted for its innovative designs; the other's designs never change. One has quality problems; the other is noted for its high quality. One is a low-cost producer, the other has high costs. One sells locally but sources its parts globally; the other sells worldwide but sources its parts locally. Overlapping research in fuel cells and accident avoidance systems can be eliminated, and the company will be able to tap easily into the basic research being done in both America and Germany. Downturns in sales are unlikely to occur at the same time in all of their combined markets. When Europe is down, America will be up.

If the human problems of putting together two very different cultures can be overcome, someone is going to get rich on the deal. But these human problems are very large and may be impossible to solve. Do they use American or German pay scales? Chrysler's CEO got $18 million per year; Mercedes' CEO got $2 million per year. The details of how German and American firms use their engineering forces are very different. Do the American unions get the co-determination in America that the German unions have in Germany?

As noted earlier, with economic globalization, national governments are losing many of their abilities to control their own economies. Consider the market where globalization first happened—finance. Financial wealth can easily be held outside the jurisdiction of one's own government. The desire to do so is why the Grand Cayman Islands are now the world's fifth biggest banking center. Whatever the physical location, everyone now essentially borrows in the same global capital market. The local American home mortgage is bundled with other similar mortgages, securitized, and sold in the New York financial markets—perhaps to a Japanese insurance company. The local bank only manages the paperwork. The buyer doesn't know who provides the money. The lenders never see the properties they are financing.

By adopting legislation in 1998 to isolate and control his national capital market to stop the activities of international financial speculators, the prime minister of Malaysia posed an interesting test of how far government powers have diminished. Will he succeed in cutting off the activities of international currency speculators? Can he really stop financiers from taking their money out of the country without a two-year wait? Or will global financial markets cut Malaysia off from the funds and technologies it needs to develop? Mainland China has never allowed free currency movements, yet in 1998 it lost more than $60 billion in currency reserves. Exporters just didn't bring their earnings back to China. Effectively China could not lock the door. A betting man would choose global financial markets over Malalysia.

If one takes a wide definition of culture (all leisure activities), culture is the world's biggest industry. People become billionaires running cruise lines and making movies. A soccer team, Manchester United, was sold for more than a billion dollars. The cultural world is a winner-take-all society, where the best are paid to perform for everyone (Pavarotti on CDs, Michael Jordan on the basketball court) and the second and third best have no market value.

Culture used to be older generations teaching younger generations the traditions of their society. Culture now skips older generations and jumps directly to the young. Foreigners see this as a dangerous invasion by American culture, but although much of this culture is produced in America (recently the top five movies playing in France were American), what is being exported is not traditional American values. Americans, just as much as non-Americans, see this change as a threat to their traditional culture. The distinguishing characteristic of this new culture is that the young will pay to buy it. If a particular facet of it doesn't sell, the electronic media aren't interested, and whatever that facet's intrinsic value, it will not be passed on to the next generation.

Governments can pass laws against pornography, but with global communications they cannot enforce them. Pornography comes up on the Internet from some other part of the globe where it isn't illegal—or even regarded as pornography. In the

Persian Gulf a women with bare arms is considered pornographic. Will America allow its firms to be prosecuted for releasing this kind of pornography in their advertisements? Obviously not. But similarly, what Americans regard as pornography isn't so regarded in Finland. Who would have believed just a short time ago that half of the pay movies in most American hotel rooms would be pornographic—that pornography would become a mainline hotel profit center?

With high-quality teaching available electronically, there are similar changes (opportunities, threats) ahead in education. No one can beat old-line industry leaders such as Harvard in traditional higher education, but they may be beatable in high-quality distance electronic education. Educational leadership in the twenty-first century is in play.

Profit-making business firms rather than nonprofit universities may well be best positioned to be the prime educational institutions of the future. Electronic education has a lot of up-front costs that few schools or universities will be able to afford—think of the cost of producing *Sesame Street* versus the cost of the local kindergarten—and even if they could afford it, they probably would not be willing to change their traditional production techniques. Meanwhile, what Otis Elevator learns in the electronic training of its global maintenance forces it can employ in other forms of for-profit education.

Maybe profit-making educational institutions won't drive nonprofit education out of business, but then again maybe they will—and very quickly. Think of the recent rapid changes in health care. An industry that had been dominated by nonprofit hospitals for a century was within a decade converted to an industry dominated by for-profit HMOs.

RULE TWO: Successful businesses must be willing to cannibalize themselves to save themselves. They must be willing to destroy the old while it is still successful

if they wish to build the new before it is successful. If they won't destroy themselves, others will destroy them.

Representative government (filtering the voters' views through congressmen and senators) was invented to compensate for the slow transportation and communication systems of postcolonial America. With modern technology, which could allow everyone to vote directly on every issue electronically, why do we need representative government? Perhaps we don't, and it too will disappear. The national equivalent of a New England town meeting may emerge to replace the U.S. Congress.

Consider the nature of warfare. A superpower (a nation with enough nuclear weapons and delivery systems to destroy the world) is replaced by a hyperpower. A hyperpower uses its satellites and other technologies to see and hear everything and to seamlessly communicate with its own forces. It can also shut down other countries' eyes, ears, and mouth so that their armed forces become blind, deaf, and dumb. During the Cold War there were two superpowers—the United States and the U.S.S.R. Today there is only one hyperpower—the United States.

But military deaths in real time on the TV set are not the equivalent of reported deaths in the newspaper. Citizen-voters care a lot more about the first than the second. In Somalia, a few local warlords and a small number of deaths (18) chased the world's only hyperpower out—even though the hyperpower had a professional army made up of volunteers who joined wanting to fight and knowing the risks. America is not alone.[27] Death rates that used to be acceptable are not acceptable in either Russia or Israel.

Peter Arnett was alone in Baghdad during the Persian Gulf War. But the $500,000 communication system he was using then is now available for less than $5,000 (less than $3,000 if you don't need solar cells to generate your own electricity). In the next Persian Gulf-type war there are going to be thousands of one's own reporters in the city being bombed. One's own reporters are going to get bombed. The public is going to have to watch *Saving Private Ryan*'s invasion of Omaha Beach in real time.

Some will hate it, some will love it, but biotechnology is inevitably leading to a world in which plants, animals, and human beings are going to be partly man-made. The process will start by curing genetic diseases and go on to make bigger, smarter, more beautiful, better human beings. Giving genetic dwarfs normal height is no different from making normal children into basketball players. Suppose parents could add 30 points to their children's IQs. Wouldn't you want to do it? And if you don't, your neighbors will, and your child will be the stupidest child in the neighborhood. Microbiology is just one of the technologies making the world very different—and in the process creating billionaires.

As in the second industrial revolution a hundred years ago, the third industrial revolution is creating opportunities for great wealth to emerge. New technologies mean change. Change means disequilibrium. Disequilibrium conditions create high-return, high-growth opportunities. The winners understand the new technologies, are lucky enough to be in the right place at the right time, and have the skills to take advantage of these new situations. They become rich.

Disequilibrium situations usually depend upon radical changes in technology, but sometimes entrepreneurs can create disequilibriums by seeing sociological opportunities to change human habits. Starbucks persuaded Americans to replace a 50¢ cup of coffee bought at a local restaurant with a $2.50 cup of coffee bought at a coffee bar. They made a competitive commodity with widely distributed points of sale out of which no one made much money into a noncompetitive differentiated product and created a rapidly growing industry with high rates of return where billionaires could emerge.

The founders of cruise lines took advantage of a sociological shift in demographics. They noticed that the relative purchasing power of the elderly had doubled in a quarter of a century. The seventy-year-olds that twenty years earlier had cash incomes 40 percent below those of thirty-year-olds suddenly had cash incomes 20 percent above those of thirty-year-olds. Cruises, a technology known at least since the days of Cleopatra, were the perfect vacation for the elderly. We move you; you don't move. Cruise lines made billions.

In both cases entrepreneurs created what might be called sociological disequilibriums, as opposed to technological disequilibriums.

The problem with wealth generated from sociological disequilibriums is that it usually reflects more a transfer of existing wealth than a generation of new wealth. Those who were selling conventional cups of coffee sold fewer cups of coffee and thousands of mom-and-pop restaurants made less money, while the extra $2 per cup that went to Starbucks came out of someone else's sales elsewhere in the economy.

A third form of disequilibrium is what one might call developmental. These opportunities exist whenever there are countries at very different income levels and entrepreneurs can replicate the activities of the developed world in the underdeveloped world.

The China–Hong Kong border provides a good illustration. A year or so before the Hong Kong handover, I was sitting in the lounge at the Hong Kong airport eavesdropping on a conversation between two rich Chinese businessmen on their way to spend six months in Vancouver to get a Canadian passport—their insurance policy in case things went wrong in Hong Kong. They were complaining about having to spend the six months in Vancouver because they could see no way to use their time to make money. To hear them describe it, Vancouver was an economic desert. Why? Vancouver is richer than Hong Kong.

The answer is to be found in the absence of developmental disequilibriums in Canada. In Hong Kong these two businessmen had become rich by exploiting the differences between the developed world and the poor but now open mainland Chinese environment.

They simply copied what was done in the developed world and replicated it in China. What were commodity operations with low rates of return and low growth prospects in the developed world were high-return, high-growth opportunities in China. Their business skills consisted of being good at replication and knowing the exact time when mainland Chinese conditions were ripe for the movement of any particular activity.

In Vancouver there were no similar opportunities for these businessmen. All of the normal first world activities already existed. To get rich in Vancouver one needed new breakthrough technologies or new sociological concepts. The two rich Chinese businessmen had neither. For them Vancouver truly was an economic desert.

But developmental disequilibriums don't exist everywhere in the developing world. If Africa starts to develop, Africans will undoubtedly want many of the goods and services now being supplied in the developed world; new markets for what the developed world sees as old products will explode in Africa; and African entrepreneurs will get rich. But Africa is not getting richer. Its per capita gross domestic product (GDP) is below where it was in 1965. Unless its incomes start to rise, there are no opportunities for replicating the activities common in the developed world. The skilled entrepreneurs operating across the disequilibriums between Hong Kong and mainland China could not operate in Africa. The conditions aren't right. Africa, like Vancouver, is an economic desert.

In Asia one can get rich if one is skilled at replication and understanding when conditions and timing are right (right education levels, right incomes, right supporting infrastructure, right governments) to move normal first world activities into areas where they have not previously existed. This is of course why the explosion of billionaires in America was being matched by a similar explosion in Asia until these billionaires were destroyed in Asia's financial meltdown. The Asian billionaires were taking advantage of developmental disequilibriums. With the meltdown, what had been forty-one Japanese billionaires fell to only nine at the most recent count.

But when it comes to generating billionaires, the mystery is not in America, Asia, or Africa. The mystery is in Europe. Why have the Europeans been able to exploit neither the Asian-style developmental disequilibrium opportunities that exist between Western and Eastern Europe nor the American-style technological disequilibrium opportunities that exist because of new technologies? Why haven't they invented some new sociological disquilibriums? The case of the missing European billionaires is a mystery to be solved later in this book.

RULE THREE: Businesses that would grow rapidly with high profit margins must take advantage of technological disequilibriums, exploit developmental disequilibriums, or create sociological disequilibriums. All other activities are slow-growth, low-rate-of-return commodity businesses.

The Worst of Times

While billionaires and market wealth dominate the headlines, there is another way to look at wealth creation that could generate a very different set of headlines if anyone wanted to pay attention. Real wealth is the ability to produce more with less—to generate a flow of goods and services without having to sacrifice something else of equal value. The real wealth of an individual who sacrifices his leisure time to work and generate a flow of income is not measured by the capitalized value of the income earned. The value of the extra time sacrificed has to be subtracted from that new market wealth to determine if gains in real wealth have occurred. The

United States, for example, is first in the world in terms of GDP per person but ninth in terms of GDP per hour of work.[28] Americans have more money because they have less leisure.

Looking at GDP per hour of work rather than per person lowers Japan's position from third in the world to eighteenth. Conversely, Belgium moves up from tenth in the world in terms of GDP per person to first in terms of GDP per hour of work.

If the leisure time sacrificed is more valuable than the new goods bought, the individual has become poorer despite having more market wealth. Real wealth is not created by taking time away from other activities and devoting it to money-making activities. Real wealth is ultimately created by increases in what economists call labor productivity: the same time spent working generates more income (and hence wealth) than it did in the past.

But the same is true of wealth created by investment in plant and equipment. If consumption is sacrificed to invest, a subtraction must be made from the flow of income from those new investments. The consumption goods lost represent a subtraction from real wealth. Here too real wealth is ultimately not created by taking income away from consumption and devoting it to investment. Wealth flows from increases in capital productivity—getting more out of the same capital resources or using fewer capital resources to generate the old levels of market wealth.

When the sacrifice of both time and capital is taken into account, economists talk about *total factor productivity*. Less time and less capital must be sacrificed to get old income levels. Or old levels of sacrifice generate new higher levels of income. Simply put, wealthier societies are higher total factor productivity societies.

Similarly, gaining market wealth by exhausting natural resources or polluting the environment does not generate real wealth. Real wealth flows from enhanced natural and environmental resources. Are products made with the use of fewer natural resources? Are products being made and used in more environmentally friendly ways? If so, the economy's natural and environmental resource productivity has risen and real wealth has been generated. Natural resource usage and environmental quality are often not included in measures of total factor productivity because of the technical problems of measuring them, but they always should be.

Productivity is the real treasure to be found within the wealth pyramid. Without productivity growth, the outside of the pyramid is simply an impressive facade. Productivity growth determines what is happening to the total output available to be divided. A slowly growing economic pie can be redivided to generate great wealth at the top. But only a rapidly growing economic pie can create wealthy societies where everyone can be a participant in wealth creation. Wages for the many cannot be growing at the bottom without vigorous productivity growth.

Here lies a central mystery. No one denies that the last decade has produced more market wealth and generated greater fortunes than any other decade in American history. The outside of the pyramid is the most impressive mankind has ever seen. Yet when the inside of the pyramid is explored, the last decade has been the worst decade in the history of American productivity growth. Labor productivity has grown at only 1.1 percent per year—one-third the 1960s' 3.2 percent per year. Even with a slight speedup from 1996 to 1998, this is the worst performance in American history. Even during the Great Depression, from 1929 to 1939, productivity was growing at 1.6 percent per year. Measured from a labor productivity perspective, wealth creation has been far below normal. The technological change that has felt rapid has in fact been slow.

In the last ten years, total factor productivity has not grown at all. Measured from a total factor productivity perspective, no real wealth has been created in the decade. The inside of the pyramid is empty. The glitter on the outside is fool's gold. There are no real treasures to be found.

Which perspective is real: the rapid technological change we feel, see, and smell, or the slow productivity growth we measure?

This gap between senses and measurements has led those who lead with their senses to maintain that something must be wrong with the productivity statistics. Those who lead with their heads want proof that these unmeasured productivity improvements could be large enough to eliminate the paradox between what we see and what we measure. Thus far no one has been able to give them the proof they want.

Those who believe in unmeasured productivity gains point out that if inflation is being overestimated, as a government commission (the Boskin Commission) and Federal Reserve Board Chairman Greenspan argue, then real output is being underestimated because it is being overdeflated, and actual productivity growth is higher than what is being reported.

This argument faces two problems. Even if there is a 1 percentage point exaggeration in inflation and a consequent underestimation of output, this explains only half of the 2 percentage point decline in productivity growth. What explains the other half? And the argument does not solve the problem at all unless one argues that inflation is being overestimated in the 1990s but was not being overestimated in the 1960s. No one, not even those on the Boskin Commission, has been willing to make this argument. There is simply no reason to believe that it is so.

There is also a counterargument. Productivity growth may be even worse than the official numbers indicate. Private surveys find that workers are working many more hours per week than are being recorded in the official statistics.[29] Using these alternative higher estimates of hours worked brings the rate of growth of labor productivity to zero and makes the rate of growth of total factor productivity *negative*.

Others point to inadequately measured quality improvements in the service sector. America's statistical procedures were established when services were a small fraction of total output, not the 70 percent they are today, and the efforts to measure quality improvements focus almost exclusively on the goods sector.

Much of the time the productivity statistics assume that there are no gains in productivity in the service sector. But clearly there are. The benefits, for example, of being able to get money out of a bank's ATM machines twenty-four hours a day 365 days a year have never been factored into the productivity statistics as a quality improvement.

But better measures of service productivity may also turn up a lot of negative productivity growth. In the last two decades, life expectancy has increased 4 percent in America, but spending on health care has increased 500 percent. Americans spend twice as much on health care as either the Japanese or the British, yet on all measures of health are less healthy than either.[30] If we measured automobile services, we might find that greater congestion and time spent commuting has offset the benefits of better cars needing less maintenance.

In the United States, the number of public and private policemen and investments in locks and alarms have both expanded enormously in the last twenty-five years. All of those baggage inspectors didn't used to exist at our airports. They increase the number of hours of work necessary to generate a mile of travel and lower productivity. Americans are spending time and resources on protecting their standard of living rather than on increasing it.

Most improvements in service output, quality, and hence productivity are measurable, but doing so costs money, and the United States has simply not been willing to spend the sums necessary to get better statistics. If Americans really want to know where they are in the search for productivity, they are going to build the right economic global positioning system. But thus far we would rather argue about the truth than spend the money to determine what it is. Without those expenditures and that effort, it is not obvious that better measures of service productivity would eliminate the productivity slowdown. They could well increase it.

There is a genuine mystery. It is not a figment of the data. For some unknown reason the third industrial revolution has simultaneously created great market wealth and a miserable productivity performance.

Perhaps current stock market values are just a bubble, much like tulip mania 360 years ago. Then one black tulip bulb bought a nice five-story row house along the canals in Amsterdam. The tulip billionaires lasted for a few years but then disappeared. Perhaps our billionaires will also fade into the history books as a glorious saga—but a story with no greater long-term economic significance than that of the tulip.

Alternatively, perhaps the new great fortunes represent the mobilization of more resources (more leisure time lost, more current consumption sacrificed, more natural resources used up, more of the environment degraded) and the transfer of existing wealth from the many to the few. Profits and stock market values have gone up on the financial exchanges because wages have gone down on the factory floor. To some extent there is supporting evidence for each of these suggestions.

In the last twenty-five years, the share of total wealth held by the top 5 percent of the population has risen from 16.7 to 21.4 percent of total wealth. That top 5 percent now owns as much market wealth as the bottom 60 percent. For the middle 20 percent of families, both their share of total wealth and their inflation-adjusted absolute levels of wealth are down from 1989 to 1997 (10 percent and 3 percent respectively).[31]

Over the past quarter of a century, the inflation-adjusted real per capita GDP has risen more than 55 percent. At the same time the median American household has been on an income roller coaster to nowhere—up 4.8 percent from 1969 to 1979, down 5.0 percent from 1979 to 1983, up 11.1 percent from 1983 to 1989, down 8.0 percent from 1989 to 1993, and up 4.5 percent from 1993 to 1996. In 1998 the median household was 3 percent above where it was in 1973 and 4 percent below where it was in 1989. The young have been hit particularly hard. Families whose head of household is less than twenty-five years of age have median incomes 25 percent below where they were in 1973, and those twenty-five to thirty-four years of age are down 8 percent.[32]

Both in the long run (since 1973) and in the intermediate run (since 1989) real wages have been flat or falling for the bottom 80 percent of the male labor force. Today's young males are making less than earlier cohorts at every education level up to and including college graduates. Only those with advanced degrees have rising real wages.[33] Among women the wage declines have been smaller and have affected fewer workers—only the bottom 50 percent of the workforce has been losing out. The middle of the earnings distribution is being particularly hard hit—the proportion of persons making between half and twice the median earnings is down from 71 to 62 percent of the total workforce.[34]

In 1997 and 1998, with very low unemployment and a sharp rise in the minumum wage, these trends were interrupted and there was a gain in real wages for those who had been losing ground. Whether this will continue remains to be seen. Since 1973 there have been several other years when wages rose but then resumed their downward trend. Even the turnaround in 1997 and 1998 could not alter the distributional pattern of wage gains, however. Wages continued to rise faster at the top than at the bottom and least in the middle. Among men, the top 10 percent of the workforce gained 6.2 percent, the middle 10 percent gained 4.0 percent, and the bottom 10 percent gained 4.8 percent.[35]

Underneath these bad numbers the real news is worse. In the median and below-median households, average levels of education are up for both husband and wife. High school degrees have more than doubled and college degrees have risen by a factor of almost four. Being better educated, these families should be earning more, but they aren't.

Wives have also substantially upped their work effort. The proportion of year-round full-time working wives has doubled for those families with children and increased 50 percent for those without children. Hours of work for husband-wife couples were up by 617 hours per year, or more than fifteen weeks of full-time work, from 1979 to 1996.[36] But this extra work isn't leading to higher household incomes. Wives have had to work much longer to compensate for the lower wages of their husbands.

The symbol, but not the principal source, of this rising inequality is CEOs' pay—up from 44 to 212 times the pay of the average American worker in thirty years.[37] Even more strikingly, CEOs' pay is up substantially vis-à-vis the number-two person in their own corporations and up relative to those who run equally large companies elsewhere. CEOs' wages are 34 percent higher in the United States than in Britain, 106 percent higher than in France, 155 percent higher than in Japan, and 169 percent higher than in Germany.[38]

It is possible to argue that wealth is up at the top because wealth is being taken away from those at the bottom, because earnings are being shifted to profits, and because leisure is being sacrificed to increase output. But even together these factors are not large enough to fully explain how productivity growth could be dramatically slowing while at the same time the generation of great wealth is dramatically rising. Much of the loss in labor's earnings, for example, is being transferred not to the wealthy but to the elderly in the form of higher pensions.

Outside of the United States, pressures are rising to increase wage inequalities in both Europe and Japan. High European unemployment rates can be directly traced to wages that are too high for European workers with lesser skills. The same skills can be bought for less elsewhere, and as a result, businesses, even European businesses, are expanding their employment outside of Europe. Mercedes and BMW are expanding production in lower-cost America rather than in higher-cost Europe.

At the same time, governments everywhere are losing their ability to help those who cannot compete successfully in the new economic game. Welfare has essentially ended for economic failures in America. They must accept compulsory work—and work for very low wages—or at least in theory starve. The Organization for Economic Cooperation and Development (OECD), the international club of the world's richest countries, regularly advises Europeans to cut social welfare spending.[39] In the twenty-first century, economic losers cannot be helped if societies want to have economic winners, or so it is said.

In some sense, government welfare has also ended for companies. They can no longer be shielded from foreign competitors with tariffs or quotas. They can no longer be given state subsidies. If countries attempt to protect their companies in home markets, their companies are increasingly shut out of global markets, and for most big companies global markets are now more important than home markets.

Among companies, the gap between the successful and the unsuccessful is also widening. In America the number of firms going out of business in any given year is almost as large (88 percent) as the number of firms coming into business. Those who advise on corporate strategies see room only for huge global players or small niche players. Merge to get global size or shed divisions to get fast reaction times. The midsized national corporation is in trouble—doomed to extinction. It will go out of business (Gimbels) or be taken over (Rolls-Royce).

The same is true for countries. Per capita income differences were narrowing among countries in the 1950s, 1960s, and 1970s, but they are now widening. In what used to be the second world (communist countries with midrange incomes), falling per capita GDPs have dropped most back to third world status. Elsewhere, much of the globe has per capita incomes well below their previous peaks. In most of Africa, per capita incomes are below where they were in 1965. In much of Latin America, they are below where they were in 1980. Large parts of Asia are now well below where they were in 1997. In some countries, such as Indonesia, all of the previous three decades of gains have been lost. The great exception, of course, is China. And it is a great exception—rapid growth is raising living standards for more than one-fifth of humanity.

Within the first world, post–World War II equalization has clearly ended, although since Japan had pulled ahead of Europe, its economic decline can be seen as a perverse form of equalization. America's superior economic performance in the 1990s, however, moves the country with the highest per capita GDP among major countries even further ahead. For example, the gap between the national incomes of the United States and Canada has expanded by a third during the 1990s.

For those who would reduce the rising economic inequality between individuals, between companies, and between countries, nothing is more important than understanding how a wealth pyramid is constructed in a knowledge-based economy. Trying to defend what exists—the wealth pyramid created during the second industrial revolution—is impossible. The forces of the third industrial revolution, as we shall see, can be channeled so that they do not increase inequalities, but governments cannot defeat them in a head-to-head battle.

Part Two
The Archaeology
of a Wealth Pyramid

4.   Social Organization

The wealth pyramid begins with social organization. Social organization constitutes the great building stones at the bottom of the pyramid. Think of any of the world's poorest countries—Haiti, Bangladesh, central Africa, Albania. All are characterized by chaos, disorder, and an inability to organize themselves socially. They cannot maintain public order. They cannot build or repair infrastructure. They cannot organize and staff village schools. They cannot deliver health services.

In human history, rich areas of the globe have always coexisted with poor areas. Even today those living in poor parts of the world outnumber those living in rich parts by five to one. Building a wealth pyramid is not easy at any time. Most groups of humans never learn how.

Even having once learned how to get rich doesn't mean that an area will stay rich. Historically the same geographic areas have gone from poor to rich to poor to rich. Around the Mediterranean, per capita incomes began to rise in Egypt five thousand years ago. They peaked in Imperial Rome in about 350 A.D. Six hundred years later, in the middle of the Dark Ages, they had fallen 90 percent. In the next thousand years they would rise again. While Europe was poor in the midst of the Dark Ages, the Middle East and China were rich.

In the nineteenth century the reverse was true. Maintaining a wealth pyramid over time is almost as difficult as building one in the first place. Both require a high degree of social organization.

Social organization is the starting point at the bottom of the wealth pyramid, but it is also an essential building block at every stage of wealth creation. All successful societies periodically confront new problems that their old institutions cannot solve. If they are to remain successful, they have to reinvent themselves. Yet social systems are very resistant to change and have an enormous ability to tolerate, rather than solve, problems. The path of least resistance—simply allowing problems to fester—all too often ends up pulling down even the greatest of societies. The actions that must be taken to resolve any of society's problems are seldom in doubt. The issue is always how a society with festering problems can force itself to act before there is a crisis that may take the system down with it.

The ability to change socially is now being tested in each of the three major economic areas of the globe. What was the fastest-growing economy in the industrial world, Japan, has to reinvent itself to confront and vanquish a financial meltdown that has created a decade of stagnation. It has to learn how to make big technological breakthroughs and not just extensions of existing practices. European entrepreneurs started the first and were major participants in the second industrial revolution, but they have seemingly vanished in the third. Europe has to reinvent itself to allow entrepreneurs to reemerge. The Americans invented mass universal public education, were its leaders for a century, and used it to create their twentieth century success. But an educational system that once led the world is no longer world-class. America has to reinvent itself if it doesn't want falling wages for a poorly skilled bottom two-thirds of its workforce.

Each of the three may fail. Argentina and Chile were rich in 1880 and poor in 1980. Or all may succeed. The Egyptians kept their economic success going for thousands of years.

Economic development starts with the organizational ability to mobilize resources. Nineteenth century America had an abundance of natural resources but a shortage of workers. The prime task was to mobilize labor. Labor was actively recruited from abroad. Long hours were worked in the new factories. Manufacturing jobs averaged more than three thousand hours of work annually—more than twice what the average American now works. Average annual hours of work lengthened dramatically as people moved from agriculture to industry. In cold climates farmers work far less than three thousand hours per year. They work intensively during the planting and harvesting seasons but very little between those times and almost not at all in the winter.

With lots of labor and few natural resources in the last half of the twentieth century, Asia mobilized capital. Government controls and incentives forced savings rates to levels never before seen. Singapore's savings rate exceeded 50 percent. China, as poor as it is, saved 30 percent of its national income. Rapid growth followed in the wake of huge inputs of plant and equipment.

In this initial mobilization phase of development, productivity growth is minimal. Inputs are going up as fast as outputs. Productivity growth comes only, and should come only, after labor and capital resources are fully mobilized.

The second stage of economic development involves copying-to-catch-up. In the nineteenth century the United States copied, refined, and eventually improved on British textile mills, steel mills, and coal mines. Similarly in the twentieth century Japan copied, refined, and improved on American technology in industries such as consumer electronics. At this stage of economic development, human skills are central. The United States outdid Britain with Britain's own technologies because it was better educated than Britain. With a more skilled workforce, the same equipment working in America and Britain produced more output in America. Japan in the 1980s was similarly outdoing America in many industries because it had a better skilled workforce. The same physical equipment working in America and Japan produced more output in Japan.

In the second stage of economic development, productivity growth begins to occur.

In the third stage of economic development, advancing knowledge is central to economic success. Big technological breakthroughs lead to big jumps in productivity. New products with undreamed-of capabilities are invented. New processes for revolutionizing the production of old products emerge. Rapid change becomes the norm. Productivity growth accelerates.

New technologies transform the nature of the wealth pyramid as they emerge. In ancient times the issue was land. Wealth came from having an agricultural base that could produce a food surplus big enough to feed an urban population that could then devote itself to building cities and fighting wars—conquering more land. This is what all the ancient civilization—Egypt, Rome, China, Mexico, Peru, and Cambodia—had in common.

In the first industrial revolution, coal was the essential ingredient. Coal was too heavy and expensive to move given the technology of the time, and the steam revolution could not occur in places where coal was not available. England's easily accessible coal supplies were part of the reason the industrial revolution began there. Its two initial challengers, America and Germany, had almost equally accessible reserves of coal.

In the second industrial revolution, mass production requiring large amounts of capital was the route to economic success. The winners were those with the most capital—Carnegie at the beginning of the century, Ford in the 1920s, American corporations in the 1950s, and Japanese corporations in the 1980s.

The third industrial revolution is reordering and reassembling the basic building blocks of the wealth pyramid. Exactly how the game should be played is uncertain. The winners will be those who first figure out the nature of the wealth pyramid in a knowledge-based economy.

The United States of America

No organization does everything well. All, without exception, have strengths—things they do well—and weaknesses—things they do poorly. The central question is whether the organization is adapted to the times. The successful are those whose inherent strengths match the strengths needed to solve the critical problems of their times and whose inherent weaknesses are irrelevant or not important to the times.

The dominant economic position of the United States at the end of the 1990s is a good illustration of these principles. In the mid-1980s many books such as *Made in America* (where I was one of a dozen different authors) analyzed the decline of American industry.[40] Those books were not wrong. In industry after industry American firms were being eclipsed by Japanese and European firms. The American consumer electronics industry was completely gone; for the first time in history America was not the world's largest car maker; and the Americans had been surpassed by the Japanese in the production of semiconductor chips. The European and Japanese press openly talked about American economic decline and the end of the American century.

To some extent America's turnaround can be traced to firms that worked hard to correct their weaknesses. Efforts to eliminate the quality gaps between themselves and their foreign competitors were particularly impressive. Companies helped design and participated in programs such as Leaders for Manufacturing at MIT. American firms ruthlessly downsized, restructured, and moved offshore. They became among the world's lowest-cost producers. For American workers the costs of regaining America's competitive edge were high. Two-thirds of the workforce took 20 percent cuts in their real wages.

But even today many of the weaknesses identified in the 1980s still exist. Defects per car are down in both Japan and America, and the defect gap between American-made cars and Japanese-made cars has been cut substantially, but the average number of defects per car is still slightly higher in American-made cars (including those made in Japanese-owned plants) than in Japanese cars made in Japan. Americans have not completely cured their weaknesses.

What happened is that the times changed, and these different times demanded a set of characteristics that more closely matched America's strengths. With the onset of the third industrial revolution, the ability to rapidly open up the new and close down the old became the central characteristic needed for economic success. The American system was built to open up the new and close down the old. That is what it does best. America's weaknesses are still there. It does not focus well on grinding out marginal improvements in mature technologies where lots of patience, training, and capital are required. But that isn't what was required in the early phases of the third industrial revolution.

Intel, the world's dominant marketer of semiconductor chips today, is a good illustration of the American turnaround. In the mid-1980s it looked as if it might go out of business. Its designs were good, but it could not competitively manufacture DRAMs (dynamic random access memories)—its defect rates were too high. The future looked dismal. IBM sold its 20 percent stake in Intel—a stake that if still owned today would raise IBM's total market value by almost 30 percent. Layoffs and downsizings were necessary to survive.

But then Intel invented the microprocessor. A big technological breakthrough put it back in business. Intel never did recover its markets for DRAMs, but having learned from its previous mistakes, it became a world-class manufacturer of microprocessors as well as a superb design house that could consistently keep one jump ahead of the competition. Having a unique, rapidly changing product, it could charge high prices. By the time its designs had been copied by others and that generation of microprocessors had become a low-profit commodity operation, it had moved on to higher powered microprocessors.

At the end of the 1990s every Japanese personal computer had "Intel Inside" written on its outside. It was the Japanese, locked into a money-losing battle with the Koreans for dominance in what had become a commodity business—the production of DRAMs—who worried about bankruptcy.

America is very good at opening up the new. Its elite science and engineering educations emphasize creativity. They are not very interested in incremental improvements. Venture capital is plentiful. Young engineers and managers are constantly looking for opportunities to go into business for themselves. They have lots of role models around them. When they do go into business for themselves, their old employers wish them well and are glad to buy components and services from them. They are not treated as traitors. If they fail, and many do, existing employers are anxious to hire them back. Having tried to set up one's own business, even if one fails, is the mark of a good potential employee—works hard, creative, takes risks, knows how the world works. The risks of failure are much lower in America than they are in societies where those who leave are considered traitors, where a business failure is seen as a personal failure, and where reemployment at a good firm is difficult if not impossible if one has left to start up one's own business.

But even in the semiconductor business, America's genetic weaknesses are evident. There are two places in the industry where American firms are not even players because of these inherent weaknesses.

The production of the pure silicon wafers on which semiconductor chips are made is completely in the hands of Japanese and European firms. The last two American producers, Monsanto and Texas Instruments, both sold out to foreign firms in the 1990s. The production of ever purer silicon wafers is a mature technology where profits are thin, where investments are high, and where a lot of patience and labor force training are required to make wafers in ever more careful ways. It isn't an activity at which Americans excel.

World-class semiconductor manufacturing facilities cost billions of dollars. American firms are very good at designing new semiconductor chips, but if every American design firm had to have its own manufacturing facilities there would be very few American design firms, since few could afford the necessary investments in production facilities. What are called semiconductor foundries arose to fill the gap. Foundries build semiconductor chips to other people's designs. They do not design their own chips. All of the world's foundries are owned by Taiwanese or Singaporians. Billions of dollars are required to be in the foundry business, and only countries with very high savings rates could hope to raise the necessary funds. Americans couldn't raise and weren't willing to risk the huge amounts of money required to get up and running in this part of the semiconductor business.

Because the American system is highly decentralized, it is very difficult for the old to politically or economically stop the new from coming into existence. AT&T, despite its huge size and entrenched position, could not squelch new competitors in the telecommunications business. American laws, such as the antitrust laws, are on the side of the little guy. Judge Green in the AT&T antitrust case simply believed that big was bad, and nothing AT&T presented in the way of evidence was going to change his mind. New telephone companies were successfully coming into business in America decades before they could do so in the rest of the world.

But America's greatest strength is not its ability to open up the new. It is its ability to shut down the old. Downsizing is always painful, but in America it can be done. Nowhere in the world, even in underdeveloped countries, are workers easier to fire. Legally no notice must be given. No reasons must be offered. No severance pay is required. As a dean at MIT, I once fired someone and had them off the MIT premises in less than an hour.

While the times are playing to America's strengths to a great extent, America is up because the rest of the world is down. America's 2.7 percent growth rate during the 1990s is below the

3.2 percent rate of the 1970s. Looking only at bottom-line economic performance, America has in fact had a subpar performance in the 1990s. But the rest of the world did far worse.

Looking forward in the aftermath of German reunification in 1990, no one would have believed a prediction that the German Bundesbank would impose a decade of tight monetary policies and slow growth on Europe in a fight against an inflationary enemy that didn't exist. No one would have believed that Europeans would politically put up with double-digit unemployment rates and come to regard them as normal.

What the Germans did was completely unnecessary. Without a scorched-earth antiinflationary policy, America ended up with an inflationary performance better than that of Europe at the end of the decade. But those policies made European economies far smaller and weaker than they would otherwise have been.

Even less would anyone have believed in 1990 a prediction that Japan's growth rate would be just 0.4 percent per year in the 1990s and that Japan would be entering the second millennium with two consecutive years of negative growth, in 1998 and 1999.

Occasionally I am asked where I have been most wrong in earlier writings. In a 1991 book, *Head to Head,* about the coming economic battles among America, Europe, and Japan, I didn't even mention the 1990s stock market crash in Japan.[41] I assumed that the Japanese would easily and quickly clean up the mess, just as America cleaned up its saving and loan mess in the 1980s. I could not have been more wrong.

Japan and the Asian Meltdowns

In many ways Japan's economic decline in the 1990s is an even more vivid illustration than America's recovery that social systems that work well in some environments work horribly in others. In the aftermath of World War II the Japanese organized an

economic system that was demonstrably the world's best at promoting economic growth. But it could not deal with financial
meltdowns. The weaknesses that caused Japan's current problems
were always there, but they were irrelevant until the stock and
property markets crashed in 1990. Because of this weakness, its
strength–the ability to generate fast economic growth–disappeared. Suddenly the system that worked so well in the sixties,
seventies, and eighties wasn't working in the nineties.

Capitalism itself is no exception to the rule that all social systems
come with strengths and weaknesses. Since the first industrial revolution, no other economic system has been able to generate consistent economic growth. No system has ever been better at catering to
individual wants. Those are its great strengths. But capitalism also
comes with two major defects—recessions and financial meltdowns.
Both are permanently embedded in capitalism's genetic code.

Booms and recessions happen because investment depends upon
the rate of growth of consumption, and even slight changes in the
rate of growth of consumption can cause big upward or downward
movements in investment. Greed—the individual desire for more—is
what drives capitalism forward, but it is also what pushes asset prices
up to levels that cannot be sustained. Once these levels have been
reached, crashes are inevitable. The only question is when.

The names of the really big meltdowns ring down through history: tulip mania in Holland in the 1620s, the South Sea Bubble
in Britain and the Mississippi Scheme in France in the 1720s, and
the great crash of 1929 in America. Dozens of smaller unremembered crashes litter economic history.[42] We remember those that
lead to disasters such as the Great Depression of the 1930s.

Financial meltdowns are not caused by globalization. They
existed long before globalization was possible. They were also
contagious long before globalization arrived. From its initial
starting points in the collapse of the Credit Anstalt in Austria and
the 1929 American stock market crash, the Great Depression
spread to much of the world.

Past infections do not provide future immunity. Despite numerous crashes in the 1800s and the great crash of 1929, America in the 1970s and 1980s saw the bankruptcy of its largest city, the need for a government bailout of one of its largest corporations (Chrysler), the collapse of its entire savings and loan banking industry, a 25 percent decline in stock market values in three days in October 1987, and a sharp fall in property prices at the end of the decade. Meltdowns happen. Any capitalistic society that cannot cope with meltdowns is in trouble.

If Japan is to restore its economic performance, it will have to rebuild its social and economic system so that it can deal with financial meltdowns. Historically, the current problems are testing the Japanese social system's ability to change just as the Great Depression tested the American social system's ability to change. If the Japanese fail, historians will write about their social inflexibility.

When societies cannot cope with the realities of their environment, wealth disappears. The Japanese meltdown reduced what had been forty-one Japanese billionaires to nine in less than a decade. The same happened in the rest of Asia and elsewhere in the developing world. There are still billionaires in the developing world—twenty in Asia excluding Japan, fifteen in Latin America, fourteen in the Middle East, and two in Africa—but their numbers have been falling rapidly in the financial crises of the late 1990s. In 1994 there were twenty-four billionaires in Mexico alone.

Individual failure and corporate failure inevitably follow social failure. Wealthy individuals and high-value corporations won't reappear in Japan unless it can reorganize itself to cope with financial meltdowns. Before the crisis, seven of the ten biggest companies in the world were Japanese. Only two American companies and one European company were on the list. Eight years later, with the crisis not yet resolved, none of the world's ten largest companies were Japanese. Nine were American and one was European.[43] No Japanese company came close to being on the list in 1998. Only one Japanese company remains among the world's top twenty-five.[44]

RULE FOUR: Understanding, recognizing, and accepting the limits imposed by their genetic weaknesses is the beginning of wisdom for all organizations. The secret of success is finding places to employ one's resources where those weaknesses are irrelevant.

The decline in Japan's economic position wasn't caused entirely by its financial meltdown. Even if none of the seven Japanese corporations on the list of the world's ten largest in 1990 had seen their stock market values slide later in the decade, none of them would have come close to making the 1998 list. Japanese corporations were systematically missing the big opportunities of the third industrial revolution. But Japan cannot begin to deal with its creativity problem (with its lack of the ability to make big breakthroughs in technology) until it learns how to clean up the mess of a financial meltdown.

The real (inflation- and deflation-corrected) fall in Japan's stock market from 39,000 to 13,000 on the Nikkei Index in 1990 was actually bigger than the one that occurred between 1929 and 1932 in the United States. Japanese property prices promptly followed the stock market down with even larger declines (70 percent by 1998). Eight years later the stock market has yet to recover and property prices are still falling 5 percent per year.

The sharp declines in gross domestic product (GDP) seen in the Great Depression are impossible today. Deposit insurance prevents collapsing banks from depriving their depositors of their money. Government spending is a much larger fraction of GDP than it was in the 1920s, does not fall in the face of economic meltdowns, and serves as an economic flywheel. But as Japan demonstrates, an unwillingness to deal with the problems of a financial meltdown can lead to long periods of very limited

growth—what might be called in Japan's case the Great Stagnation.

Details differ, but in broad terms all of the speculative melt-downs over the last 370 years have had similar causes and similar cures. The good news is that the world has a lot of experience with picking up the pieces at the end of a speculative bubble. It knows precisely what must be done to restart economic activity. All of the possible options have been explored. What does not work is equally well known. Technically the cures are not hard to implement. Japan could easily return to its previous pattern of vigorous economic growth.

The bad news is that what must be done involves some painful economic restructuring. Debts must be written off and the losses allocated to someone. Companies and banks have to be closed down. Unprofitable divisions have to be sold. Managers and workers must lose their jobs. In the economic cleanup after a financial collapse, it must rain on the just and the unjust alike.

What must be done is much like pulling a thornbush from the ground with your bare hands. The bush must be grabbed ruthlessly and pulled quickly with great strength. There will be an initial jolt of pain but it will quickly pass. Given a strong grip, the bush can easily be pulled from the ground to clear the area for more productive plants. After pulling the bush from the ground, you wipe the blood from your hands and move on to other activities. The wounds from the thorns are not deep and quickly heal.

The gardener who tries to grab a thornbush timidly, however, won't have a grip strong enough to pull it from the earth. Each attempt to grab it will lead to more wounds, and the wounds won't get a chance to heal. The pain will go on forever. The ground will never be cleared for a new burst of productive growth. The unproductive thornbush will just grow bigger, stronger, and harder to remove the longer the period of timidity lasts.

The great crash of 1929 became the Great Depression of the 193 because a timid President Hoover was unable to come to grips w

the situation. Early in 1930 everyone thought the worst was over because the stock market had recovered much of what it had lost in October of 1929. But then in March of 1930 the banks started to go broke and the Hoover administration did nothing to stop the banking crash from accelerating. Without quick, effective restructuring, the banking problems simply grew worse and worse. After almost three years of inaction the banking system was in its death throes at the end of 1932. In the process the Hoover administration lost all of its credibility and all of its ability to solve the problems.

The sequence of events in a meltdown is well known. Some assets rise in value to levels far above economic sustainability. At the peak of tulip mania, one black tulip bulb bought one of those nice five-story row houses that line the canals in Amsterdam. The price was crazy and everyone knew it, but prices were just as crazy when six tulip bulbs bought one house, and those who got out of the tulip market when it was six to one missed a chance to multiply their wealth by a factor of six. Short-run opportunities to make a lot of money overwhelm well-known long-run economic realities.

All investors (no one thinks of himself or herself as a speculator) imagine that they will be able to see the end coming and get out in time—but few do. In the South Sea Bubble in Great Britain, Sir Isaac Newton, one of the smartest men ever, was one of those who thought he could get out before the end. He couldn't and he ended up losing a lot of money. Great intelligence is no protection against greed.

It is impossible for governments to stop prices from rising to unsustainable levels. Once such prices exist, it is equally impossible for governments to stop them from falling. All governments can do is stand by waiting to do damage control after such events have run their course.

As asset prices fall, adequate collateral becomes inadequate collateral. What had been good loans become bad loans. Inadequately collateralized loans are called. Short of liquidity and fearful of defaults, banks don't renew short-term loans that normally would

be automatically rolled over. Credit markets freeze up. Suppliers, fearful of not being paid, demand cash before delivery rather than being willing to wait the normal ninety days for payment. (Within hours of the news of the Korean crisis, boats loaded with raw materials bound for Korea were halted off the coast waiting for payments to clear before unloading.) Even financially sound firms find that they cannot pay their bills since they are suddenly asked to make unexpected loan repayments and prepay suppliers. Business firms that cannot finance themselves go broke. Their customers don't get the supplies they need.

Worried about preserving their wealth, everyone wants to sell their local currency and buy currencies not expected to depreciate. Naval officers are taught that the brave go down with the ship. No one has ever heard a capitalist investor say that he wants to go down with the ship. Capitalists are by nature cowards and jump off the ship whenever they fear their wealth is in jeopardy. That instinct is built into the genes of the capitalist beast. They were bred to protect their capital. The stability of the system is someone else's worry.

Global speculators run in panic—much like a herd of antelope. Sometimes the antelope run because they see lions in the grass. Sometimes they run because they see other antelope running. Sometimes they run because they see the grass moving in the wind and imagine lions where there are none. But if you are an antelope or a global financier, it is always safer to run than to wait to see if the dangers are real. The last to run is always the most likely to be eaten or to lose money. If there are no lions, one can always return to graze on the green grass that still exists.

Vast amounts of money leave the country, and the central bank eventually runs out of foreign exchange reserves. With the local central bank out of international reserves, even companies with enough local funds to repay their international loans cannot get the necessary foreign currencies to repay their loans. The local currency plunges in value. With currency values down, the local income that must be earned to repay foreign currency loans sky-rockets.

In the process a financial crisis becomes a business crisis and then a national crisis.

The problem before the meltdown is not in knowing that unsustainable prices will eventually fall but in predicting the timing and speed of the downturn. Economic models are very good on fundamental forces and pressures, but they are horrible on timing. They in fact say nothing about timing. In this sense economics is much like geology. Geologists have a very good general understanding of the plate tectonics that underlie the San Andreas Fault in California. They know with absolute certainty that there will be a big earthquake in California. But they don't know whether it will be one second or a thousand years from now. All geologists can do is chart the faults and understand the probabilities. Humans go ahead and build houses right on the San Andreas Fault, sure that it won't happen in their lifetime.

The big economic fault lines on the Pacific Rim have long been well known.

In the long run, land values have to reflect the underlying earning capacities—the rents that can be collected from the economic activities carried out on them. When the property value of the Emperor's Palace in central Tokyo exceeds the total value of the state of California, as it did, something is fundamentally wrong. That is the equivalent of tulip mania, and everyone knows it—or should know it. The GDP of California cannot be produced on a land area the size of the Emperor's Palace.

It is a basic axiom of economics taught in every introductory class on international trade that no country can forever run a large trade deficit where its foreign indebtedness grows faster than its GDP. Foreign currencies have to be borrowed to finance trade deficits and to pay interest on previous years' loans. Eventually the sums get too big to be repaid. At some point the size of the already existing outstanding loans causes lenders to conclude that more loans are too risky (repayment is unlikely) and credit markets shut down.

The Asian countries melting down in 1997 all had large trade deficits—$8 billion in Indonesia, $4 billion in Malaysia, $10 billion in Thailand, $4 billion in the Philippines, and $19 billion in Korea. Ten years earlier those same countries all had substantial trade surpluses. Their swing from surplus to deficit is directly traceable to mainland China's decision to play the export-led growth game. Since it offered better educated but cheaper workers than Southeast Asia along with a much bigger internal market, it pulled export activities away from other Asian countries and quickly gained a $50 billion trade surplus. To get out of China's way economically, these countries needed to go upscale in technology very rapidly, but they were not well educated enough to do so.

The Koreans are much better educated than the Chinese, so Korea properly moved its low-wage export manufacturing facilities to China but then found that it could not replace those exports with high-wage manufacturing exports because of Japanese competition. As has so often happened in its history, Korea was once again squeezed between its two huge neighbors.

In capitalism, stock market prices sooner or later have to be justified by earnings. In Japan they weren't. Price/earnings (P/E) multiples exceeded 100. Not surprisingly, stock prices eventually fell. Many argued in 1998 that there was a bubble on Wall Street, yet even at 13,000 on the Nikkei the P/E multiples in Japan exceeded those on Wall Street. The profits just weren't there to justify these low share prices, much less a market at 39,000.

The Japanese argued that market share, not profits, was the name of their game. Market share maximization works as long as stock market values are rising. Investors cannot expect dividends since there are few profits, but they can get wealthy on rising stock market values. But what happens if the stock market goes down and stays down? Why should any potential investor now invest? The Japanese didn't have an answer to this question since they thought they would never have to answer it.

Projects were being built that everyone knew would lose money. The two tallest buildings in the world were built in Kuala Lumpur despite the fact that such buildings are known to be uneconomic. The Sears Tower in Chicago was sold at half its replacement cost in 1997, and in 1998 the World Trade Center in New York was sold for even less relative to replacement costs. Too much space goes into elevators and other support activities when buildings rise to these heights, and no transportation system can economically get so many people (120,000 in the case of New York's World Trade Center buildings) to one location at nine o'clock in the morning. But after a string of boom years, megalomania sets in and ordinary economic rules that apply to others do not apply to you. The Japanese built and bought real estate projects that were less spectacular but no less uneconomic than those of the Malaysians.

Crashes are never triggered by outside speculators who see internal weaknesses and attack. The first investors out the door are always the local investors who have the best information. Indonesian industrialists get their money out of Indonesia first, since their contacts tell them that the Indonesian central bank is about to run out of foreign currency. Property developers in Manila are the first to know that the new buildings are not being successfully rented. The Korean industrialist with a cousin working at the central bank is the first to know that the statistics published by the central bank about the size of its reserves are false. The Thai banker is the first to know about the phony bookkeeping in the companies to which his bank has been lending money. Knowing what is happening, they all run for the exits financially.

Outsiders are always the last to know. By the time international speculators join the flight, the panic is well under way. But those international speculators are like piranha in the Amazon. When they smell blood in the water they attack, and they can move very large sums of money—sums so large that they dwarf the reserves of even the biggest of countries. World currency markets move between $1,500 billion and $2,000 billion per day, and Japan, the country with the most reserves, has only $200 billion. In an hour of concerted attack, the world's capital markets could bankrupt Japan.

The western financial press talks as if these events would not have occurred if Asia's financial markets had been more open—more like America's. The Asian financial press talks as if these events would not have occurred if their markets had been more controlled by government—more Asian style. Both are wrong. If American-style financial markets prevented meltdowns, American history would not be littered with meltdowns. Mexico managed to melt down in 1982 when its banking system was completely owned and controlled by the government. It also managed to melt down in the winter of 1994–95 when it had completely privatized its banking system and was operating with wide-open American-style financial markets. Liberalization of financial markets is generally a good thing, but it is not an insurance policy against meltdowns.

Fiscal soundness is also not an antidote. The governments of Asia were all running budget surpluses—Korea had a large one. Mexico melted down in 1982 when its government was running large budget deficits, but it also melted down in 1994–95 when its government was running a budget surplus.

The longer it takes to clean up the mess after a financial meltdown, the worse the problems become. After eight years of minimal growth in Japan, what have been low-profit firms are becoming money-losing firms. In the fall of 1998 even world-class firms like Toshiba and Hitachi were reporting losses. Only 27 percent of Japan's small and medium-sized companies were in the black.[45] Banks find that their outstanding portfolio of nonperforming loans is growing and stop lending. The Japanese government pushed interest rates down to 0.15 percent in 1998, but few companies could get loans or even roll over their old loans. Japanese consumers cannot afford to buy cars, and Japanese auto sales fell more than 50 percent because eighteen million families are paying off mortgages on homes that are worth less than the value of their outstanding mortgages. Since the Japanese can't give the keys to their house back to the bank and walk away from their debts, as Americans do, these families face a lifetime of debt repayment with nothing of equivalent value awaiting them at the end of it.

A vicious downward spiral emerges. Profits aren't going to recover without growth. Growth can't recover with everyone drowning in bad debts. With no mechanism for eliminating debt, retrenchment is the only option. Everyone sits waiting for effective social action.

Is the Japanese government the modern equivalent of Herbert Hoover, or can it act?

The Rest of the World

The answer to this question is relevant not just to the Japanese. If Japan cannot act, it can bring others in the global economy down with it. The richest country in Asia should be orchestrating rescues for its neighbors. Instead it needs its own internal rescue. Weaknesses reverberate to become even bigger weaknesses. At the December 1997 Asian summit, Japan tells its neighbors not to count on Japan as a market for their products. Without those Japanese markets, more firms go broke in Korea and Southeast Asia, and the Japanese banks that were bankrupt based on their loans to Japanese firms are even more bankrupt based on their loans to Korea and Southeast Asia.

Russia has also melted down. But if it were not for Russia's thousands of nuclear weapons, no one would even be taking its economic problems seriously. It's a very small economy (smaller than Brazil, smaller than Indonesia) with even smaller linkages to the rest of the world. In one week in August 1998, the Japanese stock market lost more market value than the Russian economy produces in a year. Western banks may have $30 billion at risk in Russia, but this is a very small sum by the standards of global capital markets.

Russia is important only because if its economy completely collapses there are Russians who will try to recoup their personal positions by selling nuclear weapons and their delivery systems to the highest bidders. That is a major political problem, not an economic one. The answer is for the CIA to buy the missiles and nuclear weapons as they come up for sale on the black market. America has a lot more money than either Iraq or Iran and can simply pay higher prices. In the end, doing so will be cheaper than giving Russia money, when the Russians have publicly admitted that Western aid disappears into bank accounts in Switzerland with no payoff in terms of helping Russia or ordinary Russians.

But this is the past. These countries have already melted down. Looking forward, the big worry is China. It is the key to whether the Asian meltdown will become a general third world meltdown.

China has an important effect on the global spiral since it is everyone else's competition in the third world. If China melted down and devalued its currency, everyone in the third world would be forced to follow it down with lower currency values of their own. As a result the world anxiously watches China's growth rate to see if it too will slide into a recession.

China reports that its 1998 growth rate fell as a result of Asia's problems but only to 8 percent, which is a very healthy growth rate—and if that were true, there would be no worries about China joining the meltdown. But these official numbers cannot be correct. Economies do not grow at 8 percent if their electricity production is rising only by 2.6 percent.[46] Hong Kong is the economic capital of southern China, and it reported a 5 percent negative growth rate for 1998. If China were growing at 8 percent, Hong Kong could not be declining at a 5 percent rate. In addition, the GITIC, the largest investment bank in southern China, collapsed in 1998 with debts that were twice its assets.[47] In early 1999 a large investment bank in the north of China did the same. Investment banks do not collapse in 8 percent growth environments. Bottom line, China's real growth rate is substantially less than the reported 8 percent. At the end of the year, China's prime minister as much as admitted this reality when he accused local officials of reporting overly optimistic data.

But whatever China's real growth rate, positive or negative, China is not the key determinant of whether the Asian meltdown will become a global meltdown. China and the third world are not the locomotives that keep the world economy moving. Those locomotives are found in the first world.

In a global world economy, the inability of one part of the world to cope with its problems can create problems for the rest of the world. The threat starts with Japan, but it is important to understand the exact nature of the threat.

Neither Europe nor North America is dependent upon Asian demands to keep their economies going. Each exports only about 2.5 percent of their GDP to Asia. An Asian collapse that cut those exports in half would make very little difference to the world's two biggest economies. Many U.S. plants in Asia are also offshore manufacturing sites with their major markets back in the United States. Firms export U.S.-made components to their Asian assembly plants, which then export completed products back to America for final sale. These component exports to Asia will not go down. Such firms will end up making money out of the Asian crisis because of their much lower costs of production in Asia.

The threat to the world economy does not come from stock market contagion and falling share prices either. Both Europe and America know how to contain stock market collapses. They did so successfully in October 1987 when the U.S. stock market lost 25 percent of its value in three days.

The problems start from Asian and Japanese strategies that call for exporting their way out of their current problems. To do this, they will have to lower prices and increase their market shares in America or Europe. As a result, there will be big negative effects on those European or American industries that compete with Asian or Japanese exporters. Selling prices, profits, and output will fall.

The shape of what is about to happen is already visible in American industries such as steel. Selling prices are down 25 percent since the onset of the Asian meltdown.[48] In the twelve months of 1998, steel imports into the United States surged (Korea up 56 percent, Australia up 98 percent, Japan up 219 percent, and China up 245 percent) and American production fell 25 percent.[49] Similar surges are expected in many other industries.

What sounds sensible (export more) when heard separately in each country becomes nonsense when aggregated around the world. The Asian countries that melted down in 1997 need to bring their earlier trade deficits to an end and have some funds to repay their outstanding loans. They need at least another $75 billion in net exports to do so. Brazil needs and plans on $15 billion in net exports. Argentina and Mexico each want another $10 to $15 billion. The list goes on and on. Russia and all the countries of middle Europe need more exports to get back on their feet and to repay loans. Japan cannot officially admit that it is planning to use exports as a vehicle for recovery, but implicitly the Japanese government is counting on at least another $100 billion in net exports to jump-start its economy. Add up the net exports that governments of the world are counting on to get themselves out of their current crises and the total exceeds $250 billion.

But no one can have more net exports unless someone else has more net imports. If we are talking about $250 billion in net exports, there are only three places to look for sums that large— Japan, Europe, and America. Japan needs its own increase in exports and has already told the other countries of Asia that they should not look to it as an export market. Europe has come to look and sound much like Japan. It has never been a big market for manufactured products from the developing world, but it is now also dependent upon a $120 billion trade surplus (mostly with the United States) for its own prosperity. With the Russian crisis in Eastern Europe threatening to spread to middle Europe, all of its limited willingness to tolerate higher imports and lower domestic demand is going to go to its Eastern European neighbors. That leaves the United States as the focal point for all of the world's planned exports. It is in effect everyone's first, last, and only export market.

These plans would become impossible if the United States were to have a major slowdown or a recession. Exports to America, far from rising, would fall. Negative effects would reverberate back and forth around the globe and in the process get stronger, much like a hurricane picking up strength as it whirls across the water. But even without a recession there are major problems with such a strategy.

1: As imports roll into the United States, they force domestic prices down. As selling prices fall, American corporate profits vanish. The aggregate demand effects of more imports could be overcome with easier monetary and fiscal policies to maintain employment, but the price effects cannot be contained. With prices down and profits disappearing, stock markets inevitably fall. Feeling and being less wealthy and starting with negative savings rates, Americans cut back on their consumption purchases and the economy enters a recession. Instead of rising, American imports fall.

2: The United States was already running an annual current account deficit of $160 billion before the 1997 Asian meltdown began. Add another $250 billion to that sum and the deficit has to get scary to international investors who do not want to lose money on their American investments. Moving money out of dollars has to look attractive as they watch those growing trade deficits. A Mexican-style run on the dollar becomes possible.

3:    While it is an axiom of international economics that no country can forever run a large trade deficit that must be financed with international borrowing, this axiom has not applied to the United States because it has provided the world's reserve currency. It borrowed what must be borrowed in loans denominated in its own currency. Since it can print dollars, there were no default risks. Lenders may get dollars back that are worth less, but they will be repaid no matter what happens. In financial terms, America wasn't really an international borrower since it did not have debts denominated in other countries' currencies.

American exceptionalism came to an end on January 1, 1999, when the EURO came into existence. For the first time since World War II there is now a good place to go if one wants to get out of dollars. Formerly each European currency was too small and Japanese financial markets were too regulated for either to be real competition for the dollar. But that all changed with the advent of the EURO. The dollar now has to compete with the EURO for the role of the world's reserve currency.

Consider the choices for those looking for the best place to hold their international reserves. Remember that they are not looking for good investment opportunities—only for safety. One of the possibilities, the American bank, runs a trade deficit expected to approach $350 billion in late 1999. It is a net debtor, with foreigners owning $1,500 billion more assets in America than Americans own in the rest of the world. The other possibility, the European bank, runs a $120 billion plus trade surplus with the rest of the world and is a net creditor with the rest of the world. In which bank would you rather hold your money?

To ask the question is to answer it. Lots of the world is going to want to get out of dollars. European countries and companies with ten less intra-European currency transactions to make will need a lot less reserves for transaction purposes. These transaction reserves are now held in dollars. Countries like Saudi Arabia, which buy a lot from Europe and sell a lot of their oil in Europe, will sensibly want to hold part of their reserves and price part of their oil in EUROs. Simple risk avoidance and hedging call for a shift away from dollars. Four days after trading in the EURO started, Egypt announced that it would convert a major part of its reserves from dollars to EUROs.[50] Japanese insurance companies similarly announced that they were planning to gradually shift 20 percent of their assets from dollars to EURO investments.[51]

So just when the world is expecting the United States to run truly large trade deficits, the United States is about to lose much of its ability to run trade deficits.

4:   If America is to accept what the rest of the world needs to export, it must be willing to accept the displacement of a lot of its workforce from their current jobs. Every $50 billion increase in the trade deficit means that about one million American workers lose their jobs. They may find work elsewhere, but import-competing industries such as autos or steel are high-wage industries, and the jobs the laid-off workers will find in the service sector pay substantially lower wages. A surge in exports of anything like what is to be expected is going to generate enormous political pressures to restrict imports in America.

As the trade deficit rises to higher and higher levels, what happens first? Americans revolt politically at their loss of good jobs. Foreigners panic and flee from the dollar. No one knows where the breaking points are, but both of these breaking points exist.

Maybe the export-to-America strategy for keeping the world economy moving will work. But maybe it won't. What happens if it doesn't?

The biggest threat to world prosperity comes not from a slow-down in the United States but from deflation. Once started, systematic deflation almost guarantees negative GDP growth. In the last century, no country has been able to combine deflation with growth. That same historical record also tells us that deflation is extremely difficult to stop once started.

While general price declines have not been seen since the 1930s, the smell of deflation is in the air. In Japan, producer's price indexes have been negative for some time—falling between 2 and 4 percent per year in the last two years. Globally, energy and raw material prices have taken particularly sharp drops. Selling prices are falling dramatically in some industries such as microelectronics.

In the United States, measured inflation rates are still slightly positive, although America's major price indexes (the Producer's Price Index, the Consumer's Price Index, and the GDP Deflator) have had months and even sequences of months when prices were falling. But these indexes are known to exaggerate inflation and underestimate deflation. A national commission (the Boskin Commission) reported that a general underestimation of quality improvements leads America's price indexes to exaggerate inflation by 1 to 3 percentage points. Federal Reserve Board Chairman Alan Greenspan agreed.

But if one wants to understand what is happening in the normal business world, it is also necessary to remove the costs of health care from the indexes. Health care disguises what is happening to the prices facing normal business firms. In the health care sector, expensive new treatments raise costs and prices. In most cases no adjustments are made in our price indexes for the quality improvements in health care that these new treatments bring. But even if these quality improvements were not occurring, health care is just a very nonrepresentative, disconnected, separate part of the economy. Health care could be suffering from inflation while the rest of the economy was suffering from deflation. Subtracting health care inflation from the normal price indexes reduces them by another 1 to 2 percentage points.

If these two corrections were made, American inflation indexes would show annual price declines for the last few years. New technologies are partly responsible for falling prices, but a wide variety of other factors are also at work.

Globalization is forcing prices down. Production is being moved from high-cost locations to low-cost locations, and as a result, prices are falling. Name any product, add up the amounts the world could produce if all the world's factories were operating at capacity, subtract what the world is going to buy, and one finds that the world's production potential exceeds the world's expected consumption by at least one-third—often by far more. Autos, semiconductor chips, and oil are but three examples. With such an excess of production capacity, falling prices are no mystery. Firms have an enormous incentive to lower prices in an attempt to keep their facilities operating closer to capacity.

Globalization also allows pressures to be brought to bear to change work practices, raise productivity, and lower wages. BMW used its ability to set up a car manufacturing plant in the United States as leverage with its unions to change work practices in Germany.[52] Flexible shifts were introduced so that the plants could be worked on weekends and intensively when sales demand was high. This allowed capital costs to be cut by one-quarter. Workers essentially have a bank account where their hours of work on weekends or at the end of a normal shift can be deposited. When sales demand is low, BMW can lay off workers without pay and workers draw on the accumulated hours of work in their bank accounts. Overtime is not paid unless it is clear that total hours of work will exceed those of the standard working year. The company is now spreading these practices to its U.K. Rover plants. The British workers have been told that they must cut the 30 percent productivity gap between themselves and the Germans. BMW does not have to say explicitly that if they don't, production will be moved elsewhere. Everyone knows that. When costs did not come down fast enough at Rover, the German CEO of BMW was fired. But if costs can be forced down, prices must eventually start to fall.

The Asian meltdown substantially increases these downward price pressures. Countries in the meltdown such as Indonesia and

Thailand have to export more and can do so only by lowering prices. If their global competitors, mostly in the third world, do not want to lose market share, they have no choice but to match the price declines. In the developed world, similar competitive downward price pressures come from Korea and Japan.

Downsizing and outsourcing have also played a role in reducing prices. It is common practice in America for companies to sign contracts with their suppliers that require annual price reductions. Auto parts manufacturers, for example, have signed contracts with the major auto producers calling for 3 percent annual price reductions. Outsourcing plays a big role in these tough contracts, since it is easier to get tough on prices with an outside supplier than it is with an inside supplier. If an outside supplier doesn't make any money with the new lower prices, that's his problem. But if an inside supplier doesn't make any money, what the corporation gains in one of its buying divisions it loses in one of its selling divisions and there is no gain in aggregate profits. Such practices led to new car prices falling in the United States in 1998 for the first time since the Great Depression.

Manufacturing, mining, and construction can easily hold prices down because they have huge reserves of low-cost labor. Many of the laborers now working in the service sector would be delighted to quit their low-wage jobs and move into higher paying jobs in these sectors. As a result, even record low unemployment rates have not led to wage increases and inflation as they did in the past.

Unemployment rates have become misleading indicators of labor market tightness and pressures to increase wages. In 1994 the U.S. unemployment rate hit 6 percent, and many economists, including those at the Federal Reserve Board, said inflation would reemerge. It did not happen. There were simply a lot more potential workers waiting to be employed than the statistics indicated. From 1994 through the end of 1998, two million people left the unemployment rolls, but employment grew by nine million. This happened because seven million new workers entered the labor force despite the fact that the U.S. adult population was in a period of very slow growth. Some of these potential workers were immigrants (legal and illegal) and some were native-born Americans who did not meet the Labor Department's tests for being unemployed, but they were all in fact anxious to take jobs when jobs could be found. What was measured officially as a 6 percent unemployment rate in 1994 would in reality have been closer to 11 percent if all those who were actually willing to take jobs had been counted.[53] A hidden reserve army of the unemployed was holding wages and prices down.

Systematic deflation is not a certainty, but it is now likely enough to make it worth thinking about how standard economic operating procedures change when selling prices start to fall. In a deflationary world, debt is to be avoided at all costs because debts have to be repaid in dollars of greater value than were originally borrowed. Those who have debts want to repay them as quickly as possible, since debt burdens automatically grow larger in real terms as time passes. If prices fall 10 percent, a $100 debt effectively becomes a $110 debt. But if debt reduction is the number one priority, no one is investing in the things that cause growth.

Since money interest rates cannot go below zero, real interest rates are very high in deflationary periods. If prices are falling 10 percent, a 1 percent rate of interest becomes an 11 percent real rate of interest.

Since the value of money is going up while the value of other assets is going down, holding cash (doing nothing) becomes the smartest investment anyone can make. A dollar held today buys more tomorrow. One does not rush out to buy, because whatever one wants will be cheaper next year. Whenever possible, one postpones purchases. But if everyone is postponing, growth does not occur.

In a deflationary world, business firms cannot afford to hold inventory. Anything built now and sold in the future will have to be sold for less than it can be sold for today. The Dell Computer build-to-order-only-after-the-computer-has-been-paid-for model of business becomes the only profitable business model. In a world of systematic deflation, the auto companies, for example, will have to get rid of their normal 120 selling days' worth of inventories if they want to remain profitable. Selling prices four months in the future will be essentially lower than today's production costs, and losses will accrue because of the delay between production and sales.

Since getting costs down is the name of the game in a deflationary world, firms have no choice but to lower the wages of their employees. If they don't, the real wages of their employees effectively rise (prices are falling) and they price themselves out of their markets. The winners are those who can push wages down faster than the rate of deflation. But the harder they push wages down, the faster prices fall.

Governments find that tax revenues fall, since incomes and profits are down. While their costs of buying goods and services are also down, other obligations, such as monthly Social Security checks to the elderly and their employees' wages, are politically difficult to reduce. This leads governments to cut spending on the goods and services they buy from the private economy to avoid having to make more politically painful cuts.

Individuals postpone their purchases and repay debts. Businesses cut their inventories and repay debts. Governments cut purchases and repay debts. Deflation and economic growth simply do not go together in modern economies. In the Great Depression of the 1930s, a vicious cycle emerged as falling prices led to falling GDPs and a falling GDP led to falling prices.

Stopping deflation is not easy. In the 1930s a wide variety of actions were tried (minimum selling prices, government price supports), and all failed. As with many diseases, the right policy is prevention. There are no easy cures once the disease has been contracted.

RULE FIVE: Humans have discovered how to operate successful capitalist economies in the midst of modest

inflation, but not how to operate them in the midst of even mild deflation. Given a choice between the same rate of inflation or deflation, take the inflation every time.

Prevention brings us back to Japan. Because of its economic size, Japan is the key. If Japan cannot restart its economy reasonably rapidly, deflation is a real danger, not a low probability event. Our economic systems have become interdependent. In 1964 a friend and I wrote the chapter of the "Economic Report of the President" forecasting 1965's economic performance. We did not mention the rest of the world. It did not matter. In 1999 that same chapter does little but talk about events in the rest of the world. The failure to make necessary changes in one part of the world can destroy economic success in other parts of the world. The economic policy keys to a successful American economy at the beginning of the second millennium are to be found in Japan—not in America.

Conclusion

Whereas once nations needed the ability to organize themselves to be successful, it is now the world that has to organize itself to allow nations to be successful. But it cannot. No one has been given the powers to do the job. Instead the world will sit waiting, watching what Japan does, dependent upon what Japan does, unable to affect what Japan does. Later in this book we will look at what Japan has to do to restart economic growth, but in the end it is only the Japanese who can organize themselves to do what must be done. If they fail, others will fail with them.

Detailed criticisms can be made of the policies of the International Monetary Fund, but at best it is a sideshow to the real problems.[54] The key to global problems is in Japan, and the IMF has no leverage in Japan since Japan does not need IMF loans. The IMF is not even being asked for its recommendations on Japan. It is out of the decision-making loop.

Outside of Japan, the IMF's ability to affect events is limited at best. It has to deal indirectly through national governments, and when they are ineffective, as they are in Russia and Indonesia, its solutions remain unimplemented regardless of whether they are right or wrong. The IMF is run by smart individuals who understand international economics. It can and has made mistakes, but when the IMF systematically fails to stem a widespread decline, as it has in Asia, it is because it is being asked to a job that it does not have the tools to do.

Operating indirectly through national governments the IMF can only fail. It might succeed if it could deal directly with the banks and industrial firms in the countries that have melted down, but that is a power neither the developed nor the underdeveloped world is about to let it have.

5.   Entrepreneurial Skills

Seemingly polar opposites but in fact closely linked, entrepreneurs and social organization go together to form the base of the pyramid. Change requires individuals who recognize that new things can be done and who take the initiative to get them done. Entrepreneurs are needed to see the economic possibilities of new technologies, such as Internet retailing, and break the old barriers that will attempt to prevent them from happening. The existing bureaucracies, public and private, will not take on the job of changing what is. In fact, the existing bureaucracies are often what needs to be changed. They have too much of a vested interest in what is to allow change to happen.

Today in some European countries—Germany and France in particular—fears are voiced about biotechnology and restrictions are imposed on the invention and use of new biotech products that sound an awful lot like the fears and restrictions imposed in China five hundred years ago when it closed its doors to outside influences. Genetically modified foods cannot be imported and should not be eaten. Research on genetically modifying plants, animals, and human beings shouldn't be done and, if done, has to be done with "safety" restrictions so onerous that economically they are almost equivalent to saying that research cannot be done.

The attitudes have much in common: "We cannot learn about that, it's too dangerous." "We cannot use that, there are too many unknowns." Both imagine monsters if they step outside their traditional modes of behavior. The old (crossbreeding plants to change genetic structures) is OK; the new (inserting genes to change genetic structures) is not.

Societies dominated by the fearful are never wealthy societies. Wealthy societies allow individuals with explorer mentalities to flourish. No one ever knows what is possible or whether monsters really exist unless they are willing to take risks, venture out, and explore. Occasionally the doubters and the fearful are right, but most often they are wrong.

Individual enterprise does not occur evenly across time or space. Some times and societies have it. Others do not. Societies have to be organized, or reorganized, so that entrepreneurship can flourish.

Capitalism is a process of creative destruction. The new destroys the old. Both the creation and the destruction are essential to driving the economy forward. Television throws the movie industry into a big economic decline until it is revived by the invention of the VCR. Entrepreneurs are central to the process of creative destruction, since they are the individuals who bring the new technologies and the new concepts into active commercial use. They are the change agents of capitalism.

Old patterns of powerful vested interests must be broken if the new is to exist, but those with vested interests in the old system fight back. They do not willingly and quietly fade into the pages of history. Entrepreneurs built the national companies that destroyed local companies at the end of the nineteenth century and they are building the global companies that are destroying national companies at the end of the twentieth century.

Very occasionally entrepreneurs are the inventors of the new technologies that make change possible—but not often. Edwin Land of Polaroid and Walt Disney of Disney were two great exceptions, but they are exceptions. Entrepreneurs are risk takers, organizers, and doers, not usually thinkers and inventors. The characteristics needed to create new knowledge are very different from the characteristics necessary to bring that knowledge into active use. J. P. Morgan built his companies around Thomas Edison's many inventions. Bill Gates has invented no new technologies and was never a creative software programmer. He is, however, an entrepreneur and a builder.

History teaches us that it is only too easy to stamp out entrepreneurship. It is a latent human characteristic that despite its creative and destructive powers is extremely fragile. In most times and most places, entrepreneurs do not exist. The same economic possibilities exist, but they are not seen, the energy to bring them to market is lacking, or the risks they involve are seen as too great to be accepted.

When societies aren't organized so that the old vested interests can be brushed aside, entrepreneurs cannot emerge. They are much like hibernating bears in the middle of winter—perhaps they are there, but no one knows where they are until the snow melts and spring rolls around. Social systems have to be built that give entrepreneurs room to destroy the old. Yet destroying the old is all too easily seen as leading to chaos. Societies aren't ready to break with the past. Therefore they aren't willing to let entrepreneurs come into existence and destroy the past.

Successful societies are willing to take the risks of destroying what they have to make themselves into something different, bigger, and stronger in the future. The new does not adapt to them. They adopt the new and then adapt to it. Societies won't have entrepreneurs unless they themselves are willing to change.

The changes that must be accepted are seldom limited to the economic sphere. Today there are worldwide worries that the Internet will change local cultures and traditional patterns of behavior. It isn't guaranteed that something better will emerge. It will be different. But those used to the old patterns of behavior are unlikely to see the new patterns as better, even if new generations used to the new patterns of behavior see them as an improvement.

Sociology almost always dominates technology. Ideas often lie unused because people do not want to use them. The fact that something is possible does not mean that it will happen. Time lags are long and great persistence is needed to bring a truly new idea into the market. Steam toys have been unearthed in the archaeological exploration of ancient Greece, and the ancient Egyptians had steam-powered temple doors, yet the steam engine did not emerge as a source of power for economic production until the eighteenth century.[55] The right sociology had to be in place for revolutionary new products to emerge.

Europe

Europe provides a good example of the importance of entrepreneurship. Europe saves and invests a lot, it is well educated, and it has a strong technological base. But nowhere is it a leader in creating the new man-made brainpower industries of the twenty-first century. In 1998 the production arm of its last indigenous computer manufacturer, Siemens Nixdorf, was sold to Acer of Taiwan. How can a region be a leader in the twenty-first century and be completely out of the computer business? The entrepreneurs that should exist aren't there.

Consider Europe as a man from outer space might see it. It is an area roughly equivalent to China in size (about 10 percent bigger). Its population is somewhat smaller—from 850 to 900 million depending upon whether all or only part of the Turkish population is allocated to Europe—but not a lot smaller. If one were playing global economic chess and given the choice of any contiguous piece of the globe with approximately a billion people, everyone would choose to play with the European position. It has a far stronger position on the global economic chessboard than any equivalently sized group of people in the world.

Nowhere on earth are there almost a billion contiguous people who are as rich. No one even comes close. Nowhere on earth are there a billion people better educated or better skilled. No one even comes close. Nowhere on earth are there a billion people with better infrastructure. No one even comes close.

Europe is composed of peoples with great track records of achievement. European science and engineering are world-class. There are areas where Europe dominates in the creation of new knowledge (high-energy physics) and there are no major technologies that it has not mastered. Russia has demonstrated its ability to compete with the United States in space, military technologies, and high science (physics and math). Despite wages and fringe benefits 50 percent above those of the United States, Germany has a large export surplus. London dominates in the trading of international currencies. Italy and France have a flare for fashion and design unmatched in the world. No one is better at starting good small companies than the Italians. French engineering is among the world's best. Eastern Europe offers workers with Western educational skills at wage levels found only among unskilled workers in underdeveloped countries elsewhere.

A skill-intensive technological shift is under way. Sustainable long-run competitive advantage can be had only through an advantage in skills, education, and knowledge. Yet this is precisely where Europe has its greatest comparative advantage. If ratings were given for top to bottom skills, Europe would get the best ratings. It is more creative at the top than Japan and better educated at the bottom than America. Relative to any comparably sized group in the rest of the world it is the best educated. Europe is a continent rich in human capital. Why, then, is it a laggard when it comes to the creation of wealth?

No one should be better at playing the new global game than Europe. Only Europe has a more-than-forty-year history of moving toward economic integration. The European Common Market widens as new countries are added and deepens as it harmonizes its rules and regulations. It has learned how to work across national, linguistic, and cultural lines. Europe has a momentum on its side that no other part of the world can match. A major step forward was just taken with the introduction of the EURO It is much harder to jump from a national to a global economy, as the rest of the world is trying to do, than to make a two-stage jump, first to a regional economy and then to a global economy, as Europe is doing.

Europe's purchasing power parity GDP equals that of the United States and is almost three times that of Japan. Both of Europe's two major industrial competitors also have major weaknesses.

Japan cannot put together a major trading region with itself at the center. APEC (Asia-Pacific Economic Cooperation) meets and talks but cannot decide anything. Differences in levels of development and size are too great for the countries on the Pacific Rim to have a common agenda, harmonize rules and regulations, or share decision-making. When it comes to actually doing something, consensus is impossible and it has no power to force its members to act. Even if APEC were to get decision-making power, Japan would have to share the benefits and the leadership with China and the United States.

Japan's economic system is stuck, unable to deal with its post-meltdown problems. Furthermore, Japan, as the Japanese themselves recognize, has a creativity problem. It has yet to demonstrate that it can make the big breakthroughs in technology that lead to the new industries of the future. Until it demonstrates this ability, Japan will forever be playing catch-up, never the world's economic leader.

The United States' seeming strength is to some extent an imposing facade with major weaknesses. The bottom two-thirds of its labor force is poorly educated and skilled by world standards. Its rapidly rising earnings gap between the top and bottom quintiles of the workforce is in the long run unsustainable. Its productivity growth (1.1 percent per year) in the last decade is the lowest in its own history, and far lower than those of Japan or Europe. It is a low savings and investment society (Europe invests 45 percent more) that cannot balance its trading accounts (in 1998 its trade deficit was almost $250 billion) despite having some of the lowest wages in the developed world. The European Community, in contrast, has a trade surplus ($120 billion in 1998) with the rest of the world.

Much like those who whistle in the dark to keep ghosts away, a recent official German government report itemized America's weaknesses.[56] In its view America has been growing with unsustainable rates of consumption (negative savings rates), unsustainable trade deficits ($2,000 billion over the last seventeen years), and unsustainable increases in hours of work by women. By contrast, Germany has been growing with high personal savings rates (between 12 and 14 percent), high investment rates (22 percent of GDP versus 15 percent in the United States), and faster productivity growth (up from 52 percent of the U.S. level in 1960 to 101 percent in 1995). Its manufacturing productivity growth rate is 50 percent better than that of the United States.[57]

In the 1990s the inflation-corrected GDP growth rates of the fifteen countries in the European Union have been lower than that of the United States (2.1 versus 2.7 percent), but with slower population growth rates, real per capita GDP growth rates in Europe have been equal to those in America. Viewed from a cosmic perspective, European pessimism about its future economic position seems unwarranted.

The actual pessimism arises, of course, from Europe's inability to create jobs. While America created 11 million jobs in the first seven years of the 1990s, the European Union created only 71,000—none in the private sector.

Economically there are only two ways to create more jobs: grow faster to raise the demand for labor or lower wages to raise the demand for labor. With lower wages, firms find it profitable to operate facilities with lower capital-to labor ratios. Working with less capital, labor's productivity falls and more labor has to be hired. The United States has chosen the second option. Europe has chosen to do neither.

Groups like the Organization for Economic Cooperation and Development periodically recommend that Western Europe deal with its problems of high unemployment by restoring labor market flexibility—a politically correct code phrase for reducing wages. Suppose that Western Europe were to introduce an unlimited American-style right to fire labor—no notice, no severance pay, no justification necessary. On day number one of this new regime, millions of Western European workers would be fired as companies eliminated all of the unneeded workers now on their payrolls and those they have long wanted to fire. European businesses would probably fire even more workers than they really want to fire. They would suspect, probably rightly, that their new right to fire would not last very long.

In the short run, unemployment would go up substantially in Western Europe if American labor market flexibility were suddenly introduced. Unemployment would fall only if the increased competition among workers for jobs resulting from these higher unemployment rates led to reductions in real wage rates. With lower wages, business would gradually move to less capital-intensive forms of production and into labor-intensive businesses that cannot profitably operate at the current wage rates. For example, with lower wages, America uses many more guards and attendants in its parking lots than higher wage Europe, where it is more profitable to use card readers and automatic gates.

All of America's employment growth has occurred in the service sector. Services serve as an American job generation machine, but at wage rates below the levels of Western European unemployment insurance benefits. It generates jobs Western Europeans don't want and would not take. Any calculation of how much

Western Europe would have to reduce its wage rates to restore full employment if this were the only measure taken is going to produce a very large number.

Another answer to high European unemployment is to recognize that Europe lives in a deflationary world in the mid-1990s and the monetary policies that might have been appropriate for the inflationary world of the 1970s and early 1980s are now not only unnecessary but counterproductive. Western Europe's central banks seem stuck in the early 1980s—unable to understand that the world has changed. In contrast, America's Federal Reserve Board has at least partially adjusted to this new reality.

Western Europe has not solved its unemployment problem because it won't adopt policies to accelerate growth or to lower wages. It is looking for a magic third option, which does not exist. As a result Western Europe talks about reducing unemployment but does nothing to reduce it. All talk, no action.

High unemployment is Western Europe's most pressing problem politically, but its real economic problem is something quite different. The real danger to Europe's economic future flows from the fact that it is missing out on the sociological, technological, and developmental disequilibriums that are creating wealth elsewhere. Behind Western Europe's real problem is a lack of change agents—entrepreneurs. Or to push the level of causation back one more stage, perhaps the problem is societies that do not want to change and that therefore prevent entrepreneurs from coming into existence.

To say that Europe has all of the ingredients necessary for success is not to say that it will be successful. In addition to having the necessary inputs, it must skillfully play the game that is being played. One cannot spend time wishing that it were a different game.

Part of the game is being able to quickly close, open, and move production facilities.

In areas where becoming world-class is impossible or where world-class levels of productivity are intrinsically low, there are major gains to be made by those who are willing to close ineffi-cient low-wage, labor-intensive industries. What the Japanese call strategic economic retreats are important to economic advance-ment. Average productivity rises as low-productivity industries are eliminated. The country imports what it used to make and moves its own labor into new higher value-added opportunities. Western Europe won't retreat and therefore it cannot advance. Nowhere is this clearer than in its relations with Eastern Europe.

As the 1.9 billion people (one-third of humanity) who used to live under communism join the global capitalist market economy, they are fundamentally changing the economic geography of who does what where on the face of the globe. Eastern Europe is not a drag on Western Europe. It is a tremendous opportunity. Labor-intensive products expensively made in Western Europe ought to be moved to Eastern Europe, where they could be made much more cheaply. Eastern Europe could then earn the funds it needs to buy the high value-added products of Western Europe by selling those low-wage, labor-intensive products in Western Europe. Western Europe should be replacing the industries that move east with the capital equipment industries, high-tech products, and headquarters func-tions (marketing, technology development, global contacts) that Eastern Europe needs to participate in the global economy and catch up with the per capita incomes of Western Europe.

For those with the necessary flexibility, tremendous opportuni-ties exist if they can quickly move the industries that should be moved and quickly expand industries that should be expanded. In this context Western Europeans ought to be to Eastern Europe what the overseas Chinese are to China. Conversely Eastern Europe ought to present the booming growth opportunities to Western Europe that China does to the overseas Chinese busi-nessmen. But the process starts, as the overseas Chinese know, by shutting down old activities in Taiwan and moving them to main-land China. Opportunities to exploit the discontinuities between Eastern and Western Europe are being wasted.

The south side of the Mediterranean should once again effectively be part of Europe as it was in ancient times. North Africa can do for Europe what Mexico does for the United States—provide large supplies of very low-cost labor easily integrated with the high-wage, high-skill labor just next door to the north. North Africa's wages are lower than those in either Mexico or Asia. Combining simple low-cost components from North Africa with sophisticated components from Europe could be an unbeatable combination. But it requires the ability to shut down old activities in Europe and quickly move them to the south side of the Mediterranean to get the process started.

Europe can, if it wants, have its own NAFTA, its own internal overseas Chinese, as well as its own unique expanding common market. No one else has this set of opportunities. There is nothing to prevent this scenario from happening except a lack of imagination and risk-taking in Europe.

Western Europe is also failing to exploit the technological breakthroughs that have been helping North America. Exciting technologies lie unused. A real chance for European economic leadership is being lost.

RULE SIX: There are no institutional substitutes for individual entrepreneurial change agents. The entrepreneur winners of the game become wealthy and powerful, but without entrepreneurs, economies become poor and weak. The old will not exit; the new cannot enter.

To be a leader, countries and regions must be willing to improve the performance of industries that are inefficient and lagging behind the best practices to be found in the rest of the world. Copying-to-catch-up is simply the fastest way to advance. This is easy to say but difficult to do. Most societies resist copying. The process starts by having to admit that there is something to learn. Someone else does it better. Believing that if it wasn't invented here, it can't be worth copying is a universal human failing. Western Europe has resisted benchmarking with either Asia or the United States. They don't want to be the cowboy capitalists of America or the economic rabbits of Japan. In contrast, in the 1980s American firms closed the manufacturing quality gap with the Japanese by shamelessly copying them.

Exiting and copying are precursors to advancing.

If Western Europe wants to compete successfully in the new growth industries such as microelectronics, it needs to enhance its abilities to form and quickly grow new companies into large companies using new breakthrough technologies. To do this it needs industrial flexibility. If it is willing to create the needed flexibility, the entrepreneurs to take advantage of that flexibility will quickly come out of hibernation.

In contrast to America, where eight of the twenty-five biggest companies in 1998 did not exist or were very small in 1960, all of Western Europe's twenty-five biggest corporations in 1998 were already large corporations in 1960. In contrast to America, which in less than a decade went from having two to having nine of the world's ten largest companies, Europe started with one and ended with one—the same one, Royal Dutch Shell. Europe has been completely unable to grow new companies into big companies in the last forty years.

Some European countries offer better environments than others for starting up small high-tech companies. Italy is very good at setting up small technology companies. Other countries such as France rarely see new high-tech business start-ups. But no one in Europe, including the United Kingdom with its American-style capital markets, has been able to rapidly grow new big companies. Small companies that remain small aren't very interesting economically. They don't produce a lot of GDP. They don't do research and development. They don't pay high wages. They don't export. By definition they are not pioneering exciting new breakthrough technologies. If they were, they would be rapidly growing into big companies.

From the point of view of technological expertise it does not make sense that Korea makes more semiconductor chips than are made in all of Europe.[58] Companies like Siemens or Phillips were much stronger technologically when these new technologies first emerged. But sociologically Korea's dominance is easy to understand. America's old-line electrical equipment companies, General Electric, Westinghouse, and RCA, did not succeed in making the transition from vacuum tubes to semiconductors either. America needed new big firms such as Intel to seize economic leadership in semiconductors.

Old large firms usually don't recognize the value that can be created in new technologies. None of the world's leading pharmaceutical companies played a leading role in the development of biotechnology. They all had to end up buying new biotech companies rather than growing them at home. Yet they all knew what was happening in the science of microbiology.

In a knowledge-based economy, successful regions have to have the ability to grow new big companies rapidly.

By definition an economy is the area over which capitalists arbitrage prices and wages looking to buy at the lowest possible cost and to sell at the highest possible price. Businesses now arbitrage the globe. That is what creates a global economy. With global arbitrage, wages depend more upon worldwide supplies and demands for labor and less upon national supplies and demands. The market for software engineers is a good illustration. Those in Bangalore, India, are paid a little less than those in the Netherlands, but the gap is closing quickly. Skills rather than geographic location become the prime determinant of wages. The pressures of what economists call *factor price equalization* mount.

Since there are more unskilled and fewer skilled workers in the global economy than there are in the wealthy industrial world, the wages of the unskilled in the developed world should be expected to fall relative to those of the skilled in the developed world. Similarly, since the whole world has a lower capital-to-labor ratio than the wealthy industrial world, the returns to capital should be expected to rise in a global economy. All of these expected trends are visible in the United States. The earnings gap between the bottom and top quintiles of workers has expanded sharply. Capital's share of total national income is up.

In Western Europe this reality is less real because of better skill levels at the bottom of the workforce. While the needed changes would be much smaller than those America has already seen, government regulations and social practices have prevented the wages of Western Europe's unskilled from falling to the necessary levels. With wages out of line with the rest of the world, it should come as no surprise that business firms do not want to expand employment in Western Europe.

Average manufacturing wages in Germany are twenty-five times those in the Czech Republic. Existing productivity differences are not large enough to justify such large wage differentials. Volkswagen reports that productivity in its Skoda works is 90 percent that of its German plants. In this context any rational profit-making company will decrease its German employment and expand its Czech employment as fast as the law and social realities allow. If the law and social realities interfere to slow the process too much, German companies will simply lose market share to companies in the rest of the world that are not subject to these restrictions.

When Volkswagen moves some of its auto production to Czechoslovakia or Mercedes and BMW move to America, Western Europe does not just lose assembly-line jobs. It also loses some of the managerial, engineering, and other skilled high-wage jobs that go together with those assembly-line jobs. In the end Western Europe loses more total earnings than it would lose if it let unskilled wages fall and then taxed the earnings of the employed to compensate those whose wages had to be reduced.

In the century after the second industrial revolution, individuals living in rich countries with high levels of productivity could expect high pay and generous fringe benefits even if they were not very skilled. Living in a rich country, they would work with more capital equipment per worker, enjoy more and better natural resources, and have more skilled coworkers than those with similar skills in poor countries. Their national economy isolated them from having to compete with lower wage workers elsewhere in the global economy. In addition, high-productivity individuals could be taxed to fund generous social welfare benefits for low-productivity individuals. National governments could and did equalize market outcomes.

But those national economies are gone. Multinational companies take both their technologies and their capital to whatever part of the globe serves them best. With world capital markets, high-tech capital-intensive facilities can be built in poor as well as rich countries. Natural resources are less important to economic success, are sold on world markets, and are easily transportable. Korea and Japan have world-class steel industries, although neither has high-quality coal or iron ore deposits. Production can be globally sourced so that a skilled worker in the developed world is essentially working with an unskilled workmate in the developing world. Put bluntly, the unskilled in the first world can no longer automatically expect first world incomes.

Companies that do not want to pay taxes to support generous fringe benefits for the unemployed (or retirees) can move to other locations where they do not have to pay those taxes. As the Scandinavians are finding, if they want their foreign executives to spend time working at their company headquarters, they have to move those headquarters to lower tax countries. If they don't, they cannot hire high-quality foreign executives, who simply aren't going to pay Scandinavian taxes. Ordinary workers who do not want to pay social charges (payroll taxes) to finance social benefits disappear into the underground economy, where they do not pay taxes. In the United States, where payroll taxes are low, the underground economy is small. In Western Europe, where payroll taxes are high, the underground economy is large.

No country's taxes can get too far out of line with those in the rest of the world. If they do, businesses simply leave and individuals opt out. That is, of course, why the current left-wing German government is pushing so hard for tax harmonization. They know that they cannot for long provide the benefits they want to provide unless their neighbors do the same.

Western Europe will have to adjust to the realities of a global economy—play the game that is there to be played. Wishing for a different game is a waste of time.

Conclusion

In the century ahead the economic game will be played on three levels.

If any nation wants all of its citizens to have first world earnings, it has to ensure that each of its citizens is as well skilled and educated as any in the world. These individually well-skilled workers will have to have access to a world-class infrastructure telecommunications and transportation. If they are to participate in the new man-made brainpower industries of the future, their countries will have to be leaders in research and development and have the entrepreneurs to develop some of the big breakthrough ideas into actual products.

Companies will play the game based upon the skills they employ, the capital investments they make, their technical prowess, and their ability to globally source and sell new products. New start-ups that rapidly grow to become big multinationals will be an important part of success. These new, rapidly growing start-ups won't appear without entrepreneurs. Social regulations and attitudes will have to permit industrial flexibility if entrepreneurs and new companies are to emerge.

Individuals will play the game based upon their education and skills—and their willingness to change.

There is no reason to believe that Western Europe cannot play this three-dimensional game. But it has to want to lead change rather than be dragged unwillingly into the very different twenty-first century economy. It has to want entrepreneurs and be willing to reorganize itself to allow them to come into existence. It has to be willing to threaten what is, in the belief that whatever follows will be better.

We end where we began. No other billion people start with a better position on the global economic chessboard. If it plays its existing position with skill, Europe can be the biggest and most important economic area on earth in the next century. But there is no guarantee that it will be able to change to take advantage of its inherent strengths. To do so, it needs entrepreneurs. Later we will look at what Europe must do to build the entrepreneurial level of its wealth pyramid, but only the Europeans can decide whether they are willing to do what is necessary to lift the entrepreneurial stones of the wealth pyramid into place.

6.   Creating Knowledge

For thousands of years, agricultural land came next after social organization and entrepreneurship (usually in the form of military leadership) as the basic building block at the bottom of the wealth pyramid. After the first industrial revolution, energy resources replaced land as the basic building block underlying wealth. With the third industrial revolution, knowledge moves into the position previously held by land and energy.

Knowledge generates the basic breakthroughs in technology that create the disequilibrium conditions in which high returns and high growth rates are possible. Knowledge allows new things suddenly to be done in new ways. The automobile and the assembly line change the world. Old activities can be done in ways so different that they essentially become new products. The microprocessor allows the laptop computer to do anything IBM mainframes could do thirty years earlier, but because of the dramatic cut in cost and physical size, the laptop allows a whole new set of computing activities to occur.

If enough new technologies arise at the same time, or if one really big breakthrough occurs, historians talk about economic revolutions. The industrial revolution was caused by the invention of the steam engine. Electrification led the second industrial revolution. It occurred so long ago that we don't think about it as a revolution, but in prehistoric times the shift from nomadic hunting to settled agriculture was also such a revolution. This economic revolution permitted human civilizations to emerge. There was enough time after one was fed to learn to read and write, to develop the arts, and to build monuments. Relatively large numbers of people could live in the same cities since they could be feed. Schools could be built and humans could begin to learn from each other.

In between major revolutions, inventions such as the internal combustion engine create important opportunities for great wealth (Ford, Sloan, Kettering). The internal combustion engine led to the world's biggest industry, but it did not cause an economic revolution. If the internal combustion engine had not been invented, the world might have had slightly inferior steam or electric cars and relied more on railroads, but it would look much as it now does.

Advances in basic knowledge and breakthrough technologies do not just happen. They have to be discovered and invented. Some human societies have the curiosity and willingness to invest in making these discoveries and inventions—and others do not. In Europe during the Dark Ages for a long period of time (500 to 1150 A.D.) technology was regressing and knowledge was literally being lost.

Although human talent is evenly spread around the world, inventiveness is not. The process requires a lot more than smart individuals with high IQs. Societies with uneducated people and little curiosity don't produce new technologies. Those with high per capita incomes are often not the most inventive. Switzerland comes to mind.

Inventiveness also changes over time. The United States was seen as a good copier in the nineteenth century and as a great inventor in the last half of the twentieth century. Japan was a very good copier in the last half of the twentieth century but has yet to prove that it can become a great inventor. Germany was a great inventor in the first half of the twentieth century but not in the second half.

Being curious—wondering why things work and what is beyond the next ridge of hills; wanting to explore—having the courage to go where no man has gone before; being willing to learn—getting new knowledge from others; and wishing to build—using new knowledge to make something different; while these four characteristics are embedded in human nature, they only become evident when combined with other ingredients in the right environment.

For almost a thousand years during the Dark Ages, none of these four characteristics were evident in Europe. What had been known, such as how to fertilize agricultural fields, was forgotten. Literate societies became illiterate. Knowledge declined. Standards of living fell 90 percent. People could neither build nor sustain the great cities that had been built by the Romans. Not surprisingly, there was no belief in progress. All people saw was retrogression— humans unable to attain levels of knowledge that had existed in the past. They could only stare at the Roman ruins they lived among and wonder how these could have been built.

The desire to push human knowledge forward did not die out. At the time when it was missing in Europe, it was very much in evidence in both China and the Arab world. Modern mathematics and our system of numbering come from the Arabs. At the end of the Dark Ages, Europe's knowledge of its own ancient thinkers (Aristotle, Plato) had to return to Europe via the Arab scholars. China and the Arab world were the centers of human learning for a millennium. Then again there was a sudden reversal. In the second half of the second millennium, knowledge stopped advancing and started retrogressing in both the Chinese and the Arab world while the Renaissance flowered in Europe. Europeans once again came to believe that progress was possible.

While basic IQ is equally distributed across the world's populations, the advancement of knowledge is not. On each and every measure—Nobel Prizes won, patents granted, R&D efforts undertaken, research articles written, big advances in scientific understanding made, technological leadership seized, engineering advances achieved—there are enormous variances among the globe's existing human societies. Creating technological disequilibriums is an art form that not all societies have mastered. Even within creative societies, creativity is not spread equally. American Jews win far more than their proportional share of America's Nobel Prizes. (But Israelis win almost none.) America's great research universities are not evenly spread across the country. Every area of America does not have its Silicon Valley or Route 128.

Known technologies are often not used. Pre-Columbian American Indians did not use the wheel, but wheeled toys have been found by archeologists in the Americas. Using knowledge to build is not automatic. Humility is in order. Undoubtedly there is something right in front of us today that we are missing and that will bring wonderment to the minds of those in the distant future. How could they (we) have missed it?

Consider fifteenth century China.[59] Its curiosity, its instinct for exploration, and its drive to build had created all of the technologies necessary for the industrial revolution—something that would not actually occur for another 350 years. It had the blast furnace and piston bellows for making steel (China's annual steel production in the late eleventh century would not be matched for seven hundred years); gunpowder and cannon for military conquest; the compass and rudder for exploration; paper, movable type, and the printing press for disseminating knowledge; the wheeled plow, horse collar, rotary threshing machines, and mechanical seeders to generate agricultural surpluses; the ability to drill for natural gas; and in mathematics the decimal system, negative numbers, and the concept of zero to analyze what they were doing. Large armadas (as many as 28,000 men) were exploring Africa's east coast at about the same time that Portugal and Spain were sending much smaller expeditions down the west coast of Africa. Seven major expeditions explored the Indian Ocean with ships four times as large as those of Columbus.

But the geographic explorations and the industrial revolution that could have happened technologically did not happen. The Chinese rejected, did not use, and ultimately forgot the technologies that could have given them world dominance. New technologies were perceived as threats rather than opportunities. Innovation was forbidden. Imperial edicts prohibited the building of new oceangoing ships and sailing away from the Chinese coastline. By the end of the fifteenth century, the demand for order had overridden intrinsic human curiosity, the desire to explore, and the drive to build.

China could have been the birthplace of the first industrial revolution, but it had a culture and an organizational structure that prevented it. Using the new means destroying the old, and many societies, not just China, have found that impossible to do. Change is something that most societies fear. Without the comfort of the old, chaos always seems to loom. Since chaos must be suppressed, new knowledge must be repressed. Today's fears about what biotechnology might do echo those fifteenth century Chinese fears of new technology.

On a much more trivial level, French fears about adopting English words into the French language and their regular attempts to purge their language of English contamination have overtones of fifteenth century China. In contrast, any word regularly used in English speech (menu, taxi) is an English word and where they originated is irrelevant. Such fears say something about a culture unwilling to learn, to change, to adopt and adapt.

Conversely, consider Russia in the seventy-five years before the Russian Revolution. Creativity flourished in the chaos of a dying empire. Think of all of the great authors—Tolstoy, Dostoyevsky, Chekhov, Turgenev, Gogol. The list goes on and on. In the world of music and the arts the same is true. Stravinsky, Tchaikovsky, and many others are still played in our concert halls. Kandinsky and Malevich are still admired in our museums. In science Russia was a leader. Ostwald, born in Russia, was one of the first Nobel

Prize winners in chemistry for his work on the speed of chemical reactions. Mendeleyev invented the periodic table of elements. Pavlov, also a Nobel Prize winner in 1904, is perhaps the most famous animal biologist to this day. Mathematically, Markov chains have found a wide variety of applications in physics, biology, linguistics, and economics. Lobachevsky developed non-Euclidian geometry.

Being skeptical and refusing to accept authorities are essential to scientific advancement. Living in chaos, Russians became skeptical. If one accepted the dangers of revolting against the czar, any scientific revolt against perceived wisdom seemed comparatively without risk.

Yet it was all for naught. Creativity flourished in the chaos, but without some degree of order it was impossible for the Russians to use that creativity to generate a successful Russian economy. Chaos led to more chaos and ultimately to the Russian Revolution. Order was reimposed. Creativity died.

Creativity does not occur when it has to challenge authority. Creativity occurs when there is no authority to challenge—when there is an empty space without order where creativity can grow unmolested. But to many, an empty space without order is chaos—and chaos must be suppressed.

To advance and use knowledge, a society needs the right mix of chaos and order. Too much order (China) does not work. Too much chaos (Russia) does not work. Successful societies create and manage a dynamic tension between the two opposing forces without letting either of them get out of hand. New ideas are easily frustrated if societies are not receptive to the chaos that comes from change, yet they have to maintain an appropriate degree of order to take advantage of those creative breakthroughs.

As more modern examples, consider two equally small countries—Singapore and Israel. One placed its bets on order (Singapore), and one placed its bets on individual brilliance (Israel). Both are successful, but thus far Singapore is more successful. In 1965 its per capita income was $500 while Israel's was $5,000 in today's dollars. Today Singapore's per capita income is $25,000 while Israel's is $15,000. But Singapore has exhausted the easy steps of mobilizing resources and copying to catch up. To advance its position it now needs some of Israel's individual brilliance. Will it be able to get that? Recognizing its own weakness Singapore recently announced a plan to build a graduate school of engineering in cooperation with MIT, where the emphasis will be on creativity. Meanwhile, some of Israel's individual brilliance goes to waste because it doesn't have the necessary order to fully capitalize upon it. Lack of a first-class or maybe even second-class infrastructure is but one example.

RULE SEVEN: Any society that values order above all else will not be creative, but without the right degree of order, creativity disappears as if into a black hole.

At the individual level these same forces show up as a tension between tradition and rebellion. Einstein dropped out of high school at fifteen; renounced his citizenship one year later; lived on the margins socially, economically, and morally; called himself a gypsy and was considered a bohemian by others. His life was in some sense a search for order in disorder, both scientifically and sociologically.[60] Great creativity requires hard facts, wild imagination, and nonlogical jumps forward that are then proved to be right by working backward to known principles. Only the rebellious can do it.[61]

Curiosity and the desire to explore can be enhanced. Useful curiosity requires individuals who have mastered the existing body of knowledge but are not paralyzed by it. Enhancing curiosity is what really good graduate education is all about. Societies that value and honor curiosity produce curious people.

All explorations, geographic and intellectual, need social support. Columbus could not have discovered America without

Ferdinand and Isabella. The Internet would not have been established in America without three decades of government financial support. Building (embedding something in a human society) is by its very nature a social activity, even if it needs individual innovators who break old molds. Science may be an endless frontier where there is always room to be curious, to explore, and to build, but big scientific breakthroughs are almost always expensive team efforts.

Advancing knowledge is much like drilling for oil. The intellectually curious can search for major new oil fields. This is an uncertain, highly risky activity requiring huge investments in wildcat wells. Today it means offshore drilling in very deep waters in environmentally hostile places like the North Sea, where oil exploration has not previously been possible. On land the only possibilities are in areas such as central Asia, where political and social instabilities make it equally difficult and expensive. One set of opportunities requires the development of new technological skills. How does one drill in water two miles deep? The other requires the development of political abilities to operate in environments without the rule of law and with high levels of chaos.

Consider the development of microbiology. Starting in the early 1960s without any certainty that anything would ever be found, many billions of dollars were invested over a twenty-year period before it was clear that useful technologies would emerge. Years passed between that start and the discovery of the double helix, later DNA, and much later recombinant DNA. A central part of the effort, the human genome project, is not scheduled to be completed until 2005. In the end religious hostility to the use of biotechnology to change human beings may create an environment that is just as socially hostile to the use of this technology as the lawlessness and chaos of central Asia are to the exploration of oil.

Alternatively the intellectually curious can forget about drilling wildcat wells and finding big new oil fields and make much more certain, much less risky, and much less costly investments in drilling development wells to explore and expand the perimeters of known fields. The same is true when advancing technology. In 1998 IBM announced a process for putting multiple layers of transistors on silicon semiconductor chips. It is an important development that will advance technological progress, but it is not equivalent to inventing either the transistor or the semiconductor chip. It is a developmental advance rather than a basic breakthrough.

While research and development are often lumped together for purposes of analyzing the sources of technological advance, they should not be. Research is the activity of making basic breakthroughs into new areas, such as biotechnology—deepening knowledge, if you will. Development is the expansion of technological knowledge in already existing areas—widening knowledge. In between there is an area, usually called applied research, in which the basic science is in place but some fundamental engineering breakthroughs have to take place to implement empirically what is already known scientifically. The Manhattan Project atomic bomb research during World War II was essentially applied research. Einstein and other physicists had shown that a bomb was theoretically possible, but was it practically doable?

To advance knowledge, one starts with the willingness to make the necessary investments in either research or development. Some countries are willing—others are not. The right amount to invest is not obvious. In the world's four biggest economies, R&D spending as a percentage of gross domestic product is very similar: France and Germany, 2.3 percent; Japan, 2.8 percent; and the United States, 2.5 percent. But this is more because none of them wants to let the other three get ahead of them than it is because anyone has proved that they are all spending the right amount.[62]

Levels of R&D spending are similar among the big four, but patterns are very different. Much of American spending has traditionally gone into military activities. Even with the end of the Cold War, military R&D is still 20 percent of the American total and over half of what the federal government spends. In Japan, military research and development is not significant. Americans spend much of their money on research. Japan spends almost all of its money on development. In Japan, industry finances about 75 percent of the total. Until the end of the Cold War produced cutbacks in military research, the U.S. government funded over 40 percent of total R&D spending. Today it funds 30 percent—not too different from the Japanese pattern.[63] Since the end of the Cold War, American spending has been falling as a fraction of world spending, but in 1997 and 1998 these trends reversed and U.S. spending rose faster than the rest of the world's.[64]

Other wealthy countries spend much less. Italy spends 1.2 percent and Spain, 0.8 percent. A few developing countries spend a lot (South Korea, 2.25 percent), but most do not. About 96 percent of all of R&D spending occurs in rich countries.

Among private business firms, spending differences are also large. In the United States, manufacturing firms contribute 81 percent of total private R&D spending. Most firms outside of manufacturing spend almost nothing on R&D. The need to maintain an R&D base is in fact one of the principal reasons for a country to worry about losing its manufacturing base. The reason manufacturing does most of the R&D spending is that historically it has been impossible to make money on innovations unless one made and sold the products that were the fruits of that new knowledge. Selling knowledge so that others could make the products that came from it has never been a profitable strategy.

Most of American R&D (84 percent) is done by big firms. Even among these big spenders, however, the variance in spending as a percentage of sales is large—Boeing, 4 percent; Intel, 9 percent; Lucent, 12 percent; Microsoft, 17 percent.[65] Expenditure levels depend upon the industry under consideration and whether firms in that industry believe that the basic science is in place to make real progress in developing new goods or services. All of Intel's sales come from products developed within the last three years, but only 35 percent of IBM's profits come from recently developed products.[66]

There is a simple reason why big rich companies and big rich countries do most of the spending. Here again the analogy to oil exploration holds. If a small exploration company drills two wells, it is in a highly risky business. Two dry holes and the firm is bankrupt. If a large company drills a thousand wells, simple probabilities and the law of large numbers guarantee that the company will drill some dry holes, but somewhere they will hit oil. A few dry holes at the beginning of the process won't throw them into bankruptcy.

An economy as big as the United States can afford to place reasonable bets in all areas where it looks as if technology can be pushed forward. In contrast, a country as small as Israel cannot. The U.S. research and development budget is three times the entire GDP of Israel. Israel has to focus, concentrate its money, and place its bets on a very limited number of technologies if it is to spend enough money on any one technology to have any chance of success. If it spends very small sums in all areas, it will end up wasting all of its resources. But if it must focus its bets, in what areas should it focus? No one knows. Since small countries and companies have to bet in what is an intrinsically riskier, more uncertain environment, they not surprisingly tend to bet less.

Within Western Europe, a lot of money is wasted by countries betting small amounts on different technologies but not betting enough on any one technology to make a difference. If the European Economic Community could pool its research and development spending, there is every reason to believe that the payoffs could be substantially enhanced for everyone. I would argue, for example, that Spain wastes every dollar that it puts into R&D. It doesn't spend very much, but not knowing what areas will develop into new industries, it tries to spread its money around, and in so doing, doesn't spend enough in any area to make a difference. R&D spending in an integrated Europe ought to be more productive than the same R&D spending in individual countries.

For both companies and countries, technological leadership is not the same thing as R&D spending. Europe is a big spender, but if one looks at technological leadership, its spending doesn't seem to have paid off. To pay off, spending obviously has to be followed by the activities necessary to embed the newly developed technologies into the economy. Where America outclasses Europe, for example, is not so much in R&D spending on information technology, but in investments in information hardware and software. As a fraction of GDP, U.S. investments were twice those of Germany or France in 1996.[67] What is known isn't very different, but what is being done is quite different.

Even when breakthroughs are made and technological success can be said to have occurred, risks and uncertainties are still high for those financing research and development. The payoffs are often not in the expected areas. And when something completely unexpected pops up, those paying for the R&D are often not in a position to exploit it. Perhaps the developments aren't in their line of business, or the company doesn't have the necessary expertise to take advantage of them. Many new companies get started when researchers in big companies turn up ideas that don't fit in with their employers' business plans. When their ideas are turned down by their employers, these researchers go off and set up new companies to exploit them.

Often it takes a long time to realize the importance and usefulness of what has been discovered. The patent lawyers at Bell Labs didn't want to incur the costs of patenting the laser, because optical waves didn't seem to be relevant to telecommunication.[68] Yet thirty years later, no invention is more relevant. Lasers power modern telecommunication systems. Measurement devices, navigation, surgery, music, printing, the cutting of materials from cloth to rock, and military weapons are all now based upon lasers. They are everywhere.

Often what is discovered is not useful until other things have been invented. The laser needed high-quality fiber-optic cables before it could be used in telecommunications. The compact disc was not on anyone's technological radar screen when the laser was invented. No one was thinking about microsurgery or eliminating eyeglasses. Lasers in the last twenty years, like lightbulbs and semiconductor chips before them, have dramatically fallen in cost and risen in performance. What is possible and economic now is very different from what was possible and economic at the beginning of the process.

Often inventions become useful because the costs of other factors come down. The Internet is a good example. It started in the late 1960s as a communications system between military bases using IBM mainframes that cost millions of dollars. In some sense it still uses IBM mainframes today. The only difference is that the cost and size of computing has come down. The mainframe computing power that used to cost millions and be housed in its own buildings is now available in a laptop computer for a few hundred dollars. No one predicted that decline in computing costs.

To be useful, inventions usually need a well-educated workforce that can absorb the technology and acquire the skills necessary to employ it. If this skill base does not exist, the invention lies unused. That is why well-educated inventors in the developing world often move to the United States. Because their fellow citizens are undereducated, they can't get their invention to market in their home environment.

Knowledge is slippery stuff. Studies show that research done in other countries or in other companies is about half as productive as research done for oneself.[69] That is a tremendous loss for those who are pioneers and a tremendous incentive for many to be free riders, invest little in R&D, and simply use what has been invented. If a lot of knowledge is lost, those paying to develop that new knowledge cannot get the full benefits when they sell their knowledge—either directly as patent rights or indirectly as products—and they quit paying. Pilkington's molten metal float glass technology for making plate glass moved around the world and the glass industry very fast, with few royalty payments being made to Pilkington. Those thinking about investing in research and development have an incentive to wait and see what they can get for free—skip the risky phases of investment and jump in when the development path is clear.

Capturing this free knowledge is one of the reasons that concentrations of high-tech companies exist in places like Silicon Valley and along Route 128.[70] One learns faster what one's neighbor knows if one is in fact a neighbor. Knowledge, like water, eventually equalizes its level as it flows around the world. But eventually isn't instantly. In fast-moving fields, the advantages of being inside the relevant learning communities are enormous. Companies often buy or build subsidiaries in Silicon Valley to ensure themselves a listening post. Other geographic locations have much lower operating costs, but the same information isn't available on the intellectual grapevine.

From a company standpoint, the R&D investment calculus is straightforward but complex: invest as long as the expected returns from the company's R&D budget cover the cost of capital and the expected risks and uncertainties. The cost of capital is easy to ascertain (about 6 percent for the most creditworthy big corporations), but what are the relevant risks and uncertainties? They are obviously large, but how large?

Private rates of return on R&D spending average about 24 percent.[71] Since firms are not rapidly expanding their R&D budgets, this indicates that something like this level of returns is probably necessary to cover the capital costs (6 percent) and the inevitable risks and uncertainties. By subtraction, private firms seem to think that the right risk factor is about 18 percent.

Using discounted net present values (the standard capitalist investment equations), returns in the future are discounted simply because they occur in the future. If firms discount using a 24 percent interest rate, the value of $100 in earnings ten years from now is only $12 today. This is so because $12 today put to work at a 24 percent rate of return would yield $100 ten years from now. But this means that when payoffs occur in the distant future, they are worth very little to a private firm, even if the payoffs are very large.

At the same time, social returns (total economic returns to the whole society) on R&D spending (averaging the results of eight different studies) were 66 percent, with a range from 50 to 105 percent— or almost three times as high as those 24 percent private financial returns.[72] This means that $2 of every $3 in net benefits generated did not accrue to those paying for the R&D. There are huge positive social spillovers from research and development spending.

What is also interesting about these large social returns is that no one has ever found anything but these results. They are one of the most robust conclusions in economics. Die-hard skeptics can argue that the 66 percent result isn't completely conclusive, since marginal returns on the next dollar spent in the future could be far below the average returns on dollars spent in the past. But it is highly unlikely that marginal social returns are anywhere near the 6 percent cost of capital. If they were, average returns could not come in at 66 percent.

This difference between private and social rates of return is the primary reason why governments must support R&D funding. Societies can take spillover effects into account. They can focus on that 66 percent social rate of return and not the 24 percent private rate of return. They don't have to worry about which particular firms benefits. If governments don't support R&D spending, much too little R&D will be done.

But the 66 percent returns indicate something else. In all likelihood even the big spenders such as the United States are spending too little. A 66 percent rate of return is far above the returns on investments in other areas.

RULE EIGHT: The economic payoff from more social investment in basic research is as clear as anything is ever going to be in economics.

The right strategy is to push up investment substantially, say from 3 to 4 percent of GDP, for a decade and see what happens. If good advances in knowledge aren't being made, spending can then be cut back to the old 3 percent level. If returns are still in the 66 percent range, spending should be pushed up again and again until measured returns start to fall.

Research funders also have to get the mix right between supporting creative individuals and supporting institutions. Some proportion of any country's research funds has to go to institutions to sustain long-term continuity. But in many countries, and in the case of our national military laboratories, most of the research money is automatically allocated to research institutions. All such institutions tend to be dominated by older researchers. Our national laboratories are so secret that it is impossible for an outsider to evaluate their long-term creativity, but too many countries' equivalent civilian laboratories are not highly creative. While there are obviously individual exceptions, technological breakthroughs aren't usually made by older researchers who have been looking at the same things in the same ways for long periods of time. New ways are usually conceived by those who haven't accepted the old ways. This means finding some way to get a lot of the R&D money through to younger, less well-established researchers, and this is only possible if money is allocated based upon peer-reviewed project proposals.

In the United States, a democracy where legislators are elected by geographic region, the danger is that larger and larger portions of our funds will automatically go to institutions evenly spread across America without regard for the merits of their proposed research. American history is full of programs (remember Model Cities) gutted by this natural political inclination. In the past it was prevented by the Cold War and the fear of falling behind the Soviets technologically. The Soviet military threat overrode the normal political inclination to do something for every congressman's home district.

Because private returns are apt to be much more certain if one is looking simply for an extension of existing knowledge (drilling a developmental well) than if one is looking for a major break-through (drilling a wildcat well to find a big new oil field), private firms tend to concentrate their money on the developmental end of the R&D process. Time lags are also shorter, and in the business world speed is everything.

Because of this proclivity in the private sector, governments have to focus their spending on long-tailed projects for advancing basic knowledge. This is where private firms won't invest, but it is also precisely where the breakthroughs that generate a lot of private business opportunities are made. This is why biotechnology had to be supported by the government. It is also why it did not develop in places where it was not governmentally supported (everywhere except the United States). Even if private companies had known with certainty what would occur (and they didn't and couldn't know), no private company would have made the investments made by the National Institutes of Health, because money had to go in for more than twenty-five years before any money (products sold) came out.

What an analysis of incentives would predict is only too clear from the data. While the federal government and nonprofit institutions such as universities pay for 85 percent of basic research, they pay for only 26 percent of development costs.

Funding for U.S. Research & Development [73]

Purpose Source	All	Basic	Applied	Development
Federal gov.	30%	58%	29%	25%
Industry	65	27	64	74
Nonprofits	5	15	7	1

Because of the investment calculus used by business firms, a good R&D project expected to pay off in five years or less is almost sure to find private funding. If payoffs lie ten or more years in the future, the project clearly requires government financing. For projects within a five- to ten-year time perspective, there is a case for cost-sharing, as the government and auto companies are now doing on battery research to make the electric automobile into a viable alternative to the internal combustion engine.

Who Owns What?

Capitalism began in Great Britain with the enclosure movement that converted what had been the communal agricultural lands of feudalism into privately owned land. The process was messy, unfair, and violent—much like the process of establishing who owns what in Russia today. In both cases the strong seized assets that had in the past been used to support the entire community. The strong then called upon the police powers of the state to help them protect their new ownership rights.

Whatever the process for establishing clear, enforceable property rights, capitalism does not work unless who owns what is clear.[74] The private ownership of productive assets and the ability to appropriate the output that flows from those assets lies at the heart of capitalism. This principle is what gave capitalism its name. To make capitalism function, legally enforceable ownership rights have to be established.

Consider air and water pollution. What everyone owns, no one owns. As a result everyone has an incentive to pollute—to use the free disposal system that's available and let someone else downstream or downwind bear the costs. No one has an incentive to keep the air, rivers, lakes, or oceans clean. On land that is privately owned, the pollution market works. Private owners don't let their neighbors dump wastes on their property. Someone goes into the business of opening up a dump site. The only problem with these private dump sites is that their owners in turn have an incentive to abuse the free pollution rights available in the air or in the groundwater as they dispose of the rubbish dumped there. Capitalism cannot deal with pollution because it cannot establish the ownership rights to clean air and water.

With the advent of the third industrial revolution, skills and knowledge have become the only source of sustainable long-term competitive advantage. Intellectual property lies at the center of the modern company's economic success or failure. Raw materials can be bought and moved to wherever they are needed. Financial capital is a commodity that can be borrowed in New York, Tokyo, or London. Unique pieces of equipment that cannot be obtained or are too expensive for one's competitors to buy simply don't exist. The knowledge that used to be tertiary after raw materials and capital in determining economic success is now primary. With this reality comes the need for more differentiated systems of determining who owns what intellectual property, better protection for whatever is owned, and faster systems of dispute resolution when disputes arise—as they will.

Major companies such as Microsoft (the world's most valuable company in 1998) own nothing of value except knowledge. Fighting to defend and extend the domain of their intellectual property is how they play the economic game. If the intellectual property of industries such as microelectronics, biotechnology, designer-made materials, and telecommunications can be easily copied, companies will not be able to generate either wealth for their owners or high wages for their employees. These knowledge-based industries are important in their own right, but they also enable other industries to become knowledge based in turn, as we have seen in the case of oil or retailing. The source of any retailer's future success is apt to be buried in the software of its electronic information and logistics systems rather than in its advertising or the novelty of its products. Intellectual property rights now affect almost every business.

The rising importance of intellectual property can be more

directly seen in the earnings gained from the licensing of technology. In the past, companies were willing to share their technology because it did not seem to be the source of their success, could not be sold for much anyway, and would probably be stolen if it weren't sold cheaply. But those days are gone. Polaroid and Kodak settled a patent infringement case for almost $1 billion. Texas Instruments, after shifting to an aggressive licensing program, earned more than $1.5 billion in fees. In some years its licensing fees have been bigger than its operating income. Having noticed these numbers, many other corporations are now ordering their technology-licensing officers to step up their efforts.

Increasingly, intellectual property is becoming central to strategic battle plans. Patent suits are often used to create uncertainties, time delays, and higher start-up costs for competitors. In what ended up being a futile effort to stay independent, the Digital Equipment Corporation sued Intel for infringing its patents on the alpha chip. The Digital suit was triggered by an article in the *Wall Street Journal* quoting a top-level executive on an Intel chip-research team as saying, "There's nothing left to copy." Companies such as Intel have big legal budgets to defend what they think is their intellectual property. Intel ended up paying the Digital Equipment Company $1 billion to end its patent infringement suit, partly to prevent the uncertainties, delays, and higher start-up costs the suit was designed to cause.

In a current Federal Trade Commission case, Intel stands accused of depriving customers of the use of Intel's intellectual property as a bargaining chip whenever these customers sue Intel for using the customers' intellectual property. Can it really be true that Intel does not have the right to deprive others of the right to use its intellectual property when those others are trying to deprive Intel of the right to use theirs?

Clear, easily enforceable, sellable ownership rights to intellectual property have to be established if capitalism is to work in a world where knowledge is the key to wealth. Those who pay to advance technology have to be able to own, sell, or use what they have invented. In a world of man-made brainpower industries, this means establishing a system of legally enforceable ownership rights to knowledge—a system of intellectual property rights. Reverse engineering (the politically correct phrase for copying) is a way of life in the corporate world. But where should the limits be? Whatever the answer, it's not to be found in a patent system more than a century old.

Everyone understands what it means to own land or productive equipment and how those rights can be enforced. It is not so clear, however, what it means to own knowledge or how those ownership rights can be enforced. Capitalists own the equipment their workforce uses, but can they own the knowledge their workforce uses? What part of their knowledge can employees take with them when they move to a new employer? How do employers stop employees from taking the employer's intellectual property when they go? Ownership rights to land and equipment last forever. Does the ownership of knowledge last forever? If not, how long does it last? Everyone knows the difference between public lands and private lands, but where is the dividing line between knowledge in the public domain and knowledge in the private domain? Even if the line can be defined, how is it to be enforced?

Historically, efforts to establish and enforce ownership rights to intellectual property have revolved around patents, copyrights, trademarks, and trade secrets, but new technologies are rapidly eroding the applicability of this old system, which was designed for the technology of the nineteenth century. It allows one to go to a library and browse through a book without paying the author, but is downloading a book from the Internet equivalent to browsing? If so, how can anyone sell books when one copy can be easily and cheaply scanned into a computer and then cheaply downloaded? The system has no answers for such problems because they did not exist when the system was built.

Intellectual property rights were also much less important a century ago, or even a quarter of a century ago. If the legal system protected intellectual property rights poorly, no one complained very much—economic success depended upon the ownership of natural resources and capital equipment. But intellectual property rights have moved from the periphery to the center of economic success. Without a clear, workable, enforceable system of intellectual property rights, knowledge-based capitalism is not going to work. No one is going to invest the necessary sums in research and development if they cannot garner the resulting gains.

Designed more than a hundred years ago to meet the simpler needs of an economy based upon natural resources and mechanical devices, our system of intellectual property rights is an undifferentiated, one-size-fits-all system. Consider the real case of a physician who noticed a relationship between an elevated level of a particular human hormone and a congenital birth defect. He was awarded a patent for his observation, although by itself his test had too many false positives to be useful. But later developments showed that if his test was used along with two others, they could accurately forecast whether a baby would be born with Down's syndrome. Today the physician is suing to get a $9 fee from every laboratory that uses his part of the test. If he wins, the cost of testing will more than double.

Should the physician who first observed how the existing gene works have some intellectual property rights? Probably. But they should not be the same kind of rights as those granted to someone who invents a new gene to replace the defective one. Noticing what an existing gene does is simply not equivalent to inventing a new gene. Biotechnology makes such distinctions necessary. Our patent system has no basis for making them. All patents are identical—you either get one or you don't.

The prevailing wisdom among those who earn their living within our system of intellectual property protection is that some minor tweaking here and there will fix the problem. Much of this wisdom flows from nothing more profound than the belief that to open up the system to fundamental change would be equivalent to opening Pandora's box. All can vividly see themselves as potential losers. Few consider the private and public gains that might accrue from a different system.

The prevailing wisdom is wrong. The time has come not for marginal changes but for wide-open thinking about designing a new system from the ground up. This is never going to happen if the problem is left to those who make their living operating the current system. They have too many vested interests in preserving it with the fewest possible modifications.

Technology is making intellectual property rights more important, but other factors are also contributing to the need for a better system. For most of the period since World War II, knowledge has flowed easily and cheaply around the world. The U.S. government paid for basic research (other countries' R&D budgets went mainly into development) and, with the exception of military technologies, encouraged the worldwide dissemination of whatever was discovered. During the Cold War, the economic success of other countries was seen as almost as important to the United States' strategic geopolitical position as its own internal economic success was.

Arrogance also contributed to this free flow of information. Americans believed that the rest of the world would not be able to catch up with American ingenuity. While foreigners were copying the last generation of technology, Americans would be inventing the next generation, or so the thinking went. But Americans now understand that they live in a competitive world in which America's economic dominance is long gone. Developing proprietary technologies, and the skills that go with them, is the only way to defend U.S. workers from the downward wage pressures of factor price equalization. The nation's most profitable companies are those with a lock on some form of knowledge. As a vivid sign of this need to control the flow of information, witness the call by some members of Congress to keep foreign students out of U.S. university laboratories in order to stop taxpayer-financed technologies from leaking abroad.

At the same time, the U.S. government is cutting its support for research and development—both in real dollars and as a share of total spending. What used to be a 40–60 split between government and the private sector is now a 30–70 split. Under the current budget-balancing agreement, sharper cuts lie ahead. A Democratic president has promised to cut federal R&D spending by 14 percent by 2002; a Republican Congress has promised to cut it by 20 percent. It may not happen, but it could.

In the past, U.S. antitrust laws also explicitly forced some privately financed but essentially national laboratories, such as the Bell Labs of AT&T, to share their technologies with everyone, and implicitly forced others, such as the IBM labs, to do the same. But the monopolistically funded private research laboratories doing basic research are gone. IBM and AT&T are now in competitive businesses in which they cannot afford to fund projects that lead to useful general knowledge that is then freely given away. Private companies now expect to get big money from their inventions and will vigorously defend their rights to do so. The days when private knowledge was shared are over.

For all three of these reasons, less new knowledge will be freely available in the public domain in the future. If the resulting gap is to be filled, private companies will have to be enticed through new incentives to put more private money into R&D. They aren't going to do so unless stronger systems of protection for intellectual property rights exist.

Without stronger systems of protection, companies will also defend their economic positions by keeping their knowledge secret. News articles about research papers whose publication is deliberately delayed often appear in the scientific press. Secrecy is a much bigger deterrent to the expansion of knowledge than any monopolistic system of protection for intellectual property rights. An investigator who knows what is known can go on to the next step. One who doesn't wastes time reinventing what is known or wandering in an intellectual wilderness looking for a path that someone else has already found. A recent study found that 73 percent of private patents were based on knowledge generated by public sources such as universities and nonprofit or government laboratories.[75] Private, secretly held knowledge simply does not generate the next generation of knowledge.

New technologies have both created new potential forms of intellectual property rights (can pieces of a human being be patented?) and made old rights unenforceable (when books can be downloaded from an electronic library, what does a copyright mean?). It is clear that the invention of a new gene for making human beings different or better cannot be handled in the same way as the invention of a new gearbox. What should and should not be appropriable as private property needs to be rethought.

What should be patentable? No society is going to let someone have a monopoly on the cure for cancer. Nor will biologists be allowed to clone and own human beings. But it is equally clear that companies engaging in biological research must be allowed to own pieces of human beings. Otherwise, no one will invest the funds necessary to find genetic cures for diseases such as Alzheimer's. The techniques of biotechnology are what the military calls dual-use technologies. The same techniques that cure genetic diseases can make humans taller, smarter, and more beautiful. Patents on genetic cures for diseases cannot be differentiated from patents on genetic materials that make humans better. The exact line between what is and is not allowed is going to be difficult to draw.

The differentiation must start with distinctions between fundamental advances in knowledge and logical extensions of existing knowledge. Each deserves a different kind of patent. Inventing a new piece of biology that alters the natural characteristics of plants, animals, or humans is not equivalent to discovering how an existing piece of biology works. What a patent means has to be different in those two areas.

New technologies are making the enforcement of property rights much tougher. People can use high-quality scanning technologies with optical character recognition to build electronic libraries quickly and cheaply. Electronic publishers can just as quickly and easily convert that material back into printed form. When anything can be rapidly, cheaply, and privately replicated in low volumes at high levels of quality and then distributed in whatever form the user wants, the choke points available to prevent reproduction of what used to be printed materials have essentially evaporated.

With that evaporation comes the end of the copyright system—not just for books but for all information and data systems. A system designed to allow people to browse through books from physical libraries cannot provide the right framework for dealing with the issues raised by the possibility of downloading a book from an electronic library.

What initially may seem relevant only to authors and book companies is more than that. If books can be freely downloaded, then those selling financial information will find that their databases can also be downloaded and resold by competitors whose costs are lower precisely because they did not incur the costs of creating them. Telephone book publishers try to stop this practice by inserting some phony numbers into the phone books so that they can prove in court that competitors have not independently generated their own list of names and numbers.

The future of printed materials can be seen in what is now happening in the recorded music business. Even though the equipment needed to record compact discs is too expensive to be found in every household, CD pirates may hold as much as a 20 percent share of the market. In contrast, in personal electronic publishing the equipment is as cheap and available as a personal computer plus a scanner. The fully electronic library does not yet exist, but it soon will. One is being built in Singapore. The legal system may be able to stop factories from copying and selling CDs or books in volume, but it cannot stop individuals from replicating materials for themselves or selling small numbers to their friends. One has to expect that pirated works will end up with an even bigger market share of what used to be conventionally printed materials than they now have of CDs and tapes.

RULE NINE: Knowledge-based capitalism isn't going to work without a new system for determining who owns or controls intellectual property rights. Capitalism requires clear, easy-to-enforce ownership rights.

Consider software piracy. When computer makers ship their products "naked"—that is, without an operating system—as they often do in Asia, the only reason they do so is to allow the use of pirated software. These computer makers have the tacit approval of local governments to violate patents and copyrights. In Thailand, up to 97 percent of the software in use has been illegally copied, and even in the United States the figure may be as high as 40 percent. Estimates of pirated software in Europe range from a high of 80 percent in Spain to a low of 25 percent in the United Kingdom.

Computer software provides a good illustration of what happens when patent and copyright laws do not keep up with technology. Judges end up making decisions that they should not be making. One such decision ruled that the "look and feel" of a software program could not be patented—which means, effectively, that any successful program can be legally copied. The copiers need to write their own code, but they start knowing exactly what the program is supposed to do, how the internal programming components are structured, how the final program is supposed to look and feel, and that a viable market exists for the product. As a result the copier has lower costs and faces much less market uncertainty and risk than the original writers of any successful software program. When software programs cannot be protected effectively, it is not just the Microsofts that will lose. Retailers that develop software to sell their products over the Internet will find that software copied and freely used by their competitors.

Increasingly the acquisition of knowledge is central for both catch-up states and keep-ahead states. Smart developing countries understand that reality. Operating as a monopsonist (a monopoly buyer) and dangling access to its domestic market as an enticement, China has demanded the sharing of technology from companies such as Boeing and Reuters that sell in its markets. It doesn't need their capital, since it saves 30 percent of its income and has accumulated $100 billion in international exchange reserves—but it demands their knowledge in return for the right to operate in China. Americans deplore China's demands but remember fondly from their high school history classes the clever Yankee engineer with a photographic memory who visited British textile mills in the early 1800s and then reconstructed those mills in New England. Initially Americans were equally amused in the aftermath of World War II when Japanese businessmen with their cameras were ubiquitously touring U.S. factories. They are no longer amused. Few today will let third world visitors into their plants.

Yet copying to catch up is the only way to catch up. Every country that has caught up has done it by copying. Third world countries know that unless they can acquire the necessary knowledge, they will never make it into the first world. Third world countries cannot afford to buy what they need—even if those who have the knowledge are willing to sell, and they are not. They have to copy.

Recently I heard a talk given by the managing partner of a large U.S. consulting firm. The partner urged his fellow consultants to recommend relocation to India because Indians were very good at copying, had few laws making copying illegal, and often did not enforce the laws that did exist. He remarked that India recognized patents only on the processes for making drugs, not on the drugs themselves, but then went on to say that Indians were very good at developing alternative manufacturing processes. The fact that no one checks those processes very closely to see that they are really different was left unsaid. Nor did he need to say that what was made in India could be slipped quietly into the channels of world commerce without anyone having to pay for knowledge that would be considered proprietary elsewhere.

While one can understand why developing countries do not want to pay royalties for using the drugs necessary to keep their citizens healthy, it is harder to make a similar case for why they should be allowed to pirate Madonna CDs. And India does just as much of the second as it does of the first.

The issues are not just those of where a country stands in the invention cycle or where it stands on the economic development ladder. Different cultures and different parts of the world look at intellectual property rights quite differently. The idea that people should be paid to be creative is a point of view that stems from the Judeo-Christian-Muslim belief in a God that created human-ity in his image. It has no analogue in Hindu, Buddhist, or Confucian societies. There are real differences in beliefs about what should be freely available in the public domain and what should be for sale in the private marketplace. In Asia few pieces of ancient art have the names of their creators inscribed upon them. Knowledge is seen as a free good, since there is no concept of it having to be created by human beings using expensive processes.

Yet despite these differences in economic positions, cultures, and historic practices, no system of protecting intellectual prop-erty rights can work unless most of the governments of the world agree to enforce it. A law that does not exist or is not enforced in country X is essentially a law that cannot be enforced in country Y.

If one tries to enforce the law in country Y, production simply moves to country X to escape regulation.

What different countries want, need, and should have in a system of intellectual property rights is very different depending on their level of economic development. National systems, such as that of the United States, are not going to evolve into de facto world standards. The economic game of catch-up is not the game of keep-ahead. Countries playing either game have the right to a world system that lets them succeed. Whatever system is built, it will have to be a global system that allows for this diversity of positions and beliefs.

Conclusion

In research and development, but particularly in research, there are huge incentives to free-ride the system: let someone else finance the big breakthroughs and let us focus our money on development, where big payoffs are not far away. Even among governments, there is now an incentive to free-ride and let some other government somewhere else in the world pay for the basic research. These incentives were much smaller when much of basic research was focused on defense. The United States could not afford to free-ride if there was a chance that the U.S.S.R. might invent the equivalent of the atomic bomb and overturn the existing structure of military power. After the defeat of Germany in World War II, Russia was for a few months the world's dominant military power. Its armies had been the principal force defeating the Germans. But then the United States dropped two A-bombs on the Japanese. Suddenly the U.S.S.R. lost its dominant military position. Much of the history of the next forty-five years of the Cold War consisted of the U.S.S.R. attempting to regain what it had lost in 1945. Even if a country can eventually catch up, as Russia did, no superpower wants to endure a period of time when it is not a superpower.

In the economic arena the downside risks of free-riding are much lower. Saving money may be worth the risks of falling behind, given that one can always copy to catch up. But if everyone attempts to free-ride the world's R&D system, there is no new technology for anyone.

7.   Skills

Skilled people are needed to discover new knowledge, invent new products and processes, staff the necessary production processes, ensure adequate maintenance of complicated equipment, and even to use the new products and processes that advances in knowledge permit. Literacy is a necessary precursor to computer literacy.

The creation of human capital is by its nature a social, and not an individual, process. Human skills only grow if one generation teaches the next what it has learned so that the second generation can devote itself to expanding existing knowledge and acquiring new skills rather than to rediscovering and relearning what the previous generation has already mastered. Self-education is inherently limited. "Show me a self-made man and I will show you a poorly made man." Progress requires systematic social processes for educating the young.

The invention of universal compulsory publicly funded education was mankind's greatest social invention. With it, the link was cut between family income and education, and ignorance and low income in one generation did not automatically lead to ignorance and low income in the next. The educated can count on working in a world where their workmates are educated. They do not have to spend time explaining what must be done to those who cannot read instructions. The effective use of their skills can be expanded. They have more time for creative activities.

In the end it is this system of public education that lies behind the continuous improvement in standards of living and the ever-rising levels of wealth we now take for granted. Continuous economic improvement was not even a concept, much less a reality, before universal education was invented in the nineteenth century in the United States.

In the World Bank's estimates of countries' potential productive wealth, the most productive capital per person is found in large, lightly populated, but well-educated countries such as Australia ($835,000) and Canada ($704,000). In these countries land and natural resources account for 80 percent of productive wealth and human skills account for the other 20 percent. In contrast, in a country like Japan (fifth on the list at $565,000) the proportions are exactly reversed: more than 80 percent of productive wealth is held in the form of human skills and knowledge and only 20 percent in the form of land and natural resources. The United States (at $421,000) falls in between with 60 percent of its wealth in the form of human capital and 40 percent in land and natural resources.[76] Being first in terms of actual per capita wealth and twelfth on the World Bank list, the United States is an overachiever when it comes to converting potential wealth into actual wealth. Its social willingness to change and its entrepreneurial drive make up for its fewer natural resources and lesser skills.

In the future, with knowledge replacing natural resources as the key ingredient in the third industrial revolution, the same percentage distributions of human and physical wealth will lead to different overall rankings. The value of human resources will be rising and the value of natural resources falling.

In nineteenth century capitalism, human skills weren't seen as that important. Labor was a rented, hired-and-fired, marginal factor of production. Socialism arose as a response to the secondary position of labor in capitalism, promising to give labor a central position in the economic system. This is what gave it its political appeal. Interestingly, just as socialism and communism were dying, technology was elevating humans to a more central position in the productive framework of capitalism. Capitalism was being forced to put human skills and knowledge, rather than machinery, at the heart of its system.

Building a wealth pyramid in the twenty-first century will require changes in the system of skill acquisition.

1: The skills needed to succeed will be both increasing and changing very rapidly. Few will be able to equip themselves with lifetime working skills in the first twelve or sixteen years of education. Adult education, with skill acquisition at all age levels, will have to become a reality.

2: Since the needed skills will depend upon the new fast-moving technologies being deployed, many will have to be created in a joint on-the-job training effort between employees and employers. But individuals no longer have lifetime careers with one company; companies no longer have lifetime employees. The result has been the gradual destruction of existing on-the-job training systems. In an environment without lifetime careers and lifetime employees, who invests in what skills? How does the employee know what skills to acquire? How do employers ensure that they will find the skills they need?

3: In a global economy where employers arbitrage the world looking for the lowest wages, people's pay is not based on whether they live in a rich or a poor country but upon their individual skills. The well-educated living in India make something that looks like American wages, while the uneducated living in America make something that looks like Indian wages. If unskilled first world workers don't want to be in competition with equally unskilled but lower wage third world workers, they will need much better skills. With globalization and a skill-intensive technological shift, much better skills must be delivered to the bottom two thirds of the labor force in the developed world if their wages are not to fall.

Higher and Faster Changing Skills

Human skills come in many vintages. Some skills have been known for a long time. Others are brand-new. What makes the era ahead different is the extent to which it will be dominated by recently acquired knowledge and skills. The new processes, products, and services of the third industrial revolution are causing a big change in the relative earning power of old versus new skills.

Older workers sell experience and skills of an earlier vintage. Young workers sell newly acquired skills.

Experience is just less valuable. Over the past quarter of a century the returns to experience have been going down for every level of education. For male high school graduates, the value of sixteen to twenty years of experience is down 21 percent, and for college graduates it is down 10 percent.[77]

Market earnings for different skill vintages have also shifted dramatically in the last quarter of a century. The decade of peak earnings for male college graduates dropped a decade, from forty-five through fifty-four to thirty-five through forty-four. In inflation-corrected dollars, the earnings of forty-five- to fifty-four-year-old male college graduates fell 24 percent, from $55,000 to $41,898. The same shift is visible if one looks at the exploding salaries for new M.B.A.s (up 60 percent in the last four years at MIT) and the massive downsizings of older managers. The new are worth more; the old are worth less.

FINISHED AT FORTY was the cover story of *Fortune* magazine's

February 1999 issue.[78] According to the article, fifty-five is an age when it's almost impossible to find a job in business; the doors to new jobs begin shutting at age forty, and older workers (the example is a forty-four-year-old female) should be prepared to cut their existing salaries in half to get reemployed if they are downsized. More than a quarter of age discrimination suits are now brought by workers in their forties.

Old knowledge and experience are simply much less valuable than they used to be. The data show it. News stories confirm it. Younger workers work harder, have better skills, are more flexible, and have greater potential.

In the new knowledge-based economy, only those at the highest skill levels have seen real wage increases. Among men, only those with advanced degrees (master's degrees and above) have higher real wages than they had twenty-five years ago.[79] As one goes down the education curve, the wage reductions get bigger and bigger—3 percent for college graduates, 29 percent for high school graduates, 31 percent for high school dropouts.

Not surprisingly, studies show that at the same time, the payoff to high IQ is going up: the income gap between those with high (120 and above) and low IQs (80 and down) is rising.[80] A brain-power revolution raises the value of brains.

As a result of these shifts in the payoffs to experience, education, and intelligence in the last twenty-five years, the earnings gap between those without a high school degree and those with a college degree has risen 40 percent for workers twenty-five through thirty-four years of age. What is widening is not so much the wage gap between the averagely skilled and the unskilled (the gap between the 50th and 10th percentiles is up only 7 percent), but the gap between the very skilled and the averagely skilled (the 90th to 50th percentile gap is up 17 percent). The very skilled are worth more; those with average skills are worth less.

There is a message in the observed shift in wages in America over the last twenty-five years. In the twenty-first century, no country that wishes to be rich can leave some of its citizens uneducated. This applies to women as well as men. Any society that does not educate women (the Taliban in Afghanistan) is not going to be successful. As the Aga Khan's Shia Ismailis Moslem education foundation says, "Educate a man and one educates a man. Educate a woman and one educates a family." Successful societies will educate women because they contribute needed talent to the workforce, but they will also do so because uneducated mothers seldom have well-educated sons.

A knowledge economy requires two interlocking but very different skill sets. Knowledge creation requires highly educated creative skills at the very top of the skill distribution. Knowledge deployment requires widespread high-quality skills and education in the middle and bottom of the skill distribution. The same country need not lead in both. As we have seen, in the first half of the twentieth century the United States led the world in per capita gross domestic product (it had the highest deployment of knowledge), but Germany was the world's leader in the creation of new knowledge. Superior deployment skills in the middle and lower skill ranges allowed America to generate higher levels of wealth than Germany without having Germany's creative skills at the very top.

America's superior deployment skills did not happen by accident. In the immediate aftermath of the industrial revolution, the acquisition of education and skills was left to the private marketplace. Skills weren't seen as that important to the success of capitalism in any of the nineteenth century writings about it. Capital equipment was seen as the decisive factor determining economic success or failure. Adam Smith barely mentions education in his *Wealth of Nations*. He talks about it only as an antidote to the mind-numbing boredom of factory work. Nineteenth century economists did not see why education could not be bought and sold like any other commodity in capitalism.

But nineteenth century mill owners in Massachusetts noticed that an educated person working with other educated people was more productive than the same person working with illiterates. These mill owners cared about the education of their workers' children, since the education of these children affected the mill's productivity and the owner's income. If workers can read instruction manuals, less time has to be spent teaching them to operate new equipment. Productivity and profits rise. Workers who cannot tell time or read directions waste the time of other workers. The well-educated have more time to devote to high value-added activities. In more modern times, mathematically trained workers make just-in-time inventories and statistical quality control into feasible production technologies.

Historically, those mill owners understood that relying on private education had never worked. No society has ever become widely literate without some system of publicly financed education. For all of human history, and even today, most of humanity has been illiterate. Education does not happen automatically. It has to be socially organized. Even with social organization and free provision by the taxpayer, 28 percent of young Americans age twenty-five through thirty-four have not graduated from high school.[81]

Empirically, what needs to be done doesn't get done if societies rely solely on private markets.

The reasons are simple. Education is best done starting with the very young. One can argue about whether the causes are psychological or physiological, but the young learn more quickly. "You can't teach an old dog new tricks" is an ancient expression. Also, the earlier the education, the bigger the payoff—there are simply more years of life in which the education can be used. And the young don't have to be diverted from other productive activities. Opportunity costs are low. In peasant societies where the young can work during the planting and harvesting seasons, diversion costs are high, and educational levels are always very low.

Looking at how wages rise as years of education go up, big economic payoffs exist for the first few years of education and the last few years of education, but only very small economic returns accrue per year of education in between these extremes. The reasons are simple. Those with a lot less than the average amount of education lose a lot because they are excluded from society's good jobs. Similarly those with a lot more than the average amount of education gain a lot because they get society's best jobs. But annual earnings gains are very small in the years when those being educated are moving across the crowded central parts of the education distribution, and their educational achievements remain more or less average for a long period of time. College education exhibits a similar pattern. An extra year of college education has very little positive effect on earnings if the student does not complete a degree program. From an economic perspective the right advice is "Get a degree or don't go." During the long intervals when not much is happening to market wages, acquiring more education is not going to meet private market rate-of-return criteria.

While education should rationally be directed at the young, they have neither the necessary decision-making capacity nor the money to invest in education and skills. This means that the family must pay for private education. History teaches us that most won't. Uneducated parents usually don't have the necessary funds to invest in education. But more important, uneducated parents seldom appreciate the value of education. In fact they often see education in a negative light, since it will separate them sociologically from their children. The exceptions are mostly in the Confucian world, where for thousands of years those who could pass the Mandarin examinations became important government officials. There education was the only upward path.

Without public support, education levels tend to fall. Middle-class parents may have the funds and abstractly appreciate the value of education, but the returns are so distant—twelve years to a high school degree, sixteen years to a college degree, twenty-two years to a Ph.D.—that other things seem more immediately urgent, and costs look prohibitive. In the United States, twelve years of public primary and secondary education cost the taxpayer $65,000 at the end of the 1990s. A college education costs another $80,000 to $120,000 (including the taxpayer's contribution to state universities) depending upon the quality. While going to college, the student forgoes $70,000 in earnings. Put it all together and the total cost of a college education is $200,000 to $250,000. How many families can afford to pay? How many families will pay if they have to pay it all directly? Publicly financed education spreads the costs across the entire population (not just those with children) and across each individual's lifetime. Spread out in this way, the costs don't seem so overwhelming.

The financial returns for large investments in education are there when averaged across millions and millions of individuals. A high school graduate's investment in a college education will earn a 7 to 8 percent rate of return. In their peak earning years white male college graduates will earn almost 50 percent more than white male high school graduates. But at the same time, 21 percent of all male college graduates earn less than the average male high school graduate, and 26 percent of all high school graduates earn more than the average college graduate. The private risks that education won't pay off for any particular individual are very high.

Private investments in education by their very nature compound educational inequalities. Those with more money find it easier to invest and are more willing to invest, since they see the payoff for such investments in the earnings of their friends and can afford to undertake the high risks that any particular individual's earnings will not rise with more education. Those without funds cannot afford to bet on the possibility that there will be big economic payoffs to more education and are often rightly scared by the risks of failure.

Private credit markets accentuate family income differences. Before government-guaranteed student loans, those without funds found it impossible to borrow for educational investments. Private lenders were smart enough to know that too many students would default because their individual educational investment didn't pay off, and even if the investment did pay off, debt collections would be difficult. Physical capital can always be repossessed and resold if the borrower refuses to repay. Human capital cannot be. Antislavery laws prevent it.

For all of these reasons, those nineteenth century American mill owners knew that private decision-making wasn't going to lead to the right results for them. Mandatory, taxpayer-financed public education had to be invented.

America rode this social invention to the top of the twentieth century wealth pyramid.

Skill Acquisition in a World without Lifetime Careers

Individual education has always been a high-risk investment. But recently it has become even more risky. How does one plan the investments necessary to have a career in the face of corporate downsizings from profitable firms?

For my generation of high school graduates, the concept of a career had meaning. During the 1950s in Montana (where I went to high school), high school graduates started as laborers in the copper mines. Beginning wages were good, and one could count on regular 2 or 3 percent per year annual real wage increases. There was a skill ladder. Laborers moved up to operaters, running underground trains or other kinds of heavy equipment, learning the necessary skills by working as assistants to the operators. If you demonstrated intelligence and judgment, the doors would open quickly to being a blaster, responsible for setting off underground explosions. Each promotion meant higher hourly wage rates. When a worker reached his mid-thirties, he could expect to take the last step on the earnings ladder and become a contract miner, who was paid for each foot of tunnel dug rather than by the hour. He was no longer a wage slave. A career ladder was in place, and high school graduates could produce earnings that matched those of college graduates.

But that's all gone now. Those mines were shut down. The thousands of people who worked there were laid off.

What used to be true only in declining industries (skills suddenly become valueless) is now true everywhere. Downsizing is a way of life even in good times among profitable companies. In a global economy, if skills are cheaper somewhere else in the world, companies will move to those other places and lower their production costs. They aren't tied to any particular set of workers. When new knowledge makes old skills obsolete, business firms want to employ workers who already have the new skills. They don't want to pay for retraining. In the mid and late 1990s, profitable American companies are laying off more than half a million workers each and every year.[82] The old career ladders are gone. The old lifetime employees are gone.

Explicitly or implicitly, today's high school graduate is given a message: "You are unlikely to have a lifetime career in any one company. You are going to have to learn to take responsibility for and manage your own lifetime career. Regular annual wage increases are a thing of the past. Paternalism is gone." If they are honest, employers deliver this message themselves. There is only one problem with this piece of advice. How does anyone follow it?

If career ladders don't exist within any one company, they must exist across different companies if they are to exist at all. This means that a good initial performance at company A must lead to training opportunities, a better job, and higher wages at company B. But the world doesn't work this way for most people. Companies don't tell other companies who their good employees are. Even if they have no promotion opportunities for the good employees within their organizations, they don't want to lose them. And even if they did tell other companies, they wouldn't be believed. They would be suspected of trying to get rid of their bad workers. Similarly they don't tell other companies about their bad employees They don't want to open themselves up to libel suits. If asked, and they seldom are, companies are willing to tell other companies just one thing about a worker seeking a new job: "Yes, That person did work for us."

In this context, a good work performance at company A doesn't matter, since it doesn't lead to opportunities for training and promotion at company B. When workers move from one company to another, they simply start over at another entry-level job. There is no progress up a career ladder. The rational strategy is to keep moving from employer to employer until one finds a company that still has internal career ladders. But as such companies get fewer and fewer in number, the number of high school graduates with real career opportunities ahead of them declines to the vanishing point.

The cross-company career ladder runs into other problems. After age forty-five cross-company career moves are difficult, and after age fifty-five they are impossible. Those tracking downsized workers find that after age fifty-five they never again find good jobs with good companies. Age discrimination laws can protect older employees against being unfairly dismissed by their old firms, but they cannot get them a good job at a new company. Employers get to decide whom they will hire. In a fast-changing world, older employees too often bring obsolete experience and out-of-date skills. There are always a lot of possible young employees who look better and are better. Older job seekers do not suffer from discrimination. They are objectively economically obsolete.

The lack of career opportunities is dramatically visible in earnings data. The earnings gains that high school graduates used to make from twenty to forty years of age are much smaller than they used to be. There are lots of jobs, unemployment is low, but skill acquisition opportunities and the higher wages that go with them don't exist. As a result, earnings profiles are flatter. The lack of on-the-job training opportunities is another reason why the wage gap between high school–educated workers and college-educated workers has gotten much bigger in recent years.

The issue is not jobs. It is careers. If wages fall to be commensurate with skills, jobs are always available. That is what the American experience proves. In the 1990s jobs have never been more plentiful, yet wages have been falling for more than half of the workforce. In contrast with jobs, careers are a commodity in very short supply in America.

With career ladders, ambitious workers of the 1950s or 1960s could figure out what skills they would need to advance successfully—they knew what to take in night school. But without career ladders, how can they know what skills will pay off in their career and so rationally plan their educational investment? No one wants to waste their funds on skills they won't be using. But since they don't know where they will be working and what skills will be required by an as-yet-unknown employer, they cannot determine what skills they will need.

Historically, on-the-job training has been central to skills acquisition for much of the population. But with downsizings, the days of extensive on-the-job training have ended. What replaces it? In economic textbooks workers start paying their employer for the training they used to get free. Empirically this has not happened. Knowing what skills to buy from one's employer is no simpler than knowing what skills to buy from an outside institution. Employers don't set up the necessary programs, since they aren't in the for-pay training business. Knowing these facts of modern life, 70 percent of the workforce report that they don't want to manage their careers by themselves without help. They know they cannot do so successfully.

RULE TEN: The biggest unknown for the individual in a knowledge-based economy is how to have a career in a system where there are no careers.

What is also missing from a downsizing environment is a sense of economic security. If workers are asked what factors are most important in a job, economic security always comes out as more important than maximum wages. This is not the answer that is supposed to be given by *Homo economicus*. He or she is supposed to be interested only in lifetime income maximization and not worried about the risks and uncertainties of economic life. But real live human beings like the feeling of a solid economic floor under them.

Paradoxically, just as one would think that firms would be building closer relationships with their key knowledge workers to keep them committed to the firm, they are smashing that implicit social contract also. Knowledge workers, like other workers, are now fired when they are not needed or when their skills become obsolete. In addition, their real wages are reduced when alternative cheaper workers are found elsewhere in the world. If workers are downsized when they are not needed, smart workers know that they should leave whenever an even marginally better job opportunity presents itself. Firms invest less in on-the-job skill acquisition for these knowledge workers, even when they want them to stay around, since they know that fewer of them will stay around. The cycle of underinvestment accelerates.

As job uncertainty rises, those with a strong interest in the success of their current employer decrease in number. Surveys show that while attachment to their occupation has remained constant for American workers over the last two decades, those with a strong attachment to their employer have decreased by one-fifth.[83] When more than half of the workforce report that they have no attachment to their current employer, something serious has happened. The system is evolving toward less commitment and less skill investment, just as it should be evolving in the opposite direction.

Skills for the Bottom Two-Thirds of the Workforce

While official earnings data for 1998 won't be compiled until the fall of 1999, it looks as if there was an increase in real wages for the bottom two-thirds of the workforce in 1998. This fact, if it proves to be a fact, in no way changes the basic problem. If real wages had not risen, given record low unemployment rates and tight labor markets, it would have been surprising. Since wages started to fall in 1973, there have been other years when wages rose for average workers (they did so in 1984, 1985, and 1986) but then wages resumed their decline. Even in 1998 the preliminary data indicate that the top quintile of workers were getting much larger wage increases than the bottom three quintiles.

The normal argument for educating the uneducated is political. Education is important to democracies interested in self-preservation, since they can thrive only in economies where most workers are participating in the fruits of the economy's success. If this is not happening, if at some point a majority of the voters are not benefiting from the economic system, they will, and should, vote to abolish the system that is either antithetical or oblivious to their welfare. The United States is now testing this piece of received political wisdom. Real wages are falling for the bottom two-thirds of the workforce and rising at the top. Will a political explosion in fact occur? For those interested in real world political science experiments, doing nothing makes for interesting observations. For those interested in the continued success of the American democracy, it sounds like an awfully risky experiment.

While the political arguments are well taken, there are also important economic considerations. What the Massachusetts mill owners knew in the nineteenth century is even more true in the twenty-first century: without widespread educational skills, no one can build a successful wealth pyramid. At some point my fellow workers' education becomes as important to my earnings as my own. With them uneducated a lid is placed on my potential. I become the equivalent of the Indian software engineer working in Bangalore. I make a nice income relative to those of my illiterate neighbors, but less than those in the developed world with literate neighbors. More important, I am not in charge of the system. I don't make the decisions. I am just a hired gunslinger working for an owner I have never met. I can be a marginal part of someone else's wealth pyramid, but I cannot build my own wealth pyramid.

One can argue, and economists do, about exactly how much of the observed spreading out in the distribution of earnings can be attributed to a skill-intensive technological shift and how much to the development of a global economy, but those arguments are irrelevant when it comes to discussing the cures.[84] Both causes lead to a world where the wages of the unskilled in the wealthy industrial world are going to go down unless they can substantially enhance and change their skills several times in the course of their lifetimes. And looking forward, both causes of rising inequality are going to intensify. New skills are going to become even more dominant relative to old skills, and globalization is becoming ever more of a reality.

Part of the rising inequality can be traced back to the disappearance of lifetime career opportunities. With the end of company-defined careers, on-the-job training opportunities have become much more unevenly distributed than in the past. In a downsizing world, the time necessary to learn new skills is more critical, since business firms have much shorter time horizons. They have no lifetime employees and no paternalistic urges. They know that their downsizing has implicitly taught their workforce that once trained they should leave for higher paying jobs elsewhere if they are available. As a result, if skills cannot be quickly learned, they won't be taught.

Profit-maximizing private firms award training opportunities to those who are the quickest and cheapest to train. Most of the time this means those who already have the most education and training, because the more one has already learned, the easier it is to learn. One learns how to learn. As a result, on-the-job skills go to those who have acquired off-the-job education. The net result is a private investment process whereby most skills are acquired by, or given to, those who already have the most skills. Skills lead to skills. Any country that relies on private investment in human skills will quickly find itself not just with too few skills but with a very unequal skill distribution.

Looking backward, the answer to generating the skills needed for the first industrial revolution was to cut the link between parental income and skill investments. The taxpayer's money was used to build a good skill base at the bottom of the wealth pyramid. This in turn created the middle-class earnings that gave workers an economic stake in capitalism—preventing the revolution that Marx predicted would replace capitalism with socialism.

Looking forward, the new technologies that permit globalization and change the needed skill sets have cut the link between company-organized careers and individual skill acquisition. Individuals don't know what skills they should acquire or how to personally manage their careers even if they are willing to make the necessary investments. In a knowledge-based economy, skill acquisition is not something that can be limited to formal education between the ages of five and twenty-five, yet there is no system for organizing skill acquisition after age twenty-five.

Looking downward, skills and education in the bottom two-thirds of the workforce are as important as skills and education in the top one-third. Neither can reach their potential without help from the other.

Along with recessions and financial meltdowns, capitalism has another genetic weakness: myopia. Using discounted net present values as the basis for decision-making, it has an intrinsically short time horizon. Private business firms usually use three- to five-year planning horizons. Those horizons simply aren't congruent with developing the skills that knowledge-based societies need to thrive—sixteen years for a college graduate, twenty-two years for a Ph.D. Much like a snake that sheds its old skin so that it can grow larger in a new one, the education and skills acquisition system will have to become something quite different in the twenty-first century.

Looking at the three developed regions of the world, two have education problems. Japan is superbly educated at the bottom but needs creativity at the top. America is superbly creative at the top but needs better skills at the bottom. Only Europe can claim to be well educated at the bottom and creative at the top.

Both Japan and the United States have for decades issued reports documenting what they need. In 1998 alone three Japanese reports— one by the Japanese Planning Agency, one by the University Council, and one by the Curriculum Council—called for changing school and university curriculums to increase creativity.[85] Universities that were built for the catch-up phase of development after World War II need to be rebuilt to generate the skills and attitudes necessary to make technological breakthroughs.

America has an equally well-documented set of reports on the skills problems in the bottom two-thirds of the workforce. For more than twenty years Americans have been writing reports to themselves (*A Nation at Risk, High Skills or Low Wages: America's Choice*) on the need for radical changes in their education system. As all of these reports have concluded, American workers know substantially less than those graduating from high school in Europe, Japan, and many underdeveloped nations.

But neither country has been able to act in the last twenty years. What is the answer? Clearly, writing more detailed programs is not the answer. Many of them have been developed and all of them sit on the shelves in both countries unimplemented. How do Japan and America get themselves organized to act? That brings us back to being builders—building the levels of the wealth pyramid that are necessary for twenty-first century success.

Conclusion

Problems that emerge slowly, such as the rising wage dispersion that is now visible in the United States, are difficult to solve. They never seem like a crisis. It is often easier to get used to the new reality than to change it. Certainly that's what has been happening in America for the last twenty-five years. Successful societies notice such changes and prevent the impending problems from emerging. They don't wait for revolts, since by then it's usually too late to adopt sensible solutions. Reskilling the bottom two-thirds of the labor force is not something that can be done quickly. The current incentive structure took decades to create today's problems. New incentive structures would similarly take substantial amounts of time to reverse those effects. There is no time to wait for policies to work once a political revolt is under way.

To do nothing, effectively returning skill investments to the vagaries of individual decision-making, is essentially to abandon the skill level of the wealth pyramid to the economic jungle. The ensuing neglect will eventually bring the American wealth pyramid down—just as the real jungle brought down the real Mayan pyramids in Central America or the real Cambodian pyramids at Angkor Wat.

8.   Tools

Physical investments in factories, office buildings, equipment, housing, and infrastructure form the next level of the wealth pyramid. Capitalism took its name from the ownership of these capital structures since, in the century after the industrial revolution, capital equipment was seen as the vital ingredient in economic success. Economic progress and wealth were direct functions of capital investment.

Investments by their very nature require a willingness to sacrifice for the future. Some animals have this willingness programmed into them. They store food and build homes for the winter. Some animals, like the beaver, even build dams and change their natural environment. But many don't. In economic terms the latter simply suffer through a period of time (winter) with a much lower standard of living. Many die of starvation or exposure. Mother Nature doesn't worry about their deaths; she solves the survival problem for these species by having enough of them born during the summer so that there is a reasonable probability that some will still be alive when the next spring rolls around. Mother Nature isn't interested in the survival of the individual. The fastest antelope may be unfortunate enough to meet up with the fastest lion and get eaten, or it may accidentally trip and get eaten by a very slow lion. Survival of the fittest and natural selection are group modes of survival and advancement. The very best individual need not be a survivor for a species to survive.

One of the things that makes humans human is that they know they have a past and a future. Because they understand that they are on a journey, they are willing to invest to improve the future even if they know that as individuals they will not be around to enjoy the fruits of those investments. Primitive peoples who don't make such future-oriented investments live lives not very far removed from that of the beaver. They build a home, they store food, and they marginally change the environment around them, but they do not advance over time because they don't systematically invest in changing the future. Primitive tribes are much like animals. They stop building when they are well fed, warm, and dry. Great civilizations, in contrast, are marked by their willingness to use and invest in new tools. That is the essence of what make them great civilizations.

Civilization is a story of being willing to spend the time to build individual and collective tools. The ancient Romans did not by accident become famous for their road-building. Building a pyramid in Egypt or Mexico requires willingness to sacrifice for a future that is far beyond the lifetime of individuals doing the building. The same long time horizon is necessary to build a modern wealth pyramid. It is a social construction necessary if individual genius is to flourish. Learning to read and write requires major investments in time on the part of both the teacher and the student. The big payoffs from learning occur not at any particular moment in time or for any particular individual, but over time as each generation gets to build on what the last generation has already discovered. Social investments in transportation and communication systems have similar long-run payoffs.

It is man's interest in building tools that ultimately allows him to create wealth. The King of the Beasts, the lion, cannot be said to be wealthy or poor. He is only well fed or hungry.

Humans progress by building more and better tools. They want more tools to generate higher, and yet higher, standards of living. Economists as late as the early 1950s worried that the Great Depression would resume after World War II because of satiated wants. Having everything he or she could imagine, the consumer would want nothing else, tool-building would stop, and economic growth would dry up. But satiated wants are not part of human nature. Unlike other animal species, we do not stop building when we are well fed, warm, and dry. Our imagination of what might be is always ahead of the reality. There is no limit to the new things we want.

Being curious, humans also build tools for the sake of satisfying their curiosity and only later think about how the tools might contribute to their standard of living. Particle accelerators used in physics to break matter into its component parts contribute to our understanding of the world around us, but it is as yet an understanding that has no practical implications. No one can even imagine how what is being discovered today might contribute to raising human standards of living tomorrow. But we build them anyway.

The human reality of wanting more and not being satisfied with what is, is in fact what drives the capitalist economic system forward.

Tool-building urges may be part of the genetic code of human beings, but what is always latent is not always present. For a thousand years during the Dark Ages, tool-building disappeared and what was, was good enough. No new tools needed to be built. Without the willingness to build new tools, economic decline set in for almost a thousand years.

Relative to the investment calculus of capitalism, all great civilizations are in fact overinvestors in tools. Capitalist companies usually insist that investments pay for themselves in a three- to five-year period of time. Great civilizations invest far beyond those limits, often making capital investments (the pyramids, the

Parthenon, Roman roads, Angkor Wat, Mayan temples, medieval cathedrals) that are deliberately designed to last forever.

Tools are basic because all other parts of the wealth pyramid require tools if these other parts of the pyramid are to be used to generate wealth and the above-the-survival-line resources necessary to create great civilizations. Successful economic systems build social tools such as communication and transportation systems. Entrepreneurs pioneer the introduction of new tools. The compass, the rudder, and the keel allowed Europeans to explore and conquer the world. To be useful, knowledge must be embedded in tools. Without his furnace, Besssemer could not have made steel. Without tools, few skills can be employed. Imagine computer programmers without computers. Tools make the extraction of natural resources possible (multibillion-dollar offshore platforms are necessary for deep-water drilling) and produce the essential elements of high-quality environments (filtration plants give us drinkable water). Under capitalism those who own tools are the decision-makers, and market wealth consists of the ownership of tools and the output that flows from them.

Tool-building depends upon an interest in the future. Individuals and organizations take some of the resources and time they could have devoted to today's consumption (defer today's gratification—i.e., save) and use them to build tools (invest) so that in the future they can produce more than they could have produced if they had not stopped to build tools. With their new tools they can employ the latest knowledge, amplify skills, expand natural resource availabilities, and ultimately create more wealth. In the process they amplify their consumption possibilities and move some of their consumption from the present to the future.

In 1997 Americans worked with $24,883 billion worth of tools. Each worker had $191,000 worth of tools. Each $1 of gross domestic product generated required $3 worth of tools. Business plant and equipment and residential structures each accounted for 35 percent of this total, public tools (e.g., roads, sewers, schools, airports, military equipment) accounted for another 20 percent, and consumer durables (e.g., cars, household equipment) the remaining 10 percent.[86]

When it comes to investments in tools there are three critical questions. (1) What is the right total amount to invest? Or equivalently, how many of today's resources should be devoted to the future? (2) What is the right mix of investment between private tools and social tools? (3) Are investments being made and used in the most efficient manner possible, or could new technologies or new modes of social organization allow us to get more output from our existing tools?

The Right Number of Tools

While some categories of tools are growing rapidly relative to the growth in hours of work (information-processing tools are increasing four times faster than tools in general), aggregate investment in physical tools has been slowing down in America. The capital-to-labor ratio grew four times as fast in the 1960s as it did in the decade from 1987 to 1997.

When it comes to interest in the future and a willingness to defer consumption to build tools, Americans are nothing if not consistent. Right across the board in their private, corporate, and public lives they are investing less. Between the decade of the 1960s and the most recent decade, individual tool-building fell 33 percent for consumer durables and 40 percent for residential structures. Business tool-building—additions to the stock of plant and equipment—fell 47 percent. Government infrastructure investments fell even faster, down 49 percent.[87]

The declines have been particularly sharp for federal investments in public tools—down 74 percent. Current consumption expenditures on the health care and pensions of the elderly (over

50 percent of the federal budget now goes to the elderly) are driving investment spending out of the federal budget. While they are unlikely to be carried out exactly as written, the budget agreements that have been reached between the Democratic president and the Republican Congress call for further sharp reductions in public infrastructure investments over the next ten years to make room for the spending that will go to an ever-increasing number of elderly Americans.[88]

Americans are building fewer tools—investing less—than they did in the past and less than either Western Europe or Japan. But this does not necessarily mean that Americans are investing too little from the perspective of hard-nosed capitalism. If Americans do not choose to save to have more tools, and others do—so be it. Americans because they save less will have a higher standard of living in the present, and the rest of the wealthy industrial world because they save more will have a higher standard of living in the future. Each individual decision-maker is simply making a choice that rationally maximizes his or her own lifetime welfare, and what all of this adds up to for the nation as a whole is irrelevant. Individuals have a right not to save if they wish. What will be, will be.

While certainly in accordance with capitalist economic theory, something is fundamentally wrong with this analysis. In September 1998 the American personal savings rate became negative for the first time in sixty-five years. In 1933, during the Great Depression, when this last happened, earnings had collapsed, almost one-third of the labor force was unemployed, unemployment benefits had yet to be invented, welfare payments did not exist, and people had to sell their assets (dissave) to keep from starving. In contrast, in the fall of 1998 Americans were spending more than they earned because the stock market made them feel rich. Feeling rich, they wanted to consume more.

But this desire creates a social problem. Rising stock market values cannot be used to finance investment in new tools. The money received by those who sell stock must be equal to the money given up by those who buy stock. It is a zero-sum transaction as far as investments are concerned. It generates no new funds for building tools. Only holding consumption below earnings can provide the necessary resources to build tools.

Can any society afford to be completely laissez-faire and let the market mechanism produce what it has produced—a negative saving rate—for any period of time? No society can survive without tool-building. Letting the market decide to dissave is effectively a decision to fail socially. If war is too important to be left to the generals, tool-building is too important to be left to individual preferences and the market alone. There are societal interests that transcend individual interests in higher current standards of living. If individuals will not voluntarily think about the future, then the community collectively must do so.

This is especially true in a society full of social pressures and advertising encouraging people to consume more, with few countervailing social pressures and no advertising to encourage investment in tool-building. The social pressures to consume are enormous. Many have been persuaded. Over the last thirty years personal debts have risen from 59 to 85 percent of Americans' disposable income. Two-thirds of the debt service on this sum goes to consumer debt.[89] With 1.4 million bankruptcies in 1998, Americans are clearly being persuaded to consume more than they can afford to consume.[90]

While Americans are investing less in tools than their neighbors are, the conventionally cited comparative cross-country personal savings rates exaggerate how little Americans save. They are often cited only because they are easily available. In 1997 Americans saved 4 percent of their disposable income while the Japanese were saving 22 percent and the Germans were saving 13 percent.[92] In 1999 the American rate is predicted to fall to 1 percent.[93] But personal savings rates do not tell us what we want to know for several reasons.

First, they treat consumer durables as consumption, not as investment. As we have seen, consumer durables account for 10 percent of the American stock of tools, and Americans probably invest more in consumer durables than the Europeans or the Japanese do.

Second, resources invested in housing construction are statistically counted as saving and investment, but housing construction costs per meter of space are lower in the United States than they are in either Japan or Europe. As a result, Americans have more square feet of housing space per person than either the Japanese or the Europeans. When making cross-country comparisons, some adjustment has to be made for differences in the costs of building housing.

Third, personal savings rates by definition exclude the savings done by business firms and governments. While American individuals tend to save less than their Japanese or European counterparts, American businesses tend to save more. While many governments make a distinction between their investment activities and their consumption activities in a capital budget, the American government does not. Technically our public spending is all counted as if it were consumption in our standard statistical data. It is not: 20 percent of America's tools are public tools.

In comparative measures of national savings, American budget deficits are statistically shown as lowering savings rates. Tech-nically they only subtract from the total funds available for private investment, since some of the pool of funds that could have been used for private investment is borrowed by the government to finance its deficit. If deficits are being run to finance public investments, total investment does not fall despite the deficits.

Trade deficits can also be a source of more investment if imported goods are investment goods. Essentially funds are borrowed from the rest of the world to finance tools for American workers. Americans are tapping into higher savings rates in the rest of the world. One of the ways this happens is that foreign companies buy or build companies in America and make tools available to be used by their American workers.

RULE ELEVEN: Only those interested in the future build tools. Whatever they might say, those who build few tools are not interested in the future.

Local savings rates tell us who the ultimate owners and controllers of the capitalist system will be, but they don't tell us how many tools a particular workforce will have. To put it in a slightly oversimplistic way, Mercedes buys Chrysler rather than Chrysler buying Mercedes because Germans save more than Americans. But what counts on the productivity front in a global economy is not local savings rates but the total sums available to provide tools for a country's workforce.

While data are not available that would allow comparisons of the total stock of tools between countries, the best simple alternative is to look at nonresidential plant and equipment investment rates. In 1997 Japan invested 16 percent of its GDP in nonresidential plant and equipment, Germany 13 percent, and the United States 11 percent. Since the acquisition price of information hardware has been falling much faster than that of other types of equipment, and America buys a lot more information hardware than either Japan or Germany, the real investment spending gaps may also be smaller than these numbers indicate.

The lower rate of American plant and equipment tool-building relative to that of our wealthy competitors is also to some extent offset by higher efficiency. In normal times the U.S. rate of return on stockholder equity (the funds equity shareholders have invested in tool-building) is about three times that found in Japan and twice that found in Europe.[93] Some of what America loses in quantity it makes up by using its tools more efficiently.

Skeptics about private business efficiency can, of course, argue that high measured rates of return are due to the fact that Americans invest less. Lower investment rates lead to higher returns, since with a lower capital stock, tools are scarcer and can be rented for more. There is some truth in this argument, but it is not the whole truth. Some of those higher returns are due to higher efficiency. No one doubts that Americans are more ruthless when it comes to downsizing and closing money-losing activities.

Judgmentally, in the last two decades the Americans have probably invested too little and the Japanese too much—their rate of return on stockholder equity had dropped to less than 4 percent before the meltdown. The Europeans, who invested less than the Japanese but more than the Americans and who earn more than the Japanese but less than the Americans, probably come closest to hitting the golden mean. It's not hard, or controversial, to come to the conclusion that Americans save and invest too little.

Some of the problem lies with the theology of capitalism, which holds that investments are made only if the higher consumption received tomorrow is more valuable than the consumption forgone today. Investment demands that gratification be deferred and consumption postponed. But capitalism's investment calculus runs into problems in a society where growth is expected and most consumers know they will be wealthier tomorrow than they are today. Why would anyone want to lower their consumption today when they are relatively poor to raise their consumption tomorrow when they will be relatively rich? With any normal set of human consumption desires, they should not want to deprive themselves in the present.

In capitalism it is also expected that one will dissave toward the end of one's life to match lifetime consumption with lifetime earnings. The young rationally save and the old rationally dissave. But when societies have more old than young people, how do they generate the net savings that any society needs? The theory has no answer. Theoretically, as the mix shifts toward individuals who freely decide not to save, economic growth rationally slows down. But that is not an acceptable outcome for any society that wants to survive.

When it comes to investment activities, capitalism is highly directive and very restrictive. Only those investment activities that meet the test of generating a positive net present value should be undertaken, and all of those investment activities that generate negative net present values should be discontinued. Free markets exist to enforce the dictates of economic theory.

When it comes to individual consumption activities, however, capitalism turns 180 degrees and becomes completely nondirective—open to any and all expenditure patterns. Individuals have the right to spend their money on whatever they will. No individual can label any other individual's expenditure patterns stupid or foolish. Individuals themselves can say that they made a mistake and bought something not consistent with their preferences, but no one else can accuse them of error.

Capitalism is not a system that thrives, or even survives, however, in environments of persistent decline with falling investment. It's like a bicycle—easy to ride forward but impossible to ride backward. The possibilities of operating a capitalist economic system in the midst of persistent decline were tested in the Great Depression and almost finished off capitalism itself. A capitalism that cannot generate growth is a capitalism that will not survive. But this means that a capitalism that cannot generate the will to save is a capitalism that cannot replicate itself.

What is completely left out of standard economic theory is any view of human beings with the characteristics that make them human—not just another animal species. Humans are social builders who can get direct benefits—utility—from building. They can enjoy and take pride in investment goods just as in consumption goods. Whether individuals do or do not take pride in, and get utility from, those investments depends upon their social conditioning.

Capitalism comes with a built-in genetic disease—a tendency to save and invest too little. To offset this genetic tendency, building must be seen not just as an investment made to increase future consumption but as an end in and of itself. Building is a direct form of enjoyment. It is a process of creation, and humans are by nature creative. It is the equivalent of writing or reading a great book. One can measure a book's worth by its selling price, but the book lasts forever and yields benefits over and beyond its monetary costs of composition or printing. The same is true of great building projects focused on the future.

Many successful societies have existed in the past whose social conditioning led to investments being more important than consumption. Imperial Rome was one such society. Private citizens competed for the honor of building public buildings. But these large investments require an ideology extolling investment. They don't happen unless such an ideology is invented and sustained. Urges to build have to be supported so that they are at least coequal with urges to consume.

In America, all of our social conditioning is now leading not just toward the primacy of individual consumption but toward the view that nothing else matters at all. Billions are spent advertising the benefits of different consumption goods. Little or nothing is spent advertising the importance of investment goods.

When he first came into office in 1992, President Clinton was debating whether his new administration should focus on health care, education, or infrastructure. He chose health care, a form of public consumption, rather than education or infrastructure, both forms of public investment. He did not just make a political mistake. He focused Americans on a consumption problem when he should have focused them on investment problems. Even if he had succeeded in reforming health care, it was the wrong problem to address. He could and should have focused us in a very different direction.

The Public-Private Investment Mix

In all societies some tools are publicly constructed. For example, all military equipment is publicly owned. A country would not be a country if it did not own and control its own army. But roads are everywhere also a public responsibility. Road builders need to use society's power, the power of eminent domain, to force private landowners to sell their land at market prices so that roads can be built where they are needed and not where private landowners are voluntarily willing to sell their land. By definition, when someone is forced to sell, the free play of market forces—capitalism—does not exist.

Some tools are built socially because they are what economists call natural monopolies, where one common set of tools constructed for everyone's use is simply the least costly option. Once a road is built, it is efficient not to build competitive parallel roads until the first road's capacity has been reached. The same is true for airports, pipelines, and electrical and telephone transmission lines. Competitive firms cannot be organized because it is too expensive to build two or three power lines to every home.

Some tools are socially built because they need to be built ahead of market demands, and the resulting time span until they are profitable is so long that private investors will not make the necessary investments. American railroads are the classic example. East of the Mississippi River, where big cities and economic development had already occurred, every American railroad was privately financed. Railroads were profitable because they tied existing local markets together to make a national market. West of the Mississippi River railroads had to be government financed. There railroads were making economic development possible. There were no large local markets to be tied together. The function of the railroads west of the Mississippi was to create a transportation system cheap enough to allow the creation of those local markets, which could then be tied into a national market. But because the system was starting with empty space, the time necessary to recoup investments and make profits was too long for private investors. In the long run western railways were socially profitable, but in the short run they were privately unprofitable.

The Internet is a modern equivalent. Initially it was built as a communication system connecting military bases designed to survive atomic attacks. Since IBM mainframes were necessary for its use, it was far too expensive for normal civilians. With the development of powerful midsize computers it became a communication system that had other scientific uses. An upgrade of the system was financed by the National Science Foundation, and universities were tied into the Internet. Eventually, with the development of cheap personal computers that had the power of 1960s mainframes, costs fell, and private usage rose to the point where the Internet could be profitably organized, financed, and run privately. But for an initial twenty-five-year period, the Internet required up-front social investments.

These early social investments are why the Internet is an American-dominated communication system and why American companies are the leaders in electronic commerce. Other countries, whose governments did not make such investments, are now playing catch-up.

The reverse is true in the case of high-speed trains. Here the rest of the world has taken a leadership position. High-speed trains are the cheapest, safest, and most environmentally friendly way to connect major cities 100 to 400 miles apart.[94] Compared with roads, far less land has to be used and as a consequence fewer neighborhoods have to be disrupted; costs of construction for the same carrying capacity are much lower; speeds are far higher (France has trains running at 185 miles per hour and the Japanese are testing trains at 350 miles per hour, while on the Los Angeles freeways cars creep and crawl at just a few miles per hour); fewer accidents happen (it's estimated that the Tokyo-to-Osaka bullet train has saved 1,800 lives and 10,000 injuries); congestion does not exist; and pollution is minimal (100 million Americans live in cities where vehicle emissions regularly exceed federal health standards).[95] Twelve countries have high-speed trains and sixteen countries are building lines.

But America stands on the sidelines. Like those who didn't invest in the Internet, America will at some point either have to play catch-up or permanently incur the higher costs of connecting its cities with inferior, more costly transportation systems.

Bringing fiber optics from the curb to the home is another investment some countries are making and others are not. America is not, since the extra services that can now be sold to the home with a broad-band communication system aren't large enough to justify the private costs that would be necessary. The Germans in eastern Germany have made this investment on the assumption that much as the railroads opened the West, fiber optics will open the home to a wide range of services that today we cannot even imagine. At the moment it is impossible to prove either side right.

Public infrastructure investments have two big effects on wealth. First, they themselves are a form of wealth. Second, they make investments in the private sector more profitable and raise the value of private tools. Trucking company profits and the value of trucking companies went up dramatically when the interstate highway system was completed. Trucks could go farther in less time, fewer warehouses were needed, and with less stopping and starting at stoplights, truck maintenance costs fell sharply.

Economists measure investment adequacy by looking at the rate of return on new investments. If the rate of return is very high, too little is being invested. Within the economics profession there is a debate about the rate of return on public investment, since some studies have found very high rates on past investments (50 to 60 percent).[96] Since these rates are at least three times the average pretax rates of return in the private sector, if true they would provide powerful evidence that Americans are investing too little in public tools.

Critics of these studies argue that such rates are implausibly high. What they think is being found is a reverse correlation. Those areas that are already economically successful use some of their higher income to invest in more infrastructure because it adds to their well-being. High levels of infrastructure investment are the result, and not the cause, of their economic success.

Probably the strongest argument that there has been systematic underinvestment in infrastructure is that referendums on bond issues for infrastructure projects have a very high success rate (80 percent).[97] But even here one can argue that public authorities don't like to be embarrassed by bond issues that fail and that as a result they only put those projects up for a vote whose success is likely.

Ultimately these arguments back and forth are not very useful for decision-makers wondering whether they should invest more in public tools. Generalizations about over- and underspending aren't particularly useful. Public investments in infrastructure have to be judged on a case-by-case basis. While it is difficult to say whether more public investment is needed on some abstract level, it is usually not so difficult to determine the payoffs from particular projects.

The payoffs may be high in some areas and geographic locations and low in others. Military equipment requires very different judgments than schools or hospitals. Jails are yet another matter. Water and sewage systems have different payoffs (health, pollution) than investments in transportation. The payoffs from roads, high-speed trains, and airports depend on where these investments are to be made. High-speed trains aren't cost-effective when distances between major cities are less than 100 miles or more than 400 miles, and they aren't cost-effective at all in lightly populated areas. For some investments the issue is cost savings—the interstate highway system allowed big savings in driving costs and driving time for both cars and trucks. Other investments are designed to stimulate new private economic activities. The Internet can be seen in that light now but had to justified differently when first built. Buying spreaders to salt roads may be cheaper than buying plows to remove snow in the winter if one is interested only in government's costs.

But when the private damage to cars and trucks caused by salting is taken into account, plowing may be cheaper than salting for the community as a whole. A public post office that might have generated enormous externalities in terms of linking people together in colonial days may now be irrelevant to national integration in an era of television.

The place to start in improving the process of public investment is with capital budgeting. Most other countries divide public spending into consumption spending and investment spending so that the taxpayer-voter-consumer can make intelligent decisions on how much money to devote to each activity. Lumping the two types of spending together is a big mistake, since their purposes are very different.

What can be said about private investments in plant and equipment is equally relevant to public investments in infrastructure. If other equally wealthy countries are investing a lot more, and they are, then either America is making a mistake or they are. If America invested a lot more in the past (as it did), then Americans either made a mistake in the past or are making a mistake in the present. In all likelihood it is Americans in the present who are making the mistake. Public tool-building probably needs to increase even more than private tool-building, but we don't need to argue about exactly the right mix because what really needs to happen is a big increase in both.

Investing Efficiently

Both private and public investments can be inefficiently made. Whenever a company goes out of business or fails to earn a competitive rate of return on its investments, bad private investments have been made. In the private sector, failure rates are high (88 percent—almost as many businesses failed in the 1990s as were founded), and there are a lot of companies that don't earn competitive market rates of return.[98] Among the Fortune 500 companies, 31 percent failed to earn at least 4 percentage points more than the risk-free rate of return on government long-term bonds—a very modest hurdle rate.[99]

One of the arguments against America's very generous bankruptcy laws is that they don't push inefficient private investments out of the system fast enough. After Eastern Airlines filed for bankruptcy, it still went on for two years before it was finally pushed out of business. During that period it used up more than $1 billion in resources that could have been more profitably redeployed elsewhere.

In the public sector, the proportion of good and bad investments may not be much different than in the private sector (with an 88 percent private failure rate it would be hard to be higher), but mistakes in private tool-building worry us less than mistakes in public tool-building because the market automatically limits the size and length of private mistakes. Companies go out of business, and new funds aren't invested in businesses that can't make competitive rates of return. In contrast, bad public investments often seem to linger on forever. The authorities who operate the public tools enjoy a monopoly position, so that the public doesn't have the option of shifting to better, more efficient, cheaper sets of tools.

The biggest push to increase tool-building and tool-using efficiency is currently in the areas of telecommunications and electrical power. It is a push that affects both the private and public sectors. Outside of the United States, telephone and electrical power facilities have until recently been publicly built, owned, and operated. Inside the United States, these utilities have until recently been regulated monopolies—privately owned with government regulation of both prices and services. Experience has taught us that neither system works. In countries where public ownership used to be the norm, privatization is occurring. In countries where regulation was the norm, deregulation is occurring. Both are searches for more efficiency.

Public authorities don't have incentives to operate their facilities efficiently and are slow to adopt new technologies. They aren't interested in maximizing profits, and new technologies threaten their old investments. But regulation leads to the same problems. Private owners also don't have incentives to operate their facilities efficiently since they are given a guaranteed rate of return on their investments. For the same reason they are also slow to adopt new technologies. When it came to introducing cellular telephones, neither the private AT&T (the inventor of the cellular telephone) nor the public Nippon Telephone in Japan were leaders. Both had too much invested in copper wires in the ground. What they might gain by investing in a new set of tools looked smaller to them than what they would lose on the value of their old sets of tools.

But if both of the traditional methods for providing these services are wrong, what is the right way to organize such industries?

In the telecommunications sector, new technologies are making it possible for normal telephone services to become a competitive industry rather than a natural monopoly. A cellular phone can compete with one that needs copper wires in the ground. Buy some time on a satellite, and anyone can set up a long-distance phone company. The transition is cumbersome, and eliminating the cross-subsidies that existed in the old system (those who made a lot of long-distance phone calls per month subsidized those who made only a few local calls) is difficult and politically painful, but it will happen. New tools such as the Internet, however, may increase the importance of the hard wire that leads to the home. But here the cable companies can compete with the telephone companies.

In electrical power deregulation, competitive generation systems can easily be established, but the distribution system is still a natural monopoly. While the copper wires to the home form a natural monopoly, many states are now trying to establish competitive markets in which homeowners or businesses can buy power from different providers. The existing monopoly distribution net-works must then carry the power supplies of many different power providers. The key problem here is obviously to determine the right rate for renting distribution capacity to the different providers. But if someone has to regulate the price at which the distribution company carries power to the consumer, the system has not been fundamentally deregulated.

In electrical power the issue of cross-subsidies pops up in the form of "stranded" costs. The old utilities (let's say Boston Edison) have built generation facilities for institutions (let's say MIT) that no longer want to buy their power from the old utilities because they have built cheaper cogeneration plants. Who pays for the now-unused power plant—the stockholders of Boston Edison or the consumers (students and researchers) at MIT? It's a real case.

In the past, with local power companies, electricity costs varied enormously from one part of the country to another. Efficiency calls for equalizing the costs of electricity after taking into account the costs of moving power from one place to another. Power is bought cheaply in low-cost areas (raising the price there), moved and sold in high-cost areas (driving the price down). This is good news for those living in what are now high-cost areas but bad news for those living in what are now low-cost areas. Some local areas will be paying more even if on average national prices fall. Those local areas won't like it even if "efficiency" is the result.

There are equivalent problems in privatization. Looking back-ward, the earnings on what had been government-owned utilities often look very high (this was true with Britain's privatization of its public water companies), but looking backward obscures the risks that genuinely existed looking forward. It ignores the prob-lems that may have had to be surmounted to cut costs and gener-ate those high rates of return. But looking backward, the public is apt to think that it has been cheated and is being ripped off and demand reregulation.

When privatizing, governments also have an incentive to privatize in such a way that public monopolies are simply replaced by private monopolies. Assets sold as a monopoly are worth more than the same assets divided among four competing firms. British Airlines is a good example. Sold off as one firm serving the world, it brought a lot more revenue to the British government than it would have brought if it had been divided and sold off as four competing airlines. But when it is sold off as one firm, there is no reason to suspect that efficiency will result—a privately owned monopoly has replaced a publicly owned monopoly.

What is clear is that there is no simple way to organize natural monopolies. A competitive framework can't be built unless the technology permits it. Since what is sold or deregulated is often still at least partially a natural monopoly, some form of government regulation is going to remain. The solution is not to try to regulate rates of return to acceptable levels (that takes all incentives to be more efficient out of the system) but to focus on the prices of the services been sold. Start by calculating the full cost (prices charged plus tax revenue used) of the services provided by the public authority or the old regulated private utility. As long as the new system is selling these same services for less than the full costs of the old system, the taxpayer-voter-consumer is better off. If technology is advancing, it is also reasonable to demand that service prices fall by some specified amount each and every year. Regulations still exist, but they focus on the trends in service prices and not upon rates of return on capital investment. The issue should always be what is happening to the price paid by the consumer and not how much money the capitalist is making.

Another area where it's easy to see that tool-using and tool-building efficiency can be improved is in the management of public tools over their useful lifetimes. Construction and maintenance are often done by different public authorities in different budgets. Typically both are put up for bid. What gets lost in the process is the total lifetime cost (construction plus maintenance) of any project. In general too little is spent on high-quality construction, and lifetime maintenance costs are far higher than they would be if the two aspects of costs were integrated. Where possible, bidders should have to bid on a construction contract and a long-term maintenance contract jointly so that they would have an incentive to minimize total costs.

Public authorities also typically pay the interest costs on accumulated investments while projects are being built. This leaves the winning bidder (the low-cost builder) with no incentive to finish quickly. Accumulated interest charges are often a large part of the total costs of any lengthy capital-intensive infrastructure project. The builder rightly ignores them since someone else is paying them. Not surprisingly, over the last century the time to complete similar projects has lengthened substantially. The right solution is to force the builder to pay accumulated interest charges until the project is completed. The builder is then in a position to compare the relative benefits of using cheaper technologies that take longer versus those of using quicker but more expensive technologies.

Historically, public authorities have concentrated on increasing supplies and neglected lowering demands (controlling usage). On the demand side of the equation there is a lot of room for creative solutions to improve efficiency. Peak load problems—roads, electricity, airports, water—are common. It is for this reason that efficiency is higher if infrastructure investments are financed by user charges rather than general tax revenues. User charges provide an incentive to use services only when benefits exceed costs rather than to see a free good for which maximum usage is the right economic answer. For the same reason, public authorities should normally borrow part of the money to pay for major infrastructure investments. Paying off the interest and principal over time forces future users to share the cost of the investment.

Congestion is a good example of some of the issues of infrastructure efficiency. Congestion is not an externality (positive or negative) levied on someone else. Those on the road, those who cause the congestion, are the ones that must pay the price of congestion—lost time, higher energy costs, higher transportation costs, wear and tear on the physical and human systems. Everyone could individually avoid those costs if they were willing to reorganize their lives or economic activities to avoid traveling during rush hours. If they don't, it's because the benefits of avoiding congestion are not as high as the costs of reorganizing their time schedules.

Better public transit is often suggested as a solution to automobile congestion, but it isn't. The automobile has three advantages that make it impossible for public transit to compete.

First, it is far more flexible with respect to starting and ending points than any other form of transit. To get from point A to point B you don't have to get off a bus or a train and wait for another bus or train to come. You can change homes or jobs and not worry about whether the transportation system can get you between the two new points. In cities that have developed since the onset of the auto age, population densities simply aren't high enough to justify the frequency of service that makes mass transit competitive with the auto in cost or time.

Second, the auto is a personalized capsule that the owners get to custom-design in accordance with their taste and budget. It can be expensive or cheap. It can have a stereo system that plays the music you want at the volume you want. And you always get a seat.

Third, the automobile has a huge differential between average and marginal costs. The costs of owning a car that never moves are enormous—purchase price, sales tax, insurance. The marginal costs of driving the car, given that it is already owned and those costs have already been paid, is very low. Since almost everyone has a car for other uses, even if they do not commute to work, the car is marginally a very cheap form of transportation even though its total costs are very high. What counts to the driver when making a decision to commute is marginal costs. Public transit systems, which must cover average costs, cannot compete with cars, which must only cover marginal costs, even if the average costs of those public systems are below the average costs of the automobile.

Experience has also taught us that building more roads doesn't stop congestion. With more and better roads, more houses are built along those corridors and more people drive. Better roads cause people to leave for work later, and peak load rush hour congestion continues to exist. And building more roads isn't efficient, since for most the day they have a lot of idle capacity.

The right solution is to set up a pricing system that allows those who put a high value on being able to drive congestion-free during peak hours to bribe those whose travel at these time periods is not critical to move their hours of travel to some other time. With new technologies, user charges can now be collected in many places where they were formerly too cumbersome to collect. With bar codes on cars and sensors built into the streets, for example, tolls can be collected on all roads and differentiated by time of day. This new technology allows communities to solve auto pollution and congestion problems that were not previously solvable.

Being able to charge time-of-day tolls means that prices can be raised for those who want to travel at peak times to a point where their demands are just equal to the high-speed capacities of the road system. These charges can then be returned to other drivers who are willing and able to travel off-peak. Drivers during rush hour would see money deducted from their smart cards as they drove by, while drivers during off-peak hours would find funds added. Congestion tolls with cross-subsidies to those who don't drive at peak periods makes a lot more sense than trying to make public transit good enough so that people will give up driving or than building a lot more roads.

Wherever possible, private money should be used to finance public infrastructure. Public funds and public borrowing capacities should be reserved for cases where private funding will not be forthcoming because of the size, risks, or lengthy payout periods of the projects. Often private funds will not be available in the initial phases of an infrastructure project. But to say that the public has to be the initial builder and operator of some particular piece of infrastructure is not to say the public should be its lifetime operator. Here the Internet is a good example. Public funds and public management started but no longer control the system.

In general, once public infrastructure is up and running and could be run profitably, it should be turned over to the private sector, just as Britain has sold its airports to a private company. One can argue about whether public or private management will be better, but what one cannot argue about is that the sale of old infrastructure projects is one of the ways to raise the money necessary to build new infrastructure projects. Often this infrastructure will be a natural monopoly, but as we have seen in the case of electrical power, there are forms of regulation that stop monopolists from raising prices to the public without turning them into inefficient providers.

In the end social infrastructure is one of the ingredients that determine our well-being.

Conclusion

Americans have built a system that encourages personal consumption and discourages tool-building. We could easily create a system of incentives to persuade ourselves to build more tools. But we won't until we persuade ourselves that it is important to do so. Only those who see themselves as builders and who get pleasure from both building and admiring their building after it is done will deliberately adjust their systems to raise investment and lower consumption. Successful individual private builders also know that if they are to be successful, they must live in a society of builders. Good social infrastructure leads to successful private investments.

The economic distinction between those goods that directly generate utility (consumption) and those that only indirectly generate utility through their ability to permit future consumption is not as sharp as it is made out to be. One can be as proud of the tools owned by one's company or one's city (the most advanced robots, the best municipal transit system) as one is of one's personal tools (the biggest house, the fastest car).

9.   Natural and Environmental Resources

Warning: A hundred years ago our ancestors regarded wolves and mountain lions much as we regard germs and were as eager to eradicate them. A hundred years from now, with partially man-made plants, animals, and human beings long accepted realities, what it means to talk about the natural environment will be just as different. The term *genetic defects* will have a widely expanded, very different meaning. Combine this with equally dramatic breakthroughs in the material sciences that allow designer materials to be built with exactly the desired physical properties, and natural resource wealth will be seen not as a finite extractive activity but as a central area for active wealth creation.

Using nature to create wealth is a complicated business. It is not a battle between good and evil. Economic growth is not on a collision course with the environment. The interactions are much more complicated and subtle. Consider the following quotation from an environmentalist:

> In a finite world, the claim by 20 percent of the world's population to 80 percent of the world's resources makes the margin-

alization of the majority of the world inevitable. A retreat of the rich from over-consumption is thus a necessary step toward allowing space for the improvement of the lives of an increasing number of people. . . . Confronted by global warming and other environmental problems, there can be little doubt that economies are still on a collision course with the natural environment. Despite all environmental endeavors, production and consumption increasingly reduce nature to serving as a supplier of industry and a recipient of industrial waste. That is the bitter situation after 20 years of environmental politics.[100]

With a 180-degree twist of emphasis, the same statements can be heard from an antienvironmentalist:

Environmentalists are elitists living in the top 20 percent of the population whose aim it is to end rising standards of living for the bottom 80 percent of the population. Their demands mean the end of economic progress. The real enemies of the radical environmental leadership are capitalism and the American way of life.[101]

If these similar but opposite conclusions were correct, the future could consist only of natural resource exhaustion and environmental degradation. The top 20 percent are not going to voluntarily sacrifice their standard and style of living to help the bottom 80 percent. The bottom 80 percent are not going to give up their goal of higher standards of living to preserve the environment for the top 20 percent. Economic activity is going to expand in both the developed and developing world. Humans don't voluntarily contract their sphere of influence. They actively use the technologies they develop.

Fortunately, these widely held perspectives are not correct. There is a different way to look at natural and environmental resources that leads to a very different set of conclusions.

On any measure, the world is a more environmentally friendly place than it was twenty or thirty years ago. Our air and water are far cleaner than they have been in a century. Industrial wastes are much less frequently dumped into the natural environment than they were. Having to breathe secondary tobacco smoke is in many places a thing of the past. Animal species—eagles, mountain lions, whales, alligators, wolves—are rebounding.[102] There are unsolved major problems—global warming is the big one—but lots of problems have been solved or alleviated.

While natural resources are used in industrial production, technological developments have reduced their usage and increased their effective supply. Take any raw material, plot its usage relative to the gross domestic product, and one finds much less use per unit of GDP. In the last twenty-five years, energy consumption per unit of GDP is down by one-third and it would have gone down twice as fast if energy prices had not fallen to the lowest levels in human history.[103] Copper consumption per unit of GDP is down 31 percent. In the last fifteen years water consumption per capita is down 25 percent.[104] And based on what has already been achieved in other countries, it's clear that much bigger reductions are possible. Japan and Germany use half as much energy per dollar of GDP as the United States.

With changes in technology, we do not live in a finite world. There is not a fixed amount of oil. The oil that is available at any point in time depends upon the technologies that can be used to extract it. In the late 1970s at the time of the second OPEC oil shock, permanent oil shortages were predicted with oil at $100 per barrel ($160 in today's dollars). With old oil-producing technologies these predictions might have been right. But new offshore drilling technologies have proved them wrong. Suddenly the three-quarters of the globe that is covered by water and that had been off-limits to oil exploration are within those limits. The available oil supply has exploded, proven reserves of oil are at all-time highs, and oil prices in real terms are at their lowest level in human history.

Market prices measure what is happening to the relative supplies and demands of natural resources. What has happened to oil is happening across the spectrum of other energy supplies, minerals, and agricultural products. Reductions in demand plus new technologies have created a world where natural resource availability is growing far faster than demand. Everywhere prices are down. Gas prices per BTU are even lower than oil prices. All agricultural, mineral, and energy resources are now selling for prices near their historic lows. Copper prices are down. Wheat prices are down. Corn prices are down. A little of this is due to the Asian meltdown, but most of it occurred before the meltdown and is due to new technologies. Gold, the bellwether of commodities, is an example. Its price is down dramatically. With new technologies, a United States that just a few decades ago was "out of gold" has become a major gold producer. Nevada alone now produces 10 percent of the world's gold.

The materials science revolution that is now under way is also allowing us to enter a world of designer materials where high-value materials are made—not extracted from the earth. Sand is made into silicon wafers and semiconductor chips. Kevlar creates bullet-proof clothes, while Gore-Tex creates breathable waterproof clothes. Lycra seems to be in almost everything. Ceramics are simultaneously the oldest and the newest man-made materials. New medical materials are making replacement possible for many of the body's parts—artificial hips being only the most common.

The bottom 80 percent of the world's population is not falling behind—precisely the reverse. World GDP has grown faster than at any time in human history, and more of this growth has been in the developing world than at any time in human history. That growth has not been spread evenly, but standards of living have been rising dramatically for billions of people in the third world. Think about the progress in China—two decades of 8 to 10 percent growth rates have quintupled the standards of living for 1.3 billion people. Some of the developing world has in fact caught up with the developed world. Korea, Taiwan, Singapore, and Hong Kong have achieved European per capita GDPs. Until the recent financial meltdowns in much of the developing world, this was the best—not the worst—of times.

And no one in the developed world had to reduce their standard of living to make this happen.

Africa, south of the Sahara, is in fact the only place in the developing world where no progress is being made. But this lack of progress has nothing to do with greediness in the developed world. It reflects a lack of local social organization and a resulting chaos that makes internal development impossible and any outside help meaningless.

What the 80–20 distinction also ignores is that the productivity of the 80 percent must rise if their consumption is to rise. When the 80 percent have Western standards of living, they will be contributing at least as much to world GDP as they subtract. It is not possible to have American standards of living at home without at the same time having American production standards at work.

Growth is not the enemy of environmentalism. It is in fact necessary if the environment is to be improved. It is only with growth and higher standards of living that people become interested in the environment. In the jargon of economics, environmental goods like clean air and pure water are luxuries. Our demands for them rise faster than our incomes. With its much higher incomes, Hong Kong is for the first time in its history actively engaged in reforestation.[105] At lower income levels it wasn't interested. At very low levels of income, the central worry is starvation. No one cares about the environment, and no one can afford to invest in improving it. At higher levels of income, with survival worries behind us, a better environment becomes important to our future standard of living. Only the poor denude forests to provide wood for cooking fires. With higher incomes we can afford more environmentally friendly forms of heating and cooking. What wealthy people can buy privately—a very good environment—middle-class people come to demand politically (collectively) as their incomes rise.

As family incomes go up, average family size diminishes. What China has had to do with draconian measures—limit family size— happens naturally with higher family incomes. Population pressures fall with growth. In most of the developed world, birth rates are below zero population growth. The United States is almost the only exception, and its native-born population is very close to ZPG.

Since the beginning of time, the human population has risen from zero to almost six billion, yet human well-being and life expectancy are the highest they have ever been. The average life expectancies of the worst countries on the face of the globe today are above those of the best countries a century ago. The caveman used a lot less energy than modern man (2,500 calories per day versus 31,000 calories per day), but per person he undoubtedly did more environmental damage.[106] Think about what the world would look like with six billion cavemen using the technology of their day and age.

The world's human carrying capacity is important, but the right debate is not about the maximum population the world could sustain given today's food-producing technologies and fresh water availability (estimates vary from eight to twelve billion). The right debate is about the styles of life that lead to the highest human welfare given current technologies—not what is acceptable but what is desirable. What is the value of children? In an urbanized industrial society, they are certainly less valuable economically and more costly than in a poor rural community. That's why the average family has many fewer. What collective and personal choices are going to be made? If a high-quality life is to be delivered to everyone, there are limits on how large a population can exist at every point in time. But experience teaches us that those limits don't have to be imposed if people see the better lives they can have with smaller families. Technology allows us to control family size and limit the environmental pressures that come from population growth—if we so wish.

The positive role of environmental technology is clearest in the area of human health. Man's natural environment comes with diseases and a short life expectancy. High death rates, especially in the early years of life, and short life spans are perfectly consistent with the survival of the human species. Modern medicine radically changes that natural environmental reality.

Biotechnology opens up the possibility of controlling the pests and weeds that lower agricultural yields without the use of powerful pesticides and herbicides that often have negative side effects. Humans are not going to stop growing enough food to feed themselves, but they can learn to grow it in a more environmentally friendly way. Before us lie great opportunities to speed up this process with new technologies.

With biotechnology the issues of what investments should be made to improve the human environment are going to move front and center in the public debate. Biotechnology opens up the possibility of creating the plant, animal, and human environments in which we would like to live. Plants can be built that resist diseases without pesticides, use less water, and produce more edible food. Similar improvements are occurring in animals. More milk per cow leads to less pressure on grazing lands and more room for wildlife. When it comes to improving humans, the process will start by eliminating genetic diseases and move on to building better (smarter, taller, more beautiful) men and women. The biotech processes for curing existing diseases are dual-use technologies. The same techniques that allow genetic defects (very inferior genes) to be eliminated allow the replacement of slightly inferior genes with superior ones.

Technology is not a threat to the environment. Precisely the reverse, it will be the savior of the environment. A host of technological changes (new materials, better computer-aided designs) are behind the decrease in energy used per unit of GDP. No one is going to persuade the world's population to give up their automobiles. In the United Kingdom it is estimated that gasoline prices would have to rise to $12 per gallon to hold usage constant in the next decade.[107] But the hottest current area in auto technology is fuel cells. This is a proven technology used in space exploration to provide electricity from hydrogen and oxygen. Its only waste product is water. If the costs of making fuel cells could be reduced to the right level, the auto could be made into a vehicle that neither pollutes nor uses gasoline. The costs of the polymer membrane material necessary to build fuel cells have already been reduced from $750 to $5 per square foot, and a fuel cell engine that once cost a hundred times as much as an internal combustion engine now costs only ten times as much.[108] On the outside of cars, "Fuel Cells Inside" may come to be the equivalent of "Intel Inside."

Similarly, if desalinization technologies could be made cheaper, fresh water would become a man-made material—and not something in finite supply. The 2.5 percent of our total water supplies that are fresh (two-thirds of which are locked up in ice) would suddenly be augmented by the 97.5 percent of the world's water that is salty. Half of China's six hundred biggest cities wouldn't have water deficits with falling groundwater levels. Iceland would no longer have thirty thousand times as much water per capita as Djibouti or nine thousand times as much as Kuwait.

It was the dream of essentially free energy and all the good things that would flow from it that drove the initial enthusiasm for nuclear power. There are lessons to be learned from the fact that the dream did not come true. Not all technology can be perfected. Not all technologies go down the steep cost curves that we have seen with semiconductor chips. They often run into difficult, perhaps unsolvable, problems. What does one do about nuclear waste? How does one handle the cracks that long-term radiation produces in metal pipes? Is the technology too complicated for normal humans to handle? Safety issues have driven the costs of nuclear power far above those of conventional power plants.

Like all plant and animal species, humans are going to affect the world in which they live. Agriculture has probably had the biggest effect on our natural world. But with higher agricultural productivity, areas that used to be farmed can be returned to nature. New England has more forests today than it did in colonial times. Grassland parks where the deer and the buffalo roam are being created from what were cattle and wheat ranches in western North Dakota.

Logic would suggest that the development of better communication and transportation systems should be spreading economic activity out geographically, but in fact it is being concentrated on less and less of our total land area. In the United States, a little less than a thousand out of America's three thousand counties are losing population. Most of the growth is in just a few of the other two thousand. Powerful economic and social forces are pushing us into smaller and smaller portions of our land area.

One can speculate about why this is happening. Economists like to look for economic forces. One suggestion is that close human proximity facilitates the informal exchange of information. But most likely the answer lies not in some mysterious, powerful economic forces that no one can quite articulate, but in the social reality that humans are by nature herd animals and like living on top of each other. The need for food historically caused us to spread out. Nomadic hunter-gatherers and people using primitive agricultural techniques such as slash and burn need a lot of space to survive. When that need is eliminated (only 1 percent of the American population is needed to feed the other 99 percent) we concentrate on top of each other because we like to be on top of each other.

Whatever the reasons, the bottom line is clear. More empty space not needed for economic activities is being created. That space can be used to create different environments. A better environment is within the technological reach of humankind.

Conversely, environmentalism is not the enemy of growth. This can also be seen in the history of the last twenty-five years. Increasingly stringent environmental regulations have been imposed on the economy without cutting off economic growth. Economically it has been a very good twenty-five years in the developed world and an even better twenty-five years in some parts of the developing world. If standard measures of economic output were augmented with measures of the benefits of cleaner air and water and rebounding populations of mountain lions and other species, as they should be, the measured gains would be even larger than they have been.

Environmentalism and natural resource development are opposite sides of the same coin. They both contribute to higher human standards of living—a better human environment. All species affect the environment. All species benefit from the environment. All species, including humans, are part of the environment. An environment without humans is no more natural than an environment without other plants or animal species. All species change the environments in which they live—often for the better. Animals provide fertilizers for plants, and worms plow the earth for plants.

No exception, human beings change where they live. Mother Nature created a world where life expectancies were short and diseases common. Modern medicine has created a less "natural" but far better environment. Evergreens dominated colonial New England's forests until settlers cut them down and made room for the hardwoods, whose brilliant fall foliage is so beloved of tourists and local residents alike. This man-made natural environment is much more interesting and beautiful than the former "natural" environment. But either is natural or neither is natural. Nature's environments are always changing. They are not static. Deserts and forests move over time—shifting locations, sometimes expanding, sometimes contracting.

What makes humans unique among animal species is that they

can think about what creates a better environment and they have the capacity to deliberately create those environments. What they have to think about, and work toward, in the area of natural and environmental wealth is not restoring some previously existing natural environment without humankind (humans aren't going to disappear), but what good environment do we want to create for ourselves—and as a result, for other animal and plant species. Once this vision is articulated, we can then worry about how we get from here to there.

Wolves have been restored to Yellowstone National Park not because they are natural (they have been there at some points in the earth's history and not at others), but because they create a better, more interesting environment.[109] With them the herds of elk can be kept under control without starvation, with less disease, and without forest rangers herding the animals out of the park so that they can be shot by human hunters waiting at the border. An environment in which prey and predator interact is richer than an environment without predators.

Humans can create environmental wealth.

Humans learn. As a boy in school, I was taught that there were essentially inexhaustible supplies of fish protein in the world's oceans. It wasn't true. Today we worry about the end of ocean fishing and the extinction of many edible species. Supplies are exhaustible and have to be conserved. If they aren't, the result is not slow declines in fish catches but often sudden crashes in population. Off the North American Pacific coast the catch of sardines went from 500 million tons to zero in fifteen years.[110] On the New England coast, in the "land of the bean and the cod," there is no cod. Overfishing has forced closure of the last of the great cod-fishing banks.[111] There is a crisis of the commons in the world's oceans. But we also now have the technologies to monitor fish populations and prevent overfishing before such crashes occur.

Because humans think of environmental wealth as coming freely from nature, they tend not to value it, not to count it, and to waste it. They only notice that it is important to their total wealth when it is gone and it becomes a subtraction from other forms of wealth. Effectively they see it as free when it is not. Because they see it as free, they also tend to think of it as in unlimited supply. It is the tragedy of the commons. Where everyone collectively owns something, everyone has an incentive to overuse that resource until it no longer exists. Everyone drills wells into the aquifer and pumps as hard as they can so that they can get more water than their neighbor before the aquifer runs dry. No one recognizes their mutual self-interest in a sustainable water supply.

RULE TWELVE: Economic and environmental progress are synonyms—not antonyms.

Over time we have also learned how to both solve environmental problems and simultaneously make environmental regulations more effective and less intrusive. The trading of sulfur dioxide emission permits has decreased such emissions below where they would be with command and control environmental regulations.[112] Sustainable use is different from no use. Since all natural environments have some self-cleaning capacity, permits to use that capacity can be auctioned off and the proceeds used to clean up other aspects of the environment. The community essentially asserts its collective property rights to nature's self-cleaning capacity and sells those rights to finance a better environment.

Required pollution reductions can be traded so that expenditures are focused on those sources of pollution that are the cheapest to clean up. Polluters can be taxed. Subsidies for overuse can be ended.[113] Even if those who have a historic right to the cheap use of resources have to be bought out (agriculture gets 80 percent of what is expensive water in California), efficiency is improved when resources are moved from low value-added uses (agriculture produces only 10 percent of the GDP) to high value-added uses.[114]

Telling those who live in the rain forests that they should not cut their trees down isn't going to work, any more than it would have worked with the settlers who cut down most of the forests in the eastern half of the United States in the eighteenth and nineteenth centuries. In both cases people were, and are, simply trying to improve their standards of living. If we want to preserve more of the world's rain forests, however, we can easily do so if we are willing to invent new social institutions. Those who live outside the rain forests can pay taxes to make growing tropical trees much more profitable than the alternatives of burning or chopping them down. Luckily the alternative uses of the rain forests aren't that profitable. It would not take the collection of very much tax revenue to make the expansion of rain forests their most profitable form of economic activity. Space satellites could easily measure the hectares of trees, and local residents could be paid based on the acreage of trees in their region. Similarly, if we value biodiversity, there are good mechanisms that can be expanded to increase it, such as rewarding private landowners for good stewardship and the expansion of habitats for endangered species.[115]

The definitions of a good environment will change over time (today we see coyotes very differently than we did when I was a young man growing up in Montana). The definition of a good environment will not be imposed by a minority on a majority or even by a majority on a minority. It will emerge by consensus as we see the changes that will create higher standards of living for everyone. It will evolve from our individual and collective concerns about it.

In the end, environmental wealth is the ability to use constructively the environment given to us by nature, and where possible, to improve it. Clean air, clean water, and a beautiful environment are not necessary for human survival (much of the world lives without them), but they add immeasurably to our wealth if we have them.

An Insoluble Problem?

Environmentalism is no exception to the rule that every political and economic system does some things well and some things poorly. Economic incentives handle natural resource exhaustion well and can contribute to lowering environmental pollution. Political incentives lead to the control of local or national pollution as average incomes rise. No one with means to do otherwise wants to live in a polluted environment. Individually and collectively, as we grow richer we will buy a better environment and have smaller families.

But what our political and economic system does not do well is handle long-tailed, highly uncertain problems such as global warming. When fourteen of the twenty warmest years we have measured have occurred in the last twenty years, when 1997 is the hottest year on record—until 1998 is reached, and when each and every one of the first nine months of 1998 broke the all-time record for heat in the United States (the tenth fell just short of the all-time record set a year earlier), global warming has begun to sound plausible even to those not interested in scientific disputes.[116] Meteorological studies seem to indicate that events not expected until the second half of the next century are occurring now. Bad storms have increased 20 percent in the last decade.[117] The pace of the adverse changes seems to be speeding up. On a global basis, studies of tree rings and other evidence make it likely that 1998 was the hottest year in the last millennium.[118]

Horror stories can be told about the consequences of global warming.

Plant and animal species unable to move to cooler climates die out by the thousands. Human agriculture is disrupted (normal rains don't arrive) and millions starve. Ultraviolet radiation kills the plankton in the top 10 feet of the ocean and disrupts the food chain for essentially all living species. Skin cancer skyrockets. Huge erratic storms become more frequent. In short, humans find the globe a much less comfortable place to live.

The oceans were 100 meters lower during the last Ice Age, 18,000 years ago. But 120,000 years ago they were 5 to 6 meters higher. Most of humanity lives within 200 feet of sea level. If the oceans were to rise 3 meters, 30 million people would have to move in Bangladesh alone—and it is not obvious where they could go.[119] Melting at the North Pole makes little difference, just as melting ice cubes don't cause a glass of ice water to overflow, but if the east and west Antarctic ice sheets were to slide into the southern seas and be combined with thermal expansion, big changes could occur rather suddenly.

The flow of the Gulf Stream depends upon subtle differences in temperature and salinity. Northern Canada is uninhabitable, yet it is no farther north than areas of northern Europe where hundreds of millions of people live. Disrupt the Gulf Stream in the Atlantic Ocean, and Europe could become as uninhabitable as northern Canada even if the earth is warming up.

All of these horrors may occur, but if there were ever a problem humans are unlikely to solve, it is global warming. Human nature and human socioeconomic systems were simply not built to solve such distant, uncertain problems.

Horror stories may horrify but they don't lead to action.

The reality of the problem can always be denied. Whatever the weather is in any one year and any one place, it may all be due to natural statistical variance. Changes have to be huge and persistent before one knows for sure that events are outside the realm of normal statistical variability. Even two decades of hot weather or the hottest year of the millennium does not prove that global warming has arrived. There is, after all, a small chance of getting a hundred heads in a row if one is flipping coins.

And once we are sure that global warming has arrived, it is obviously too late to prevent it from arriving.

Even after it is agreed that the world is getting warmer, it may all be due to natural causes—not human activity. At various times in the past the world has been much warmer than it is now. Perhaps we are just entering a naturally warmer period. From 1940 to 1970, carbon dioxide emissions rose much faster than they have since, yet no increase in the earth's temperature was recorded.[120] To agree that the weather is warmer is not to agree that human activities are causing the weather to get warmer.

Finally, even if it is agreed that humans are causing global warming, forecasts predicting that average temperatures will be a few degrees warmer don't sound so bad to those living in the frost belt. Heating one's home is more expensive than cooling it. Snow tires cost money. Instead of their migrating to the sunbelt, the sunbelt will move to them. Humans are very good at insulating themselves from climatic effects (air-conditioning has conquered heat). We function well under very different climatic conditions. We are the only animal species that lives in tropical rain forests, deserts, and even in the glacial ice of the Arctic.

To say that agricultural conditions will get worse in some countries is to say that they must get better in others. Cold Russia and Canada might be big agricultural winners. With hotter climates and more evaporation from the oceans, more rain has to fall somewhere. Much of the world is desert in need of more rain. Some of the rain has to fall in the right places. Some areas may also become drier, but depending upon exactly where those areas are (something no one can predict), this also may not be bad news. No one in Bangladesh would think a little less water a bad thing. The world may become a better place for human beings to live.

There may be natural feedback mechanisms that prevent the predicted effects from becoming very large. Warmer weather will lead to more evaporation from the oceans and more precipitation. If this precipitation were to come down in cold climates (the Arctic or Antarctic) in the form of snow, it would reflect more sunlight back into space and stop average temperatures from rising very much even if the human causes were to continue expanding. The particulates discharged from coal-fired electrical generating plants may have radiated heat back into space and stopped temperatures from rising even though carbon dioxide emissions were rising between 1940 and 1970.[121] If pollution stopped global warming, curing that form of pollution started global warming. Straight-line extrapolations of adverse (or favorable) effects are clearly wrong. Offsets occur. There are natural and man-made feedback mechanisms—positive and negative.

What looks like a good solution may not be. Natural gas electrical generating plants are cleaner than coal- or oil-fired plants, but if even a little methane escapes into the atmosphere unburned (2 to 4 percent is enough, and the world is very close to these levels), natural gas plants are worse for global warming than coal- or oil-fired plants.[122]

The effects of warmer weather are uncertain. Many species of plants—sugar maples, for example—will have to migrate farther north to survive, but they may be surprisingly good at doing so. Pollen records are showing that trees have migrated north and south much faster than previously thought.[123]

Everyone agrees that the costs of eliminating human effects on climate will be huge, since they involve finding a cost-effective substitute for fossil fuels and the carbon dioxide they discharge when burned. Today nothing on the horizon is remotely cost-competitive. Poor people living in developing countries don't want high energy costs postponing improvements in the quality of their lives. Rich people in developed countries are not going to quit using electricity. To talk about people using their cars much less to prevent a problem that has not yet emerged is to talk about something that is not going to happen. Those who talk about reducing current standards of living to create a better environment are usually talking about changing someone else's lifestyle and not their own. Luxuries become necessities with remarkably speed for those who have them.

If there is global warming, whatever is done today won't have any positive effect for many years. The discounted net present value of a dollar's worth of disaster prevention fifty years from now is precisely zero. Spending money to prevent problems that far in the future doesn't make economic sense in capitalism. If a disaster is under way fifty years from now, spending money to reduce that disaster another fifty years further into the future will make equally little sense. The humans alive then will instead spend whatever money they have to adjust to their new realities. Cities will be abandoned and moved if necessary. The breadbaskets of the world will be located in different places. Long-term trends toward living more in man-made inside environments and less in uncontrollable outside environments will accelerate. Lifestyles will change.

Whatever the current horror stories and whatever the future disasters, it is clear that today's human beings are going to do very little about global warming unless we begin to think about it in very different ways. "Let tomorrow look after tomorrow" will be the rallying cry. Whatever the future costs, they are uncertain, amorphous, and will affect someone else anyway. Only those with the mentality of the builder are going to be willing to think about solutions.

Conclusions

Natural and environmental resources undergird the foundations of our wealth. We use them to survive. We build our civilizations upon them. Civilization began in the Nile River Valley because it was a natural environment that made agriculture easy. No plowing had to be done, since the annual flood left the fields covered with mud. With very little effort devoted to slowing the flow of water back into the Nile at the end of the flood season, an irrigation system could be built for extending the growing season. Lots of pumps and canals weren't necessary.

Our civilization is also built upon the natural environment. Man-made technologies for reducing usage and increasing economically reachable supplies have vastly expanded the natural resources that can be used effectively. We create our equivalents of the Nile River Valley in places such as Silicon Valley. Technology creates a better human environment where natural resources are more available, where environmental goods are just as important to our well-being as the goods we buy at our shopping centers, and where better environments can be built.

A revolution is under way. For the first time in human history humankind has the ability to create new materials and new biological entities. A hundred years from now, humans will look back and view the movie *Jurassic Park* much as we now view Jules Verne's *20,000 Leagues Under the Sea*. Reality has eclipsed science fiction.

Part Three
Treasure Hunters within the Wealth Pyramid

10.   Marketable Wealth

The time has come to look marketable wealth, the glittering eye at the top of the wealth pyramid, in the eye.

Market wealth consists of ownership rights to the lower levels of the pyramid and the productivity (output) that flows from them. Because it lies at the top of the pyramid, great wealth commands all of our attention, but it would not exist without the natural and environmental resources, physical capital, skills, knowledge, entrepreneurs, and social organization that lie below it. There are many social and personal reasons for wanting to enhance, expand, and augment each of these levels, but in the economic system of capitalism, using these building blocks to accumulate marketable wealth is the sole object of the game. Wealth is how capitalism keeps score.

Market wealth is important because it directly raises standards of living (home ownership), permits consumption purchases, provides financial security in times of need (unemployment, sickness, old age), and generates economic power.[124] If the focus is on great wealth, economic power is the central motivating force. Rather low levels of wealth are more than sufficient to satisfy other human motivations for accumulation.

Americans are surprisingly modest if you ask them about their needs. In 1996 an income of $30,000 per year per family was needed for "getting by," $40,000 for "comfort," and $90,000 for "dreams."[125] In the same year the median family had $42,000—two-thirds earned by the husband, one-third earned by the wife. The median household (a measure that includes everyone, not just those living in related families) had $36,000. Americans want more than they have, but with marketable wealth of just $1.3 million invested in riskless government bonds, one could have those dreams without ever having to work, without ever touching one's principal, and at death be able to leave one's children $1.3 million in wealth. When it comes to great wealth, the objective is power, prestige, immortality, and being one of the economic winners. More consumption is not the driving force.

In the United States, the Federal Reserve Board periodically calculates the level and distribution of private net worth, or marketable wealth.[126] In America we know exactly who owns what and how much. The top of the pyramid has been accurately, and officially, surveyed.

Few other countries have such data. It does not take a major cynic to come to the conclusion that most countries don't have such data because they don't want to know how unequally wealth is distributed. In all countries, wealth is much more unequally distributed than earnings. To know the actual numbers is to immediately raise the political issue of inequality—especially in countries that in the past had strong socialist parties. It's best to be ignorant of the facts. Knowing the facts might generate political pressures that would force governments to do something to change the facts.

In most other countries, someone like Bill Gates is viewed with a mixture of admiration and horror. Foreigners stand in awe of a system in which a man can create one of the world's great companies in a decade and in the process become richer than anyone can imagine. Simultaneously they are horrified by the inequalities in wealth that he represents. The net result is ambivalence. They aren't sure whether they do or do not want a Bill Gates in their country.

Because Americans are more comfortable with inequalities in

wealth than the citizens-voters of any other country, our government has been more willing to explore the distribution of wealth. When the Fed releases its latest survey of wealth every three or four years, the results are duly reported in the press, usually on the inside pages, and then forgotten. They don't lead anyone of importance to suggest that Americans ought to change the system to produce a more equal distribution of wealth.

The Federal Reserve Board's calculations of private net worth exclude public assets such as national parks and collectively owned assets such as church property, but include everything individuals can own and sell except consumer durables. Housing, other real estate, cash and bank accounts, financial securities of all types, corporate stocks and bonds, mutual funds, the ownership of private businesses, trusts, and the cash surrender value of life insurance and pension benefits are all included. All private debts—mortgage, consumer, auto, and business—are then subtracted from these asset totals to get private net worth.

When discussing individual earnings and household incomes the focus is quite rightly heavily directed toward what is happening to the median family or the median earner. But when it comes to discussing wealth, median numbers (the numbers at which 50 percent of the population have more and 50 percent have less) aren't meaningful or interesting, since most of America's wealth is held by the top 10 percent of the population. From 1983 to 1995 (the latest comprehensive Federal Reserve Board study), the wealth of the top 1 percent rose 17 percent, but the wealth of the median household fell 11 percent. Knowing what was happening to the median household would have given a very misleading view of what was really happening in the world of wealth.

In 1995 the top 1 percent of households owned 39 percent of total American wealth, and the top 20 percent owned 84 percent of total wealth—not far from what in marketing is known as a universal human rule: 20 percent of the people drink 80 percent of the beer. From 1983 to 1995 the share of the top 1 percent went up while the share of everyone else, including the next 4 percent, went down (see the table below). (Calculations updating these numbers show that by 1998 a rising stock market had pushed the share of the top 1 percent to about 41 percent of total wealth.)

Distribution of Wealth[127]

Percent of Total Wealth

Year	Top 1%	Next 4%	Next 5%	Next 10%
1983	33.8	22.3	12.1	13.1
1995	38.5	21.8	11.5	12.1

Year	Top 20%	Next 20%	Next 20%	Bottom 40%
1983	81.3	12.6	5.2	0.9
1995	83.9	11.5	4.5	0.2

Source: Federal Reserve Board

To make it into the top 1 percent (in America 1 percent is a large number—850,000 households) requires a surprisingly small amount of wealth (less than $2 million in total net worth), but to rise to the top of the group takes a surprisingly large amount (more than $83 billion at the end of 1998 to supplant Bill Gates as America's wealthiest person).[128] Even among the wealthy, wealth is very unequally distributed.

In sharp contrast, the bottom 40 percent of all households own very little—0.2 percent of total net worth, a percentage that has fallen by a factor of four in the last twelve years. The bottom 19 percent of all households actually has negative net worth—their debts exceed their assets.[129] This is why Bill Gates's wealth can be equal to that of the bottom 40 percent of Americans. What is a lot of money for one person is very little spread across 110 million people.

Looking at financial wealth, a concept that leaves out the value of owner-occupied housing, the top 1 percent owns 47 percent and the top 20 percent own 93 percent of total financial wealth. For most Americans, equity in their own home is their only significant asset. It accounts for two-thirds of total wealth for 80 percent of all households. The median household had almost no financial wealth—only $9,950 worth of net financial wealth in 1995, or enough to finance its consumption for less than four months.

Different assets are owned in very different proportions as one goes down the wealth distribution. The top 10 percent own 92 percent of all the equity in private businesses, 88 percent of all corporate shares, and 80 percent of all financial securities (see the table below). In contrast, the only thing that the bottom 90 percent own, or in this case owe, in anything close to their numbers is debt. The bottom 90 percent owe 72 percent of America's debt. Debt burdens have risen sharply—up from 30 percent of personal income in 1949 to 85 percent in 1997—with particularly large increases in consumer debt.

Holdings of Different Assets

Asset Type	Top 1%	Next 9%	Bottom 90%
Business equity	69.5	22.2	8.3
Financial securities	65.9	23.9	10.2
Trusts	49.6	38.9	11.5
Stocks & mutual funds	51.4	37.0	11.6
Nonhome real estate	35.1	43.6	21.3
Bank deposits	29.4	32.9	37.7
Pensions	17.7	44.7	37.7
Life insurance	16.4	28.5	55.1
Home real estate	7.1	24.6	68.3
Debt	9.4	18.9	71.7

Source: Federal Reserve Board

Going into debt is one of the ways to keep up with those whose wealth is rising faster than one's own. By taking on debt, consumption spending can rise faster than income. But the effort to keep up only too often gets the borrower in trouble. In the United States the result has been an explosion in personal bankruptcies—up 93 percent from 1990. In 1998 1.4 million American households went broke in a futile effort to keep up with the Joneses.[130]

Wealth inequalities were held under control in most of the post–World War II period since home values (the form of wealth most held by the bottom 80 percent of the population) were rising faster than the stock market. In the last decade inequalities in the distribution of wealth have sharply increased because the stock market has been rising rapidly while the value of home equity has actually been falling.

Stocks are overwhelmingly owned by the top 10 percent. In the run-up in stock market prices in the period from 1995 to 1998, 86 percent of the gains have gone to the top 10 percent of all households.[131] Since the bottom 60 percent of the households own no stock, they obviously cannot gain from a rising stock market.

Recently, although home prices have risen, they have not kept pace with the stock market. More important, because debts on principal residences have almost doubled from 1983 to 1995, the net equity in owner-occupied homes has been going down.

Falling equity in one's own home is also the principle reason why the wealth of the median household is going down in absolute terms. When it comes to the wealth accumulation of the median family, home equity loans (something first allowed in the mid-1980s) have been a disaster.

Stock ownership (directly in the form of shares and indirectly in the form of mutual funds) has been going up. Among the 40 percent with stock holdings, 15 percent own shares directly and another 30 percent own stock indirectly through mutual funds. But bank deposits have been decreasing. In recent years upper-middle-income families have been changing where they save their money, but their total savings have been going down.

While there is some mobility up and down the wealth distribution, it seldom carries one very far.[132] Looking at the bottom quintile of wealth, 70 percent of those who were there fifteen years ago are still there. At the top, 60 percent are where they were fifteen years earlier. Only 3 percent move more than one quintile in any five-year period. If the natural movement due to aging is taken out of the data—the old have had longer to accumulate wealth, and households naturally become richer as they grow older—real wealth mobility is much smaller than even these small numbers indicate.

Good data on wealth do not exist for much of the rest of the world, but based on the data we have, the top 5 percent in America own more than twice as much as they do in Japan, one-third more than they do in Canada or Sweden, and one-quarter more than they do in France.[133] While there is no reason to believe that any first world country has greater inequality than America, many third world countries, especially in Latin America, have much more.

The greater inequality in America can be seen in three very different lights:

1:   America is a land of opportunity where it is easier to get rich and the rich are richer. Greater opportunity explains greater inequality.

2:   America is a land of closed doors where it is harder for those below the very top to become wealthy. Big racial groups (blacks and Hispanics) suffer from discrimination and are not allowed to play the game. Those in the bottom three-quarters of the workforce are far worse educated and skilled than those at the bottom in other developed countries. A lack of opportunity for the many explains greater American inequality.

3:   Americans save much less than those in the rest of the developed world. The bottom 80 percent of American households have chosen to accumulate much less wealth than similarly situated households elsewhere. Great wealth does not depend upon personal savings, but modest wealth does. With lower savings rates in America, less wealth for those with lower savings rates should come as no surprise. Americans have a more unequal distribution of wealth because they have chosen to have more current consumption and less wealth. America's greater inequality is simply a matter of different tastes.

Any of the three explanations is consistent with the facts. All three in combination can of course be the right answer. Which one of these explanations is preferred tells a listener more about the philosophical position of the speaker expounding upon wealth inequalities than it does about the real underlying causes.

When asked, two out of three Americans think that wealth should be more evenly distributed, but they are not resentful.[134] More think that one gets wealthy by working hard (46 percent) than by exploiting others (38 percent).[135] Lack of effort (39 percent) is considered almost as important as adverse circumstances (44 percent) in explaining those without wealth.[136] With such attitudes, Americans are quite different from those in the rest of the world. In America, 50 percent more people believe that hard work leads to success than in either the United Kingdom or Japan.[137]

Luck versus Talent

To what extent are those with wealth just lucky—in the right place at the right time—and to what extent do they have some unique talent that allows them to accumulate wealth? Just looking at the data, it is impossible to determine which of these explanations is true.

Is Warren Buffett (the second wealthiest person in America) a great investor—or just lucky? Almost alone among the very wealthy, he is a stock market investor rather than a builder of new companies. If 272 million Americans were flipping coins, and twenty heads in a row were needed to get very rich, 272 Americans would get rich just by chance. The small number of very rich people in America is not inconsistent with a lucky-unlucky view of the world.

Similarly, although Bill Gates has as much wealth as the bottom 40 percent of American households, he has no known talents (IQ, business acumen, willingness to take risks) equal to the combined talents of those 110 million people. There are many other individuals just as smart, just as good businessmen, and just as good at everything else who do not have his wealth.

Acquiring great wealth is best seen as a conditional lottery. Luck is necessary. One does have to be in the right place at the right time. Great wealth is created during times of change—the second and third industrial revolutions. Capitalizing on existing disequilibriums (technological, sociological, or developmental) is the name of the game. Equally talented businessmen in the 1950s, 1960s, and 1970s did not get fabulously rich. Ability by itself is not enough.

RULE THIRTEEN: Luck is necessary. Talent, drive, and persistence by themselves aren't enough to get wealthy.

At the same time, we know that Bill Gates isn't just lucky. Being in the right place at the right time is not enough. One also has to have the talents to capitalize on good luck. There is always more than one person lucky enough to be in the right place at the right time. Which of these people win the resulting race for success is not a matter of luck. One needs to be in the right place at the right time with the right skill set. There are many who could have built Microsoft. The founders of Apple Computer are the most obvious, since they had, and have, a better computer operating system than Microsoft, but they saw themselves as a hardware company and not as a seller of software (operating systems) to other computer manufacturers. They either did not see, or could not capitalize upon, the opportunities in front of them. But while Steve Jobs, the founder of Apple, isn't as wealthy as Bill Gates, he is one of America's billionaires.

Wealth is created in the financial markets but not by the financial markets. Financial markets capitalize the value of eliminating technological, developmental, or sociological disequilibriums.

Markets are important to the process of creating new products and processes since they give investors liquidity (allowing them to sell, or exit, their investments) and mobility (allowing them to move from one investment to another) and speed up the rewards for success. In providing an easy exit, financial markets reduce the risk and increase the rewards of bringing a new idea into being. Most venture capitalists want to know where the exit is before they're willing to walk through the entrance. They don't walk in if they think the door can be locked behind them. Mobility allows those willing to take risks with their money to move quickly from mature, successful start-ups to brand-new ventures. Countries that don't have active initial public offering markets for new companies have fewer new companies. IPOs let initial investors get out faster and increase the speed with which the rewards of entrepreneurship appear, and rapid wealth is a great incentive. If you don't believe this, look at the huge increase in business school enrollments in entrepreneurial programs in the last five years.

If one wants to know how to reduce wealth inequality, there is one easy answer and one hard answer. Increasing penalties for consumption (the honest way to say increasing incentives for savings) for the bottom 80 percent of the population would substantially increase their wealth. Saving nothing, it is difficult to have any wealth. Getting wider participation in eliminating disequilibrium conditions is harder. Luck is necessary, but it cannot be given to anyone. Most are not going to be masters of exploiting technological, developmental, or sociological disequilibriums. One cannot blame the lack of wealth in the bottom 40 percent of the population upon Bill Gates. His success has nothing to do with their failure. Reducing his wealth won't bring them success. What can be done, however, is to widen the skill base so that more could, if they wished, work for entrepreneurial companies, where stock options are usually given to everyone.

Widening that skill base is a matter of social organization. It brings us back to the organizational issues of improving education in the United States, organizing an environment where little companies can be easily founded and quickly built into big companies in Europe, and reducing the personal penalties for failure in Japan so that individuals can dare to take the risks of founding new companies.

Where Have the Profits Gone?

Economic revolutions don't just create new industries and transform old ones. They change where the profits are made along the production and delivery chain of every industry. To make money, businesses have to be at very different economic locations on the value-added chain than they were in the past.

Imagine that you're John Ackers, CEO of IBM in 1990. In the previous decade your company had average profits of between $8 and $9 billion per year. (To put those numbers in context, in 1997 the two most profitable companies in the world, General Electric and Exxon, each made just a little more than $8 billion.) In 1990 IBM made between $10 and $11 billion. No company has made that kind of money before or since. You run the most profitable company in the world, have the best known brand name in the world, are the most admired company in the world, and when the brightest young people at the world's best universities are asked where they would most like to work, your company is number one.[138]

God comes to you, John Ackers, much as he did to Moses. "Come up the mountain, John. I want to show you the promised land. The era of the mainframe is over. The personal computer is here. If you don't do something dramatic to restructure IBM, in 1991 your profits will be zero, the year after that minus $9 billion, the year after that another minus $9 billion, and the year after that minus $5 billion. In the next four years your company is going to lose $23 billion—more money than any company in human history. Now, John, it is your job to go down the mountain and persuade 420,000 employees who have had the best decade and the single best year in human history that they have to rip it up and do something different."

No one could have accomplished that task. The job was impossible. It is well to remember that Moses had to go up the mountain to get the Ten Commandments twice before they were believed by the Israelites. While few will fall off a cliff as IBM did, every business is going to have an IBM-like experience. Profits will slip away to some other point in their industry, and they will have to change.

Remember that IBM at one point owned 20 percent of Intel—a company that now has a higher stock market value than IBM. IBM did not see, or did not want to see, that the profits in the computer business were moving from those assembling computers in the middle of the value-added chain to those making parts (Intel, Microsoft) at the beginning of the chain and to those selling computers (Dell, Compaq) at the end of the chain. IBM was not alone. The Digital Equipment Corporation, once the second largest company in the computer business and now absorbed into Compaq, made exactly the same errors.

With electronic ticketing, the airlines are trying to take the profits away from the travel agents. In the health care sector, the HMOs have taken a lot of what were effectively profits, hidden as very high wages for doctors in technically nonprofit hospitals, away from the doctors. In the telephone business, no one knows where the profits are going to be made; companies are regularly sewn together and ripped apart. In the oil business, will the money be made by those who own oil—the place to be for the last hundred years—or by the oil well service firms—the place many believe is the place to be in the next few decades? The electrical power industry is in the midst of deregulation, new technologies, and stranded costs. What part of the industry is the place to be? All parts will not be equally profitable.

With electronic shopping, where products are delivered to the home rather than carried home by the buyer, maybe the profits will be made by the delivery companies (UPS, Federal Express) and not by those that run the Internet stores. For what new, never-before-delivered services will people be willing to pay premium prices? What will have to be done to preserve those premium prices? Is the secret in brand names like Coca-Cola? Is the secret with Microsoft and its domination of a key node in software programming? Or is it in Intel with both a brand name ("Intel Inside") and a microprocessor that keeps one generation ahead of the competition?

In the knowledge-based economy, none of these questions have settled answers. No one knows for sure. But those who figure it out first, or who are lucky enough to be at the right place on the value-added chain, win. They are at the top of the wealth pyramid.

11.   Missing Treasures

In the long run market wealth cannot grow unless productivity grows. Productivity is the putting together of the basic building blocks of the wealth pyramid so that humans with finite lifetimes and limited energy levels can produce ever greater levels of output. New technologies are staffed with new skills organized in new ways using new tools powered by new sources of energy to make new things. The difference between output and input growth is what causes wealth to increase. More can be produced with less.

As noted earlier, the growth in labor productivity in the United States fell from 3.2 percent per year in the 1960s to 1.1 percent per year in the ten years from 1987 to 1997. The 1970s were slower than the 1960s, the 1980s were slower than the 1970s, and the 1990s have been slower than the 1980s. A 1.1 percent per year rate of growth of productivity is the worst performance in any decade of American history. If it weren't for a pickup in productivity growth at the end of this period, the numbers would be even worse. It seems that although market wealth certainly glitters at the top of the pyramid, inside the pyramid there is very little productivity growth to be found.

The treasure hunter has to explain three mysteries. First, why has productivity growth collapsed? Second, if the third industrial revolution is under way, why hasn't productivity growth accelerated? With big breakthroughs in technology, there ought to have been some big jumps in productivity growth as new processes were brought on-line to produce old products and as new products were introduced to the marketplace. Third, why hasn't downsizing paid off in higher productivity? Downsizing was invented in the 1990s. Profitable companies did not have massive layoffs in earlier decades. Before then only money-losing companies engaged in massive downsizings. Those laying off workers in the 1990s were not downsizing to avoid bankruptcy in a race where employment chases output downward but never quite catches up. They were explicitly cutting employment to raise productivity and profits as output grew. The downsizing occurred, but the productivity gains that should have flowed from it did not.

The treasures to be found inside the wealth pyramid ought to be much bigger than those found in the 1960s. Instead the treasures that have thus far been found are much smaller than expected.

Part of the answer is easy to find.

In the United States, physical investments in tool-building have slowed down while growth in hours of work has accelerated. In the high productivity growth decade of the 1960s, capital per hour of work grew 2.8 percent per year; in the low productivity growth decade of the 1990s (1987–97), capital per hour of work grew only 0.8 percent per year. Some of this decline was due to lower investments (the capital stock grew 43 percent more slowly in the 1990s than in the 1960s), but much of it was due to a greatly increased rate of growth in hours of work. Immigration, new entrants into the labor force, and many more hours of work for each female employee pushed hours up 70 percent faster than in the 1960s. Americans simply did not buy the tools necessary to equip those new workers with what they needed to be productive. On the contrary, they increased their consumption and cut back on tool-buying just when they should have been reducing their consumption and increasing their tool-buying if they wanted to keep productivity growing at the old rates.

Slower rates of growth in the capital-to-labor ratio inevitably mean slower rates of growth in productivity. Additional tools aren't expanding labor's ability to produce more output per hour of work to the same extent that they were in the past. Historical studies of economic growth have shown that a 1 percent growth in the capital-to-labor ratio leads to a 0.2 to 0.3 percent growth in per capita output. As a result, the almost fourfold slowdown in the growth of the capital-to-labor ratio between the 1960s and the 1990s should have caused a productivity slowdown of about 0.4 to 0.6 percentage points.

Similarly, skills—as measured by the years of schooling embedded in the workforce—are growing more slowly than in the past. In the 1950s and 1960s, median years of education per worker were growing at 1.1 percent per year. In the 1990s, years of education per worker grew at 0.5 percent per year—less than half as fast. Historically, a 1 percent growth in skills per worker has led to a 0.7 or 0.8 percent growth in output per worker. Using this relationship, the slowdown in the growth rate of the average worker's years of education (0.6 percent per year) explains another 0.4 to 0.6 percentage points of the slowdown in productivity growth.

Together, a slower improvement in the capital-to-labor ratio and a lesser increase in skills per worker explain about 1 percentage point of the observed 2.1 percentage point decline in the productivity growth rate between the 1960s and the 1990s. Restoring a little less than half of the expected productivity is a matter of rebuilding and strengthening the skill development and tool-building levels of the existing wealth pyramid.

Qualitatively, skills might also be blamed for a little more of the observed slowdown in productivity growth. A close examination of the extra years of education embedded in the workforce in the 1990s shows that the biggest increases have been in workers who finish high school, go on to college, but drop out or flunk out before they complete a degree program—even a two-year associates degree. Of those who go on to college, 37 percent quit without completing a degree. The proportion of the adult population in this category has grown twice as much as the proportion graduating from college.

What we know from looking at wages is that an extra year of university education that does not lead to a degree has no economic value. If it isn't worth anything, economically it should not be counted as a year of education, yet it is—instead of having twelve years of education a worker is recorded as having thirteen years of education. If these dropout/flunk-out years weren't counted, years of education per worker would have been growing even more slowly than the recorded rate of 0.5 per year.

Qualitatively, high school achievement test scores have also fallen about 5 percent since their peaks back in the late 1960s. Making some correction for this factor would also increase education's impact on slower productivity growth. Some of those two-year associates degrees should probably be counted as remedial high school education rather than as years of college.

As a result, a little more of the slowdown in productivity growth might be traced back to a lack of skill development.

Another small part of the decline might also be traced to lack of investment in public infrastructure. The quantitative impact of a slowdown in public infrastructure investment has already been included in the earlier calculations of the effects of a slower growth in capital per hour of work, since the measurement of capital in those calculations included infrastructure investments. But if public infrastructure investments have more payoff per dollar of investment than private investments in plant and equipment, then something extra should be added. [139]

Accounting for these two qualitative factors might allow us to explain a little more of the productivity slowdown, let's say another 0.1 percentage point, but they still leave us with about 1 percent of the slowdown unexplained. How can this have happened when the world is experiencing such major advances in knowledge?

Some have argued that a considerable period of time might be needed for humans to learn how to make revolutionary technologies pay off in terms of productivity growth, but time lags don't explain why an acceleration in technology would cause a deceleration in productivity. They merely explain why productivity growth might not accelerate at the same time or quite as fast as technological change.

Coincidentally there was also an unexplained 1 percentage point of productivity growth in the studies of the sources of productivity growth in the 1950s and 1960s. When additions to capital, skills, and improvements in the industrial mix were totaled at that time, productivity should have been going up by 2 percent per year, but it was actually going up 3 percent per year. (In economic jargon, there was an unexplained 1 percentage point positive residual above what would be expected given the growth in productive inputs.)

To explain that percentage point, economists came up with the concept that advances in knowledge could directly raise productivity independently of how fast skills and capital were growing. Not all advances in knowledge had to be embedded in skills and capital before they could be used. Learning how to better organize a factory using the same people and machines was one of the examples given.

What has effectively happened is that the 1 percent addition to productivity growth found in the 1960s and ascribed to advances in knowledge has vanished. Leaving it out of the analysis, productivity in the 1990s is advancing at precisely the rate that would be expected given the additions to capital and skills. But even if one ignores the mysterious disappearance of the 1960s' positive residual, there are still two remaining mysteries: why have the invention of downsizing and the revolutionary nature of current changes in technology had no impact on productivity growth?

At this point a treasure hunter has two possible anwers. Maybe the tomb never did contain treasure. Following up on this possibility, the treasure hunter goes back to examine the downsizings and shifts in technology during the 1990s to see why they have not produced the expected results. The other possibility is grave robbers: someone or something has stolen the treasures that were once buried in the wealth pyramid.

When no treasures are found in real Egyptian pyramids, archeologists know that they were robbed in ancient times. Often they find evidence of the ancient robbers in the tombs, left undisturbed for thousands of years. But even when they do not find such evidence, they still know that a robbery occurred. Treasures were originally buried in all tombs. That's just what the Egyptians did. If treasure isn't there, the tomb was robbed.

In our exploration of the wealth pyramid, we know with a similar certainty that a robbery has occurred. The downsizings are real. Millions of workers have been eliminated from the payrolls of profitable firms. The big breakthroughs in technology—the computer, the laser, the Internet, robots—are also real. Some unknown modern grave robber has been stealing the productivity growth that we should have found in an era of man-made brain-power industries.

Identifying the grave robber is the task of the treasure hunter. Restoring the treasures of productivity growth is the task of the builder.

Traces of the robbery can be found in the productivity statistics themselves. In the 1990s manufacturing productivity grew at 3.1 percent per year—just as fast as it did in the 1960s. Simple mathematics tells us that if manufacturing productivity is growing at 3.1 percent per year and total productivity is growing at only 1.1 percent per year, productivity growth must have disappeared in some other sector, pulling the whole economy down with it. With a little economic forensics, the place where productivity disappeared can be found.

Productivity growth in the private service sector has been negative in some years and has averaged only 0.4 percent over the decade from 1987 to 1997. In the 1960s, service productivity was growing faster than manufacturing productivity and was 12 percent higher than that in the rest of the private economy.[140] The private service sector provided 70 percent of the employment growth of the 1960s, but this contributed to higher national productivity growth then. These employees were being added to a sector with an above-average level of productivity and with an above-average rate of growth of productivity.

Since 1969, service productivity has been growing less than half as fast as productivity in the rest of the economy, and as a result, private service productivity is now 4 percent below that of the rest of the private economy. Combine this small adverse productivity gap with a much slower annual rate of growth of productivity, and on both counts a larger service sector now substantially slows national productivity growth.

In the 1990s to talk about employment growth is to talk about the service sector. Private services provided 89 percent of the economy's employment growth from 1970 to 1980, 104 percent from 1980 to 1990, and 119 percent from 1990 to 1998. In the 1990s almost 20 percent of the employees in the rest of the economy lost their jobs and had to find reemployment in services.

In earlier times workers moved from a low-wage shrinking sector (agriculture) into high-wage expanding sectors (mining, construction, manufacturing, and government). But in the 1990s farm employment stabilized at about 2.9 million employees, the construction and government workforces were only slowly expanding, and an ever-increasing number of workers were forced to move from high wages and high productivity in mining and manufacturing to low wages and low productivity in the service sector.

Services are like a sea anchor (a sail tied to a ship and thrown overboard), slowing the speed with which winds and currents can push a ship through the sea. A sector with slightly low and very slowly growing productivity but rapidly growing employment is offsetting the positive productivity impact of other sectors with higher and more rapidly growing productivity but shrinking employment. The algebraic and economic outcome is a big subtraction from national productivity growth. The growth in private services offsets the positive productivity effects of downsizings and faster technological change.

In examining services, it is important to understand that statistically speaking they are what might be called a "garbage" category. Statisticians carefully define agriculture, mining, construction, and manufacturing, and everything that doesn't fit into those definitions is dumped into the category called services. The result is a sector without any common denominators. Services include high-tech capital-intensive industries (such as nuclear power plants) and low-tech labor-intensive industries (such as dog-walking). They include some of the country's most skilled workers (medical doctors) and some of its least skilled workers (janitors). They pay some of the highest wages (investment bankers) yet include most of the economy's minimum-wage jobs. They even include goods-producing activities (kilowatts of electricity).

With outsourcing and the use of temporary workers, activities that used to be included in other sectors are now moving into the service sector. The graphic arts department of an auto company closes down and the company's annual report is outsourced to a graphics arts service company. The temporary employees hired on the assembly line are counted as employees of the temporary help service firm that pays their wages. Low-wage activities that used to be counted within the manufacturing sector are transferred out to the low-wage service sector, raising the wage gap between the two sectors.

Services end up being the biggest employers of part-time workers (accounting for 74 percent of total part-time employment) and contingent (temporary, on-call, or contract) workers in the economy. With the shift to part-time work come lower wages and large reductions in the fringe benefits (pensions, health care, paid vacations, and holidays) that are important parts of a good job.

Contingent workers often do as well when it comes to wages but almost always miss out when it comes to fringe benefits.

The service sector also explains how wages can be falling while output is rising and unemployment is at record lows. While service wages vary widely, average hourly wages in the goods-producing sector are 30 percent above those in the service sector. Old workers are downsized in manufacturing or mining and reemployed in services. In this shift they take a big wage cut. With employment shrinking everywhere else, new workers must find jobs in the service sector, but these jobs pay real wages below the average wages paid in the economy twenty-five years earlier.

Within the service sector, most of the lower wages are found in retail trade, a category that includes restaurants. Transportation and public utilities pay wages 15 percent above those in manufacturing, wholesale trade, and finance; insurance and real estate pay wages equal to those in manufacturing; and "other services" pay wages only 8 percent below those in manufacturing. But in retailing, average hourly wages are just 62 percent of those in manufacturing. Retailing is also the only segment of the service sector in which the wage gap with manufacturing is widening: wages fell from 27 to 38 percent below those in manufacturing from 1970 to 1996. This creates an enormous downward twist on wages because the retail trade has generated 21 percent of all the new jobs in the past ten years. In 1947 retailing's wages were only 16 percent below those in manufacturing and the downward twist was smaller.

Hours of work per week in services are also less than those in manufacturing. Since much of the growth in service employment reflects declining hours of work per week rather than output growth, it is statistical rather than real. What were full-time jobs are simply being divided into two or more part-time jobs. While weekly hours of work rose 4.3 percent in the twenty-five years from 1970 to 1995 in manufacturing, they fell 2.2 percent in finance, insurance, and real estate; 4 percent in wholesale trade;

5.8 percent in "other services"; and 14.8 percent in retail trade. Here again, by far the largest gap is with retailing (28.8 hours per week in retailing versus 41.5 hours in manufacturing). By way of contrast, in 1947 weekly hours of work in retailing (40.3 hours) were as long as those in manufacturing (40.4 hours).[141]

The shift to part-time and contingent work also results in less training, fewer skills, and reduced career ladders. These workers are not on the team and not in the future plans of the places where they work.

Higher productivity growth and a more broadly shared prosperity cannot be restored unless the private service sector, and retailing in particular, undergoes some major structural changes. Services need a new structure of employment and remuneration that will lead to a very different pattern of wage and productivity growth.

This can be done. In continental Europe a very different pattern of employment and remuneration in services explains much of the difference between U.S. and European patterns of earnings. In continental Europe there have been only small increases in the wage gap between the top and bottom quintiles and few if any workers with failing real wages. Services also explain much of Europe's better productivity performance. With service wages near those in manufacturing, continental Europeans run a much more capital-intensive service sector with much higher rates of investment. With more capital per hour of work, services have a higher level of productivity.

A Swiss ski resort, for example, operates with a very different capital-to-labor ratio than an American one. Tickets are sold electronically, the doors on cable cars open and shut automatically, the lift attendants responsible for safety watch more than one lift, and in general the organization reflects a reduced need for labor. In America wages are so low that it does not pay to make the necessary labor-saving investments.

Continental Europe clearly demonstrates that it is possible to run a profitable high-wage service sector with career ladders and skill development similar to those found in other industries such as manufacturing. While part-time and contingent workers have also been increasing in Europe, this growth has been primarily a device to avoid European restrictions on firing and not an effort to reduce wages or fringe benefits. These workers have also not been heavily concentrated in services.

But there is a price to be paid. Services also explain much of Europe's failure to create new jobs. With much higher productivity growth in the service sector and slower growth in part-time workers, service employment has grown much more slowly in Europe than in the United States, even though Europe's output growth in the service sector has followed the American pattern.

The message to the treasure hunter is simple. To find the treasures of high productivity growth within the wealth pyramid, one has to become a builder, not a treasure hunter. A very different private American service sector must be organized.

Part Four
The Builders

12.   Managing the Tensions of Wealth Creation

After the treasure hunters have found, or not found, their treasures and left, the builders' more interesting tasks begin. Builders do not accept what they find. Their goal is to build a bigger and better wealth pyramid. To do so, four intrinsic tensions must be kept in balance.

Chaos versus Order

Chaos must be balanced against order if creativity is to exist and be utilized. Too much of either one leads to disaster and stagnation, as seen in nineteenth century Russia and fifteenth century China. While neither country is as extreme, the United States and Japan are their modern analogues.

No one looking closely at the American system can miss the intrinsic chaos, or lack of central control, built into the system. There is no national curriculum or national exit examination from high school to tell teachers what they must teach or students what they must learn. On average the American high school does not turn out a student comparable in quality with those in the rest of the world, but it also does not squash those few who think in contrarian terms. It is too inefficient and chaotic to do so.

Similarly, what makes the American university system unique is its variance in quality. It ranges from institutions that are glorified high schools to the world's very best. No one controls them the way ministries of education do in the rest of the world. Variety is almost infinite. Anything can be taught. That contrarian high school student who hasn't learned very much may enter one of America's best universities based on nothing but a very high IQ. Poor past performance is ignored because the school, not the student, may be at fault. Few doors are ever completely closed.

The antitrust suit against Microsoft is a dramatic case in point. It illustrates a type of regulatory chaos that doesn't make sense in a well-ordered society. It's a suit that would not have been brought in any other country in the world. In a short period of time Microsoft has become the most valuable company in the world, with a dominant global market position. It is precisely the kind of company that every country wants. Anywhere else it would be protected like a crown jewel. Other governments would ask what they could do to help it—not what they could do to hobble it.

The suit wasn't brought because the president or the Congress carefully studied the American computer software industry and came to the conclusion that it would be stronger if Microsoft were broken up. The decision to go ahead with the suit was made by a midlevel official, the head of the antitrust division of the Justice Department, with no participation from higher authorities. His decision to bring the suit had more to do with finding a high-profile case that would make headlines and help justify his annual budget appropriation from Congress than it did with the future health of the American computer software industry. The Justice Department had not had a high-profile case since AT&T in the early 1980s, and it had five hundred antitrust lawyers to keep busy.

Whatever the outcome of the Microsoft case, in all likelihood America will lose more than it gains. An earlier antitrust case against the United Shoe Machinery Company (which once dominated the globe in the making of shoe machinery) was a big factor in America's loss of both the shoe machinery and the shoe manufacturing industries. The first antitrust case against AT&T in the 1950s produced a consent decree that transferred to Japan, essentially free of charge, the technology (the transistor) that built Japan's consumer electronics industry and drove the American industry out of business. In the second antitrust case against AT&T in the early 1980s, Judge Green believed that small was beautiful and scornfully dismissed arguments that he should consider AT&T's efficiency before acting. In the Brown Shoe case of 1962, Chief Justice Earl Warren of the Supreme Court explicitly wrote that decentralization and fragmented markets were more desirable than low prices for the consumer.[142]

But such erratic, nonsensical actions reflect a type of regulatory chaos that does create economic space for other firms—even if those other firms are apt to be in other countries. American industry has too much chaos, but too much is clearly better than too little when a country reaches America's position on the wealth pyramid.

A high degree of chaos leads to economic creativity. Economic revolutionaries can thrive in successful societies only if the leaders of those societies cannot control everything, even though they want to control everything and have all the powers of the system—legal, economic, and social—at their disposal. This can only happen when the system has a certain intrinsic level of chaos built into it, which cannot be suppressed by the powers running the system.

Chaos creates room for new ideas to grow. Chaotic environments prevent vested interests from becoming so powerful that they can stop new ideas from germinating or growing. Chaos allowed new industries such as biotechnology to get started first in the United States. No approval was needed to start manipulating plant and animal genes. Americans have a tolerance for chaos since they are accustomed to it. This permitted an early start on airline deregulation. In its early years deregulation made air travel miserable. But something happened in the United States that only now, twenty years later, is very slowly happening in Europe and Japan.

A lack of order and discipline also contributes to the lowest productivity growth rate in the developed world. Consider the criminal justice system. In the United States, 1,800,000 inmates are guarded by 300,000 public and private correctional officers. Many sit idle when they could be productive. China, a totalitarian country with five times as many people, has half a million fewer people in jail.[143] Those Americans not in jail are guarded by an additional 1 million public policemen and 900,000 private security guards. Nowhere else in the world are any of these groups as big. All of this activity represents potential output and productivity lost.

Conversely a high degree of order in Japan has led to a lack of economic creativity. In high school, students memorize enormous amounts of material so that they can pass tough exit examinations written by a central ministry of education. Those who do well on the high school exit examination will have gone to after-school school to memorize even more than those who just went to school could memorize. There is no time for creative thinking or to let one's imagination run wild. These exit examinations, without exception, determine who gets into the best universities. The universities then follow centrally prescribed curriculums. A lengthy approval process is required to open up new fields of intellectual study. The result is a workforce with skill levels in the bottom half that Americans can only admire and envy. But at the top there is a lack of creativity.

Once at work the Japanese system is well ordered. Lifetime employment leads to career paths and on-the-job skill training for everyone. But those who leave to set up their own businesses are seen as traitors whose products should not be bought and who should not be rehired if their new firms fail.

Everything is efficiently organized in Japan. There are no cracks in the system where weeds can grow, but this also means that there are no cracks in the system where flowers can grow.

Missing the microprocessor caused what had been the world's largest semiconductor industry to fall back into a fight for second place with the Koreans. The semiconductor industry was left producing what had become a commodity—DRAMS—where profits could be made only at the top of cyclical booms and where losses would be huge in cyclical troughs. Missing the microprocessor also put Japan's computer industry into a tailspin. Most of the computer industry had been built on the IBM mainframe model and went into the tank along with IBM. The Japanese were still very good at writing software for mainframes, but that wasn't where the action was. The small, innovative software firms that are the heart of most of the world's personal computer software industry were never able to come into existence. The personal computer part of the industry was left having to buy Microsoft and Intel products if it wanted to sell the computers for which the world was writing software. The Americans ended up selling the profitable components, and the Japanese ended up in low-profit personal computer assembly.

The same is true in biotechnology. Since the technology was invented in America, young Japanese had to be sent to America to study for Ph.D.s in microbiology. But those who were sent were sponsored by the old pharmaceutical firms or the government and went back to work for their old firms, as was expected—or might we say, demanded. The new firms that were the heart of this new industry in America never came into existence in Japan.

Order, however, has left the Japanese with less than 100,000 people in jail and less than 250,000 policemen.[144] Billions are not spent on locks and burglar alarms. With health care spending less than half that of the United States, every health statistic (life expectancy, measures of illness, days lost from work) is better than in the United States. The Japanese productivity growth rate before the meltdown was more than three times that of the United States.

A well-educated and broadly skilled bottom two-thirds of the population does not suffer from falling real wages. Japanese CEOs make 60 percent less, while the average worker makes 25 percent more than their American counterparts.[145] The resulting income gap between the top and bottom 30 percent of the workforce is only half as large as that in the United States.[146]

America has more than enough chaos to be creative but too little order to use its ideas in the most efficient ways. Japan has more than enough order to be efficient but too little chaos to be creative. Both could gain if they moved a little in the direction of the other.

The issue is not choosing between order and chaos. Both are necessary. The issue is keeping them in the right balance—and understanding that the right balance changes as countries grow wealthier.

Initially order is paramount. The problems of the poorest countries of the world start with an inability to organize themselves. If the police aren't paid, or are paid very low wages, they will be corrupt. In the end they have to feed their families. Infrastructure and schools don't get built. Only the rich get privately educated—usually abroad. In the midst of disorder there is only one way to get rich—the powerful take from the powerless. Often the most powerful, the military, seize control of the government to further their own personal aims. Military rule is by its very nature the ultimate form of corruption. Those who are supposed to guard society steal social control.

Order is necessary to mobilize the resources (capital, labor) that are necessary to start the development, wealth creation process. In Asia governments built systems with forced savings. The rapidly rising capital-to-labor ratios that were the consequence of that forced savings pushed economic development forward. The steel, ship-building, and auto industries that drove first Japanese and then Korean development were not the labor-intensive, low-capital industries associated with economic development in the rest of the world.

Order, but a different kind of order, is also necessary for the second phase of development—copying to catch up. Discipline and patience are needed to figure out what the world's industrial leaders are doing, to adopt and adapt so that one can carefully replicate it at home, and to then fine-tune and improve it so that one can compete with those who first invented the process or product. The later part of the copying-to-catch-up process—improving on what one has copied—requires perhaps not creativity but ingenuity. Ingenuity, like creativity, requires room to do things somewhat differently, to not be completely imprisoned by old ways of doing things.

The Japanese have enough chaos to be ingenious. There are many examples of American products or processes that they took and made better. The automobile assembly line was invented in America, but a lot of Japanese refinements made it into something that could turn out cars at a much higher quality level. In the 1980s Americans visited Japan to learn about automobile assembly.

The great nineteenth century American example of improving on what one has copied is interchangeable parts. Conceiving the concept of interchangeable parts is not difficult. What is difficult is to develop the industrial precision, attention to detail, and most of all the discipline—everyone working to exactly the same set of specifications—that make interchangeable parts a practical reality.

The development of interchangeable parts should have occurred in Great Britain, which had all of the advantages. It was far richer than the United States. Its industrial processes were far more precise. Its craftsmen were better. It should have been far easier to get everyone working to the same precise specifications in Britain. But it wasn't. The old successful order, by far the greatest economy in the world, would not permit new ways of looking at the problem. The heavy hand of history and success squashed the new approaches.

Being a world economic leader, making the big technological breakthroughs—the third stage of economic development—requires a further rebalancing of order and chaos. Completely new ways of looking at things have to be developed, yet the old ways have already proved to be the most successful in the world.

Normally revolutions occur because of dissatisfaction. A poor country occupied by a foreign colonial master is dissatisfied with the existing order, and this dissatisfaction provides the motivating force for a political revolution. But in the third stage of economic development, revolutions have to occur in precisely the countries that are already the richest and the most successful. Members of such societies cannot be dissatisfied with the existing system because it has already proved itself to be the world's best.

Those who would like to move into this top creative group of countries or companies often talk about deliberately making room for economic revolutionaries—becoming places and having resources for those with the big ideas. But it never happens. Revolutions cannot be organized from the top by those running the old system. Revolutions are always frightening to those with vested interests. Those at the top of any successful system, whether political or industrial, have vested interests.

Leaders of the old system are by nature not revolutionaries. They dislike disorder. It threatens them. The existing system has picked them to lead it, and by doing so it has proved that it is the best of all possible systems. They return the system's confidence in them by opposing anything that threatens to fundamentally change the system. Leaders are not entrepreneurs. Leaders are the order part of the system. Entrepreneurs are the chaos part of the system. Both are necessary, but neither can play the role of the other.

Creativity cannot be organized. It is a product of disorganization. In very successful societies, creativity requires some chaos, but not so much chaos that there is not enough order to use what has been invented.

Singapore is a good example of what needs to happen over the course of development. Order and resource mobilization—the world's highest savings and investment rates, more money invested in education than any other society in the world—pushed it forward. By deliberately building the infrastructure to ensure that it would be the world's best place for offshore manufacturing, Singapore persuaded the rest of the world to bring some of their best technologies to Singapore. Copying to catch up was fast, since the inventors were bribed to be the teachers. In just thirty years Singapore went from having a per capita income of $500 to having a per capita income that rivaled the world's best. Right before the Asian meltdown its per capita gross domestic product briefly surpassed that of the United States.

But will Singapore learn to make the breakthroughs in either technology or social organization that real economic leadership requires? That is a stage of development it has not yet mastered. To do so it will have to create a degree of chaos that will be difficult to introduce into what is perhaps the world's most well-ordered society. It knows what it must do. But can it be done?

The Individual versus the Community

Wealth creation requires that a degree of tension and balance must be attained and sustained between the needs of the individual and the needs of the community. One of the central weaknesses of capitalism is that it does not acknowledge that it needs healthy institutions—public or private. In the theory of capital-ism, institutions come into existence and go out of existence automatically when the market calls for them to do so. But in fact it doesn't happen that way.

Biotechnology is a good example. Enormous individual eco-nomic opportunities in biotechnology would not have opened up unless the community had been willing to invest enormous sums in research and development and in the Ph.D. training in biology and medicine that were necessary to build the foundations for this new industry. Even today, forty years after major spending started, the National Institutes of Health and the National Science Foundation are still spending billions per year.[147] In today's dollars, far more than $100 billion has gone into the effort. Billions were being spent long before anyone could prove that big payoffs would exist. Even the wealthiest individuals and corporations don't have the necessary funds or, more important, the appetite for risk and uncertainty that this effort required. The biological gold mine was there for anyone to find, but the initial prospectors had to be publicly financed.

Major public R&D spending on microbiology did not happen outside of the United States. Because the public spending did not occur, private prospectors, even those from the biggest firms, never went out to search for biological gold. As a result, everyone plays catch-up with America.

Conversely the community cannot thrive unless individual entrepreneurs exist to bring new ideas into the market. The big American pharmaceutical companies knew what was happening in biological research, but none of them were leaders in the effort to create biotechnology. In places like Japan and Germany, where starting new companies and quickly growing them into big com-panies is difficult, the biotechnology industry still isn't thriving.

Large bureaucracies, whether government or private, always have too many vested interests in the old to be pioneers of the new technologies that will destroy the old. Government-owned

British Steel sank into an economic quagmire when foreign competition and mini-mills came along, but so did privately owned U.S. Steel. Capitalism's only advantage is that death is easier if big firms are privately owned. Eleven of the twelve largest firms that opened America's twentieth century won't be around to celebrate the twenty-first. Socialism never figured out how to kill its dinosaurs; they just went on using up resources until the system collapsed. But large private firms do not go out of business as easily and smoothly as the theory maintains either. Public benefits such as unemployment insurance, health insurance, and pension guarantees make it a lot easier and smoother to shut down any private operation when the right moment for euthanasia arrives.

To build wealth, one must build communities—big companies—even if it is also necessary to kill them at the appropriate time.

Big companies are the big spenders on the development side of research and development. Without them the developmental efforts that are necessary to make real products out of good ideas and prototypes just don't happen. Government research laboratories aren't interested in working out the details of producing and marketing the results of their efforts—no matter what they say.

Small new companies usually start as spin-offs of big old companies. Relatively few come directly out of university or national research laboratories. Often these new small companies are using technologies that the big old companies developed but don't think will lead to big markets. Big companies are where managers of the new companies learn the management skills (make mistakes on other people's money) that allow them to start up their own companies with fewer mistakes.

Usually the initial markets for small companies are components used by big companies. Selling to a few business customers is much easier and cheaper than selling to millions of individual consumers. Without big companies, small companies don't have markets they can easily tap.

Big companies are the big exporters that every country needs. Exporting requires a detailed knowledge of foreign markets that small companies don't have and aren't going to get because it's too expensive for them to acquire it.

Big companies provide most of the economy's good, well-paying jobs with career ladders. Remaining an employee in a small company that is going to remain small means that the prospects for high wages are bleak.

Small is not beautiful. What is beautiful is a small firm that rapidly grows into a big firm.

Among different animal species, the individual and the community often live together in very different arrangements. Like some species (wolves) and unlike others (American mountain lions), humans are clearly pack animals. Few humans could live their lives as hermits. Those who do—like the Unibomber with his letter bombs—are usually considered mad. What is different about human pack behavior is that we construct complex societies that change over time. The pattern of dominance in a wolf pack remains the same, even if the power positions held by different wolves change. In contrast the city of the Middle Ages is not the city of today.

Social controls are what make humans human. We do not live in an individual state of nature where the strong eat the weak. When those social controls break down and the strong do eat the weak (Cambodia from 1975 to 1979 under Pot Pol), human standards of living fall very rapidly. Complete freedom to do what the individual wants—anarchy—does not work.

The Present versus the Future

Wealth creation requires that the present pay homage to the future. The future is never here and we will never live in the future. Nonetheless the future has to play an important role in our decisions. It makes demands on us. We have to make sacrifices for it. The present can destroy the future—for example, if current consumption is allowed to drive out the investments necessary for future success.

Different societies have solved the problem of how to make their citizens invest in the future in different ways. The ancient Egyptians believed that life after death was more important than life itself. The pharaohs lived in mud homes, which disappeared long ago, but were buried in stone palaces that thousands of years later are still perhaps the grandest thing ever built by men. The Romans believed that their empire would last forever and they built it to last forever. It is not by accident that the Appian Way still exists. They also believed that they were building for the empire—not for their own future consumption. Medieval man built his cathedrals for God. God demanded a permanent place for His followers to worship Him.

In the last half-century, the Cold War was the social conditioning factor that led Americans to build. All of America's great building projects were justified as military necessities—the interstate highway system in the 1950s, a big increase in the production of engineering and science Ph.D.s in the 1960s, placing a man on the moon, the Internet in the 1970s, and Star Wars in the 1980s. Capitalism and democracy were threatened by communism and totalitarianism and America needed daring investments to survive. Defense focused American attention on the need for the current community to defend the existence of the future community.

Biology is the only place where America has been willing to make major investments in the future without the impetus of the Cold War. Here the announced goal was extending life expectancy—living longer. The desire to stay alive in the present makes us willing to invest in the future. Most of what we are investing in now, such as cancer research, won't come to fruition fast enough to help us live longer if we develop cancer. But we can always hope. We collectively invest in the future in the illusion that we are making our individual personal futures longer. Unfortunately, this isn't a rationale for future investments that is applicable outside the health care sector.

Outside of health care, none of the Cold War rationales for caring about the future are now relevant. America's collective existence is not remotely threatened by anyone or anything. Yet something has to make us interested in the existence of the future after we as individuals have ceased to exist.

Humankind, alone among the animal species, has a past, a present, and a future. Perhaps it is not an accident that our current lack of interest in history (enrollments in college history courses were down 25 percent from 1990 to 1998) occurs at the same time as our lack of interest in the future (as evidenced by our low investment rates).[148] If a group of people have no sense of where they came from, it is difficult for them to have any sense of where they should go. Without a remembered past and a charted future, few humans see the journey that they are in fact taking. Not knowing that they are on a journey, they cannot and will not build the tools that will be necessary if their journey is to be successful.

Throughout their history humans have been explorers and adventurers. Geographically the exploration game has almost come to an end. There are a few depths of the ocean that humans have not yet explored, but not a lot. Unmanned space exploration will continue, but humans won't go much farther into space than they have gone. Going to the nearest star would take sixty thousand years in the space shuttle.

Our endless frontier is science. Pushing technology where it has never gone before and building what has never been built before is the way humankind will go where it has never gone before. The future requires huge investments, but the most exciting age of exploration is ahead of us—not behind us. The major unknown is how to make everyone feel that they can enjoy the excitement of going along on the journey. One can enjoy the excitement of biotechnological discoveries without having a Ph.D. in microbiology. One can make those investments knowing that this journey of exploration will help future generations much more than it will help those now paying for it.

Competition versus Cooperation

Competition and cooperation are the final pair that must be balanced in the wealth creation process. The need for both is easily proved.

The fall of communism proves that a system that focuses on community cooperation to the exclusion of individual competition does not work. Many countries tried it. It did not work anywhere.

In the 1950s and 1960s, the U.S.S.R. was held up as the model of successful economic development. It went from being a very poor country to being a world military superpower with midrange per capita incomes in just a few decades. It could marshal resources and copy to catch up, but it had no change agents and could not move beyond the second stage of economic development. Stagnation set in the 1970s and 1980s. The system collapsed in the 1990s.

Socialism and communism failed because neither had a change agent. Both deliberately banished entrepreneurs. In their view it was unfair that entrepreneurs got so rich and powerful. The central planner was supposed to replace the entrepreneur and be the change agent in socialism. But it did not work. Centrally organized economic change is theoretically possible but in practice impossible. The economic losers who already exist are always politically stronger than the potential winners who have yet to come into existence. What already exists politically captures the central planning agency, the designated change agent, and turns it into a backward-looking bureaucracy protecting the old rather than a forward-looking bureaucracy promoting the new. Without a real change agent, stagnation eventually sets in.

By way of contrast, in capitalism the winners do not have to negotiate with the losers in the planning apparatus. The winners simply push the losers ruthlessly aside in the market.

But history also teaches us that all individual competition and no community cooperation does not work. America tried survival-of-the-fittest capitalism in the 1920s. It left us with Herbert Hoover and the Great Depression. Unfettered financial markets imploded and pulled the industrial economy down with them. Public authorities, believing in nonintervention and the self-regulating, self-recuperative powers of capitalism, did nothing to clean up the mess. From October 1929 to March 1933 the economy spiraled ever downward, ending up with almost one-third of Americans unemployed and with no form of social support. Starting in March 1933 President Roosevelt introduced a wide range of social programs to end the Great Depression, but by then its grip and momentum were so great that none of the programs really worked. There was a recession within the Depression in 1938, and when World War II began in Europe in 1939 there was no light at the end of the economic tunnel. Unemployment was still over 20 percent. World War II intervened to stop the Great Depression, but without the war it might well have gone on long enough to spell the end of capitalism in America.

With the Nazi (the term is a contraction of National Socialism) conquest of continental Europe, there were only two capitalist countries left—Great Britain and the United States—and the British would vote for a socialist government as soon as the war was over. In the 1950s, all of the third world believed in the communist model of development. The U.S.S.R. had used it to become a superpower in a very short period of time. History might well have written an epitaph for capitalism in the 1930s and 1940s if events had been just slightly different.

History teaches a simple lesson. The pendulum can swing too far in either direction. Competition and cooperation have to be kept in balance.

13. Building a Wealth Pyramid

In an era of man-made brainpower industries, when knowledge is the fundamental building block underlying wealth, a new global economic game is under way. Not surprisingly, no country just by accident has all of the right building blocks in place in its wealth pyramid. No part of the globe is immune from the need to rebuild.

Japan: Cleaning Up the Mess

Japan's rebuilding job starts right on the bottom level of the pyramid with social organization. Japan needs to build a new economic structure that can cope with financial meltdowns.

Consider the frequently heard moral charges: crony capitalism, phony bookkeeping, sweetheart loans to friends and relatives, politicians on the payroll, criminal activities. What is being referred to—Japan in 1990, Asia's 1997 meltdown, Russia in 1998, or America's savings and loan crisis in the 1980s? The answer, of course, is "all of the above." Experience is clear—sooner or later everyone experiences a meltdown. Let him who has never had a crash throw the first stone.

The only relevant question is which governments are going to be good at cleaning up the mess. The big losers are those with ineffective governments that cannot do what is necessary. Viewed from the perspective of demonstrated abilities to deal with the aftermath of a bubble, Japan is the sickest country on the Pacific Rim. Japan's crash occurred in 1990, yet eight years later it has made no progress toward recovery. The result has been a long period of stagnation, with negative growth in 1998 and negative growth expected in 1999.

Bank problems still fester. With an overhang of nonperforming loans, banks cannot make new loans and cannot afford to roll over old loans, even for profitable firms. The banks need whatever money they can collect to pay their depositors and avoid going broke themselves.

When governments refuse to shut down bankrupt banks, problems only become worse. Since the banks must pay more interest to their depositors than they are collecting from their nonperforming loans, the imbalance between their assets and liabilities only becomes larger with time. Government injections of cash to cover the deficits eventually run out and have to be repeated. Bank deficits grow, and the ultimate amount that the bank deposit insurance system owes to bank depositors gets larger and larger.

There are no options: eventually the failing banks have to be shut down. But Japan is only now very slowly and with great reluctance beginning to do so.

The Japanese business firms that aren't making the required interest and principal repayments find that their unpaid interest accumulates and is added to the principal they owe. What they owe gets larger and larger with time, and they are less and less able to repay. Weak Japanese retailing and industrial firms follow weak banks into ever-weaker positions. As delays drag on, the number of business firms that must eventually be shut down grows.

Problems do not get solved with the passage of time. In the words of Shakespeare in Macbeth, "If it were done when 'tis done, then 'twere well it were done quickly." Delay only makes the problems bigger.

Much like the Hoover administration in the 1930s, the Japanese government has lost all its credibility. It talks, it debates, it promises, but it does not act. Restructuring actions that might be taken are scheduled far into the future. In 1994 Japan announced that its financial markets would be liberalized in 2001. Yet nothing was promised in 1994 that could not have been done by 1995. Long, unnecessary delays mean that the government in the end won't do what it promised. Like the promised privatization of Nippon Telephone, the process will stop before it is completed. Timid policies will become even more timid when they are implemented.

Japanese monetary policies have been timid and ineffective and are now exhausted. Sharp large interest rate reductions at the beginning of the crisis would have had very different effects from those of the many small cuts spread out over a long period of time that actually happened. Japan is caught in what Lord Keynes during the Great Depression called a liquidity trap. Money interest rates are close to zero (0.15 percent) but loans are unavailable. In a deflationary environment, real interest rates can be very high even though money interest rates are very low. Inexplicably, in late 1998 and early 1999 interest rates were allowed to rise.

Japanese fiscal policies have been even worse. Spending programs have focused on supporting land values rather than stimulating output. Timid stimulus packages come and go without major effects. Personal taxes were at one point raised when they should have been lowered.

One of the benefits of having a long history of financial crashes is that one knows what must be done to restore normalcy. Governments don't have to invent new solutions. It isn't necessary for a meltdown, even a very big one, to end up in a Great Depression or a Great Stagnation. Messes can be cleaned up. Governments need only the will to do what is necessary.

The American S&L bailout provides a good guide to what must be done. The solution starts with an honest third-party accounting that divides existing loans into those that are likely to be repaid and those that are not. Firms and banks with solid balance sheets (assets exceeding liabilities) get government-backed loans to tide them over the period during which private credit markets will be frozen—when they cannot roll over their existing short-term loans and when suppliers refuse to offer normal credit terms. Bad banks and nervous suppliers cannot be allowed to destroy good firms or good banks.

For banks whose balance sheets are underwater (liabilities exceeding assets), some government agency (America called it the Resolution Trust) has to take charge. Bank depositors have to be repaid if meltdowns are not to cause depressions. But the sale of the assets that were used to collateralize bank loans will not cover what has to be paid to the depositors. Banks with liabilities greater than assets are allowed to fail and go out of business. At the onset of the S&L crisis, the United States had thirty thousand banks. After it was over, there were fifteen thousand banks. One out of every two banks had to be shut down. Some of America's biggest banks were shut down. Even America's largest bank, Citibank, came very close to being shut down.

The Resolution Trust quickly sells the assets it has acquired from bankrupt banks to the highest bidders. It cannot hope to manage these assets profitably, since they have no common denominator other than an original owner that has gone broke. For a short time in the 1980s the Resolution Trust tried to manage the assets it had acquired and nurse them back to health so that it could get more when they were finally sold. It failed. The longer the assets were held, the lower their market value when they were eventually sold.

Taxpayers have to pick up the losses. They are not rescuing the banks, they are rescuing the system.

Priority number one: Debts must be eliminated if growth is to resume. In capitalism, every asset is a good asset at some price. A Japanese hotel group, for example, built a hotel in Hawaii that was so expensive that every single room had to be rented every single night of the year for $1,000 per night just to break even. The world's best hotel manager couldn't make that hotel profitable. Three years ago it was sold for 15 percent of the value of its mortgage debts. It quickly became a money-maker. With its old debt structure, this could never have happened. The interest and principal payments owed on it exceeded the intrinsic productivity of the property. Neither better management nor time can solve this dilemma.

Debt write-downs and debt elimination are the keys to restarting the economy. Without them nothing else works.

In the process of auctioning off the assets that the equivalent of America's Resolution Trust has acquired, equity-based capitalism replaces debt-based capitalism. Bringing equity in means letting outsiders buy. Only outsiders have equity. Insiders are drowning in debt. Inside managers have all been tainted by the previous failure. Only outsiders have the untainted management talent that can turn failure into success. At the onset of the S&L crisis in America, every bank in Texas was owned by Texans. When it was over, no bank in Texas was owned by a Texan.

Japan is unwilling to auction off assets since it is reluctant to let foreigners buy. Yet foreigners are not going to buy control of Japan if they are allowed to buy some bankrupt firms—any more than foreigners have bought control of America. In America 18 percent of the gross domestic product is produced by foreign firms; in Germany it's 24 percent. In Japan the corresponding figure is less than 1 percent. A lot of Japan can be sold to foreigners before issues of control become relevant.

In the end the taxpayer is going to incur enormous losses. There is no other option. At the height of the S&L crisis America's Resolution Trust was expected to lose $900 billion. What it finally had to pay depositors was *only* $550 billion more than it collected from the sale of foreclosed assets. If taxpayers are to be persuaded to assume this distasteful burden, they have to feel that they are not being abused. They are paying their taxes to rescue the economic system—not to rescue those who got rich in the bubble.

In the United States, four things were necessary to make the takeover of bad debts politically acceptable to the taxpayers.

First, shareholders lost all of their equity before any public funds were used. Shareholders were never rescued. Shareholders are the risk-takers in capitalism and have to be held responsible for failure.

Second, in any failing bank or business firm, all of the top management team was fired. No effort was made to determine whether the top management team was, or was not, directly responsible for the failure. They were the decision-makers, they should have prevented such disasters, and as the decision-makers they were ultimately responsible for failure regardless of the detailed causes.

Third, where criminal actions—even minor ones—had occurred, those involved were thrown in jail. Michael Milken, one of the richest men in America, went to jail for a number of years. He was not alone.

Fourth, when politicians were criminally involved, they too were thrown in jail. A number of American congressmen, including powerful committee chairmen, went to jail. When politicians were involved but not criminally implicated, they were removed from office. Six senators lost their jobs because of their involvement in the S&L crisis.

When it comes to failing industrial firms, the problems are different from those in the banking system and the solutions have to be different. When banks go out of business, not much happens to the economy other than the loss of a few jobs. Most branches remain open. Good borrowers still have their loans, since they are sold to good banks. The depositors are all protected. But in any economy there are industrial firms too large to be allowed to fail. If they were to fail, they would bring the national economy down with them. Five *chaebols* account for 37 percent of Korea's GDP and 44 percent of its exports.[149]

When big industrial firms go broke, the job losses are much larger and the serious consequences go far beyond the immediate loss of jobs. In contrast to what happens in the financial sector, those up and down the distribution chain aren't protected. The firm's suppliers go broke because they aren't paid for goods already shipped. The firm's industrial customers go broke because they can't quickly shift suppliers and get the components they need to manufacture their own products.

Big firms are going to be rescued, but where industrial rescues do occur, the top management team is replaced. Shareholders are both the first to lose their equity and the last to regain their equity during the recovery process. When a new management team is brought in, as when Lee Iacocca was selected to head Chrysler by the U.S. Treasury, they are not paid to manage. They are paid to achieve a successful turnaround. Salary? No. Stock options? Yes. Because Lee Iacocca succeeded, his stock options made him rich. If he had failed, he would have had only his salary—$1 per year.

In the case of large firms such as the Korean *chaebols*, separable pieces are auctioned to the highest bidders to pay off debts. Chrysler was forced to sell all of its foreign subsidiaries and all of its nonauto-related U.S. activities.

When the government makes industrial loans, it always gets an equity kicker. If government takes a downside risk, the taxpayer must have upside potential. The American government ended up making money on its Chrysler warrants in addition to getting interest and principal payments.

It is completely unfair, but firms too small to affect the national economy are allowed to fail. There is just no way government can replace the management in thousands of small firms, in which owners often cannot be separated from managers because they are the same people.

Buying shares, as the Hong Kong government was doing in the summer of 1998, and as the Japanese government has done in the last eight years, does not work. All government share acquisition does is let private investors get out of the market with smaller losses. The problem is not abnormally low share prices. The problem is interest and debt repayments that exceed the earnings potential of the assets that owe those debts. If debts are reduced to levels consistent with underlying earnings, the economy can be restarted and the stock market will recover to levels consistent with profits. If those excessive debts are not eliminated, there is no way to restart growth.

The same principles apply in the real estate sector. Government policies to purchase land directly or indirectly (with unneeded infrastructure projects) are a mistake. The issue is not the price of land but the debts owed on the land that rents cannot cover. Land prices cannot forever be held higher than the price dictated by the earnings of the activities carried out on the land. Stopping land prices from falling makes the banks and real estate companies look better. They do not have to write down their portfolio of assets quite so much. But it's like applying cosmetics to a seriously infected wound. It hides the damage temporarily but doesn't cure the infection. Lower land prices consistent with underlying productivity are necessary if there is to be a recovery.

Other government actions, such as stimulating demand with lower interest rates, tax cuts, or spending increases, may be required to complete a recovery, but macroeconomic policies will not work until the economy's excessive debts have been eliminated. Capitalism does not work when assets have to carry debts whose value is greater than the market value of the assets themselves. Capitalism works only when profits can be earned.

History is clear. Preventing speculative bubbles is impossible. Controlling bubbles once they have appeared is impossible. But cleaning up the mess is possible.

The reasons why Japan, and much of the rest of Asia, cannot do what is necessary are as simple as they are hard to change. Japan is a consensus society with a narrow establishment at the top. And it is impossible to get a consensus that a firm should go broke and out of business when the managers and owners of the firms that need to be liquidated are part of the group seeking a consensus. How do you get them to agree to their own liquidation? How do you throw people into bankruptcy or jail when they are your sons, your social peers, your college classmates, or your in-laws? In America our establishment is so big and diverse that the unpleasant job can be done by strangers.

Consensus doesn't work if the job is cleaning up the mess at the end of a speculative bubble. An economic czar has to be appointed with the power to close down those who are hopelessly bankrupt and sell off their assets to the highest bidder. The existing system has proved that it can't do what has to be done. Giving it more time only makes the problems worse.

When problems occur because of outside forces (such as defeat at the end of World War II), consensus societies have huge economic advantages. They're great at uniting people and directing their energy toward common solutions. But they have huge weaknesses in turbulent times when the problems are internally generated: they can't rally insiders against outsiders when the problems are caused by insiders.

Bankruptcy is also more serious in some parts of Asia than it is in the United States. It is seen as a permanent character flaw. There have been newspaper reports of creditors in Japan who expected those who had gone broke to atone by committing suicide. In America bankruptcy is seen as a mixture of bad business judgment and bad luck. It is only a slight exaggeration to say that going broke is almost a badge of respect—it shows that you're an aggressive businessman.

One must be cautious about predicting that Japan will not do what it needs to do. Japan is a country with a history of taking a long time to reach a new consensus on what to do after a disaster.

It was the last of the countries with major destruction in World War II to get back to 1939 levels of production. But once it reaches a consensus it is the world's best when it comes to implementation. The arguments suddenly stop, the resistance ends, and everyone works together toward the new goals. After 1957 Japan was the fastest-growing economy in the industrial world.

Restarting rapid economic growth in Japan and on the Pacific Rim, however, is going to require something more than the ability to clean up the mess at the end of an economic bubble. The countries that want to resume their rapid growth will have to understand that the era of export-led growth is over and implement the structural changes necessary to shift to an internally driven growth strategy.

In export-led growth strategies, the focus is on pumping up exports. If exports can grow at something like 15 percent per year, the country can then import enough to allow its domestic economy to grow at 7 to 8 percent per year. It can afford to buy the equipment, spare parts, and consumer products it needs, and it can build up its foreign exchange reserves to cover imports during the occasional export slowdowns due to recessions in its foreign markets.

But export-led growth only works when a few small countries play the game. Japan was a small country economically when it played the game in the 1960s and 1970s. The principal players in the 1970s and 1980s—South Korea, Taiwan, Hong Kong, and Singapore—together had sixty-five million people. When most of the world, including big countries such as China and Indonesia, wants to play the game, the game ends. How can every country increase exports at 15 percent per year when the world economy grows only at 2 to 2.5 percent per year? They can't.

Japan is still trying to play the export-led growth game, but it is too big. The rest of the world cannot absorb what Japan would need to jump-start its economy with exports. This would be true even if China had not joined in, but it's doubly true with China as a player.

Japan needs internally driven growth strategies similar to those used by America in the nineteenth century. These strategies require different industrial structures and different national economic policies. Internally driven growth is not a return to the failed model of quasisocialism and import substitution tried by most of the underdeveloped world in the 1950s and 1960s. Industry is neither government owned nor government financed. A competitive environment is sustained by letting foreigners enter and compete under the same set of rules that apply to the country's citizens. Foreigners are in fact encouraged to enter and drive locally owned firms out of business—if they can—to keep local firms on their toes.

In Japan, internally driven growth means changing rice land, inheritance tax, shade, eminent domain, and earthquake regulations that hold land values far too high and prevent the building of highrise apartment towers as would happen in other equally rich and densely populated countries. With the right changes in rules and regulations Japan could build residential housing consistent with its per capita income. New markets would then open up for the consumer durables needed to fill those new big apartments and homes.

What has to be done is absolutely clear. History has taught us what must be done many times. Technically it is not hard to do. With an effective national government able and willing to do it, a speedy recovery is certain. The savings and loan crisis in the United States had no short- or long-run consequences on U.S. economic performance.

If countries cannot do what is necessary, economic stagnation looms over their futures. But the causes of that stagnation are not in the economy. They lie in an unsolved political crisis—an inability to act when action is required—that leads to disastrous economic consequences.

Western Europe: Building Entrepreneurs

Western Europe's rebuilding job begins one level up on the pyramid. It must create an entrepreneurial environment if it is to succeed in a knowledge-based economy.

Understanding this reality does not mean that Europe has to cast aside completely what many continental Europeans like to call the third way (a social market economy) between Soviet communism and American survival-of-the-fittest capitalism. While some higher degree of inequality is probably inevitable in this new global knowledge-based economy, Europe can have a more egalitarian, humane economy than America. The market wages of the unskilled in Europe must fall to global levels if they are to be employed, but there is a short-run remedy that can stop their take-home pay from falling until they are reskilled and retrained.

It is what in America is known as an earned-income tax credit. With an earned-income tax credit, low-wage individuals don't pay taxes; they get a government payment based on their earnings. The lower the earnings, the greater the payment. For example, workers making a $6 per hour market wage might get a supplement of $2 per hour, bringing their take-home pay up to $8 per hour. Earned-income tax credits dominate unemployment insurance benefits on every dimension. They save jobs yet deliver benefits to low-skilled, low-wage workers. Those who receive the benefits have the dignity of earning their living rather than being idle. More important, they stay active and their existing skills don't atrophy in a long period of idleness. Those employed make more than those unemployed. The long-run solution is to raise the skills of workers whose wages must be low in a global economy if they are to be employed, but an earned-income tax credit allows time to deliver the necessary skill training without suffering through a long period of rising inequality.

Priority Number One: Increased Industrial Flexibility

More fundamentally, if Europe wants to compete successfully in the new man-made brainpower industries now emerging, it needs industrial flexibility—the ability to form and quickly grow new companies into large companies using new breakthrough technologies.

As we have seen, Western Europe has been completely unable to grow big new companies in the post–World War II period. In visiting Europe, I often talk with businessmen who are deliberately attempting to keep their companies small to stay below the radar screens of government regulation. If they remain small enough, regulations such as co-determination don't apply to them or they can cheat a little on the regulations and no one is likely to notice. Conversely if they are very large, like FIAT, and need to downsize, the government will help pay the costs imposed by the regulations because the Italian government can't afford to let FIAT collapse—it's too big. But medium-sized firms come up on government radar screens. They have to obey the government regulations, which make it difficult to grow, but they aren't big enough to be helped by government if they get into trouble because of those regulations.

To grow small firms into big firms requires easy-to-follow, equally enforced rules and regulations that apply to firms at all size levels.

Industrial flexibility does not require the wholesale dismantling of the Western European social welfare state, but it does require some labor market flexibility. American firms that have grown large in short periods of time have usually had periods when they needed to downsize. If they had not been able to downsize, they would have gone broke during their cyclical or structural downswings and not have remained in business long enough to take advantage of the great opportunities that were later to emerge. Being young, rapidly growing firms, they hadn't had time to accumulate the financial reserves necessary to employ unneeded labor over these rough periods.

Intel is a good example of this problem. It was one of the pioneers in basic DRAM semiconductor chip manufacturing but had a very rough period when Japan was conquering this market in the 1980s. Later on it would take advantage of the invention of the microprocessor and come to dominate its industry, but its pattern of growth was not consistently up. If it could not have downsized it would have gone out of business in the mid-1980s and would not have been around to be successful in the 1990s. What happened to Intel has happened to almost every new large American company.

The lesson is simple. The ability to downsize is an important part of growth.

Successful economies need small firms that rapidly grow into big firms. Big firms provide good jobs; big firms do research and development; big firms export; big firms are a training ground for future entrepreneurs. But some of those big firms have to be new firms, since old big firms are going to contract. In America from 1990 to 1995, twenty-one out of the twenty-five industrial firms that had more than a hundred thousand employees shed jobs.[150] Net, they lost three jobs for every one they produced. But it was not small companies that were creating America's new good jobs. It was another set of companies that were in the process of becoming big.

If one asks why America's two great high-tech areas, Silicon Valley and Route 128, exist, the answer is partly found in great educational institutions (Berkeley and Stanford, Harvard and MIT), but there are other places in America with great universities. Their real genesis is found in banking institutions that were willing to lend money based upon good ideas and did not require physical assets as security.

Consider my employer—the Massachusetts Institute of Technology. MIT graduates and faculty members have founded 4,000 companies employing 1.1 million people with sales of $232 billion. By themselves, MIT-founded companies would be the twenty-fourth largest economy in the world. A tradition of entrepreneurship clearly exists and has existed for a long time—some of those companies were founded before World War II.

But in the last decade, by design, that tradition has grown. The MIT patent licensing office has shifted its policy from selling its patents to taking an equity position in companies that use MIT's technologies. This makes it much less costly to start new businesses. An MIT Enterprise Forum was organized so that those who had started new businesses could provide tutoring and mentoring for those who wished to start new businesses. Students can enter a new business plan competition with a $50,000 prize to the winner. Over time the prize itself has become secondary, since many of the plans presented (including many that don't win) are now financed by the venture capitalists who monitor the competition. Five years ago MIT started to give the Lemelson-MIT prize ($30,000) to the best MIT student-inventor of the year. Several winners have already founded their own businesses. The professors who run the entrepreneurial track within the M.B.A. program at the Sloan School believe that they have a lot to teach about how to make new start-ups successful. While 80 to 95 percent of all purely technical spin-offs fail, 80 to 95 percent of those from MIT succeed when packaged with the right marketing and business skills.[151] All of these activities have buttressed and expanded an existing tradition of building new companies.

Whatever the current degree of entrepreneurial spirit, actions can be taken to enlarge it.

Although there are common problems within Europe, there are also differences from country to country. Some countries such as Italy have a good record of new start-ups. But their rules and regulations then prevent the new start-ups from quickly growing into world-scale high-tech corporations. Other countries such as Germany and France have a poor record with new start-ups. Their social systems (dislike of risks, intolerance of failure, avoidance of change) do not permit start-ups to get going. A country like Great Britain would seem to have all the ingredients of the American system (or maybe it's the reverse), yet Britain also has a poor record when it comes to start-ups and building new big corporations. What Britain lacks is what it lacked a hundred years ago when it lost its global position of economic leadership: the necessary mass base of technological manpower. Its scientists are very good but too few in number. It educates so few people technologically that the number of people necessary to run high-tech industries simply don't exist.

Israel is an interesting illustration of the British problem. Before the Russian immigration it had 60,000 engineers, and once those needed in defense were subtracted from this total, there were not enough left to run high-tech industries. But among the 800,000 Russian immigrants came 200,000 engineers, and that gave Israel the mass skill base it needed to successfully build high-tech start-ups, something it was unable to do before the Russians came.

Priority Number Two: Eliminate Payroll Taxes

Rapid growth requires competitive wages. The easiest way to start is not by a direct attack on high wages or high social welfare system benefits. The way to start is by eliminating the payroll tax that funds the social welfare system. In some countries, such as Germany, payroll taxes double the hourly wage bill. These taxes should be completely eliminated, and the revenue they now produce (about 40 percent of total revenue on the continent but half that in the United Kingdom) should be replaced with an equivalent increase in the value-added tax. While net tax collections and the existing social welfare system would remain the same, five good economic effects would flow from this shift in the tax base:

1: Since value-added taxes are rebatable on exports while payroll taxes are not, European export prices would fall dramatically.

2: Since the tax base would expand to include those who consume but who are not in the workforce (the elderly) and those whose consumption is financed with nonlabor income (the rich), the effective value-added tax rate that would yield the same revenue would be much lower than the payroll tax rate. Lower tax rates cause fewer distortions in economic decision-making.

3: Since government is using most of its tax receipts to finance pensions and health care, consumption taxes should be levied to pay for these consumption expenditures. Collecting consumption taxes to pay for consumption expenditures means that no distortions are created in the consumption-investment balance of the economy. The value-added tax is a consumption tax.

4: Most important, the shift would eliminate what economists call the tax wedge.

Today employers see wages that are far higher than the wages actually received by their workforce. When thinking about hiring, they have to think about whether a new worker's productivity justifies a $32 per hour payment (half to the worker and half to the state). At the same time workers see only the $16 minus whatever income and payroll taxes they have to pay. They see a wage much lower than that seen by their employers.

When the two sides see very different wages, inefficiency results. Employees disappear into the untaxed underground economy and quit paying taxes. Employers move to other locations where they don't have to pay high payroll taxes.

Employers and workers would see the same wage rate if a value-added tax replaced the payroll tax. Without payroll taxes the same German employer faces a $16 per hour charge and can justify hiring a lot more German workers. The worker's incentive to leave the tax-paying economy and go into the untaxed underground economy simultaneously falls.

5: The normal argument against value-added taxes is that they are regressive (effective tax rates go up as incomes go down, since middle-income people consume more of their income than rich people do). But value-added taxes are less regressive than payroll taxes. Replacing a payroll tax with a value-added tax yielding the same revenue is a progressive movement in the tax system. Value-added taxes can be made even more progressive, if desired, with offsetting refundable vanishing income tax credits, by which low-income families get all or part of their value-added taxes rebated in the form of an income tax credit that phases out as incomes go up.

While there are economic losers from such a tax shift (the tax bills of the affluent elderly who have left the workforce would go up), such a shift in the tax base provides an enormous win-win opportunity for Europe. Few policies offer more winners and fewer losers.

The conclusion is simple. Europe's financial institutions, its sociology, its social rules and regulations, its tax system, and its universities need to be reexamined from the perspective of creating a better environment for growing new large firms. The building blocks that must be added to the European wealth pyramid can be built.

The World: Intellectual Property Rights

At the knowledge level of the wealth pyramid, a new system of intellectual property rights will be needed to make knowledge-based capitalism work. This is not something that can be built by any one country and then imposed on the rest of the world. It will have to be built by the world for the world.[152]

There is reason for the world, rich and poor, to do so. As we can see by examining countries such as Taiwan, which have developed successfully, enforcement of intellectual property rights is a short-term issue. In the long run most countries will opt for a system of enforceable intellectual property rights for internal reasons. If there is no protection for computer software programs in China or India, there will be no indigenous Chinese or Indian computer software companies. Others will steal the programs they write just as fast as they now steal the programs written in the developed world. Western companies will also learn how to steal what they want in India or China and then transfer it freely back to their other operations outside of India or China.

Just as the industrial revolution began with an enclosure movement in England that abolished common land and created private land, the world now needs an organized enclosure movement for intellectual property rights. If it does not get it, the world will witness a wild scramble among the powerful to grab valuable pieces of intellectual property—just as the powerful grabbed the common lands of England three centuries ago.

In thinking about protecting intellectual property rights, one starts with an inherent tension in the system. To develop new products and processes, individuals must have a financial incentive to undertake the costs, risks, and efforts of developing new knowledge. Not surprisingly, bigger incentives lead to the production of more knowledge than do smaller incentives. A recent change allowing patents on plants, for example, has led to an explosion of new plant varieties.

The standard incentive is to give inventors a monopoly on the right to produce the products that can be created with their knowledge—a right that they can use or sell. Whether we like it or not, the corollary of fading government R&D efforts is the need for stronger private monopoly rights to increase private funding of R&D.

At the same time, once any piece of knowledge exists, the social incentives are reversed 180 degrees. The wider the use and the faster the distribution of that new knowledge, the greater the benefit to society. Free usage leads to the widest and fastest distribution. For this reason, whenever anyone has a really important patent, it is often suggested that antitrust laws or something else (like compulsory licensing) should be used to take away the monopoly rights bestowed by the patent laws.[153]

Any system of intellectual property rights must involve a trade-off between these two inherently conflicting objectives—more production versus faster distribution. There is no single right answer about how to make that trade-off. A new system must strike the right balance between the production and the distribution of new ideas. It's a judgment call.

But it's a call that should not be made by a judge. Judges don't think about what makes sense from the perspective of accelerating technological and economic progress. Their concern is with how new areas of technology can be inserted into the legal framework with the least disruption to existing legal interpretations. Such lazy law-writing practices do not make for good economics or sensible technology policies. The right approach would be to investigate the underlying economics of an industry to determine what division of incentives is necessary for its successful development. Those are socioeconomic decisions that should be made in our legislatures—not our courts.

A strong patent system is by definition a system of strong monopoly rights. But in our modern economies, private monopoly power should be less worrisome than it was when the patent system was originally set up. As alternative product and process technologies proliferate, as per capita incomes grow larger, and as more and more of what we buy are luxuries, fewer and fewer products are necessities with inelastic demand curves that would allow companies to raise their prices arbitrarily and earn monopoly returns. Today customers have many alternatives and very few products lack close substitutes. Raising prices simply leads customers to buy something else. In none of the recent antitrust suits, including the Microsoft case, has the Justice Department accused anyone of raising prices above the competitive level. Usually the charge is precisely the opposite—lowering prices too fast and stopping potential competitors from entering the market.

As monopoly power wanes, and social interest in encouraging the development of new intellectual property grows, the balance in our system should shift toward encouraging the production of new knowledge and be less concerned about the free distribution of existing knowledge. Tighter or longer-term patents and copy rights are warranted.

Laws on intellectual property rights must be enforceable. Laws can be written, but they are meaningless—and should not be written—unless a technological choke point exists to make enforcement possible. Although the need for protecting intellectual property has never been greater, the same technologies and developments that have made intellectual property rights more central to economic success have often made enforcement of those rights much more difficult. Downloading compact discs from the Internet is a good example.

Laws that cannot or will not be enforced make for neither good law nor good technology policies. The honest end up being suckers who pay more precisely because they are honest. And a law that is widely violated leads to disrespect for the law and more violations. If someone cannot think of how a legal right can be enforced, it should not be a legal right.

The system must be able to determine rights and resolve disputes quickly, efficiently, and cheaply. Many of the problems with the current patent system flow from the lack of consistent, predictable, rapid, low-cost determinations about intellectual property rights and a means of quick, cheap dispute resolution.

For inventors of technologies that have very short useful lives, making use of today's system of dispute resolution—with its delayed, lengthy, and expensive court trials—is equivalent to not having any rights. In the search for an alternative approach, the U.S. system for settling water rights disputes in dry irrigated areas might serve as a model. Because crops die quickly without water, a water master is given the authority to settle disputes quickly and allocate water in dry years.

There is another alternative. In the United States, people who file for patents pay user fees that exceed the costs incurred by the patent office. Those fees are put into the general budget, and Congress then appropriates funds—less than the amount collected in fees—to run the patent office. User fees could go directly to finance what they are supposed to finance and be set high enough to ensure enough patent examiners to get speedy decisions. The relevant agencies should be taken out of the civil service system, and salaries should be set high enough to attract and keep the people who could run the system efficiently and speedily.

One Size Doesn't Fit All

Although simplicity can be a powerful virtue, builders of a new system must reconcile a number of competing interests and allow for some critical distinctions. One is between private and public knowledge.

To accomplish society's interest in expanding knowledge as rapidly as possible, certain classes of knowledge ought to be in the public domain and freely available to everyone. The use of basic scientific knowledge is central in an era of man-made brainpower industries because it allows breakthrough technologies to be developed. But there are other reasons for keeping knowledge in the public domain. A society may determine, for example, that its interests in educating the young justify placing some types of knowledge—such as educational technologies—in the public domain. Egalitarian democracies may want lifesaving technologies to be generally available to everyone, not just to the rich.

This does not mean that patents or copyrights should be forbidden in areas where there is a social interest in allowing general access to knowledge at little or no cost. That would not work, because no one would have the incentive to produce such generally useful knowledge. Moreover, inventors who happened upon such discoveries would have an enormous incentive to keep them secret. Secrecy is far worse than monopoly rights when it comes to extending knowledge.

The answer is to ensure that those who generate knowledge in the public domain get paid for what they generate but that their knowledge is freely available. The solution to this problem could exist in the establishment of some public agency—perhaps a branch of the National Science Foundation—armed with the funds and the power of eminent domain. The agency could decide to buy knowledge for the public's general use whenever that was deemed warranted. If the seller would not agree to sell at a reasonable price, adjudication principles very similar to those used in eminent domain land-acquisition proceedings for other forms of public infrastructure could be used.

In a global economy, a global system of intellectual property rights is needed. This system must reflect the needs of both the developed and the underdeveloped world. The problem is similar to the one of which types of knowledge should be in the public domain in the developed world. While the third world needs low-cost pharmaceuticals, it does not need low-cost access to popular CDs. Any system that treats such different needs equally, as our current system does, is neither a good nor a viable system. Depending on the income level of the country and the importance of the technologies to basic human needs, different predetermined fee levels might be internationally imposed on those who want to use what others have invented.

Global enforcement of intellectual property rights is in principle simple. As in dumping cases, countervailing duties could be imposed on those who violate intellectual property rights. The duties would be high enough to offset the losses incurred, and the revenue raised would be given to those whose patents are being violated. Or countries that don't respect the intellectual property rights of others would get no respect for their intellectual property rights—no matter where they are registered.

The optimal patent system will not be the same for all industries, all types of knowledge, or all types of inventors. Individual inventors should not be treated in the same way as large corporations. Filing fees could be adjusted to reflect the income level of the applicant.

Consider, for example, the electronics industry and the pharmaceutical industry. The first wants speed and short-term protection because most of its money is earned soon after new knowledge is developed. The second wants long-term protection because most of its money is earned after a long period of testing to prove a drug's effectiveness and the absence of adverse side effects. Different types of advances in knowledge should be distinguished from one another and alternative types of patents awarded.

Finally, inventors should be able to choose from a variety of patents or copyrights. A differentiated system might offer different levels of monopoly rights. Cost, speed of issuance, and dispute-settlement factors could vary. Let those who file for patents decide what type of patent they wish to have. In no other market do we decide that everyone wants and must buy exactly the same product.

One size does not fit all. Trying to squeeze today's developments into yesterday's system of intellectual property rights won't work. The current one-dimensional system must be overhauled to create a more differentiated one.

America—Skills, Careers, High-Wage Jobs

America's prime need is to work on the skill-building blocks in its wealth pyramid. This is not so simple as improving the school system. It also involves major changes in how on-the-job training is financed and how the service sector is organized.

Despite having invented compulsory universal public education, Americans are slowly withdrawing from the system that created their own success. America invented universal compulsory public education in grades K–12 to provide the basic skills necessary for the new industrial age. America was the first to open up public state universities where tuition charges were far below costs. Perhaps it is worth remembering that neither was prompted by families politically demanding better education for their children. Both were prompted by businessmen who wanted a better educated workforce. Private charity from like-minded businessmen created private universities and allowed them to offer scholarships in what later came to be known as need-blind admissions—tuition charges adjusted to family incomes, and merit rather than wealth determining who was admitted.

Despite this history, the spirit of the times is slowly moving against government educational activities. Government spending is down, private spending is up, and total spending is holding even at about 6.5 percent of GDP in the 1990s. At the federal level, the budgetary pressures created by Social Security and Medicare for the elderly are crowding out educational spending. Federal educational spending went from 3.4 to 1.8 percent of the federal budget between 1975 and 1995. With the end of the Cold War, defense no longer provides an excuse for federal spending on education. The GI Bill of the 1950s and the National Defense Education Act of the 1960s are gone. About 50 percent fewer American Ph.D.s in science and engineering are being trained than two decades ago. Public state universities are relying less and less on public money and more and more on tuition payments from students, effectively becoming private universities. At private universities, loans have to a great extent replaced scholarships. The market is used more. Gifts are used less.

If one looks at state and local spending cutbacks in the 1991–92 recession, they were disproportionately concentrated on elementary and secondary education.

School vouchers are often suggested for central cities where educational institutions run by the state are failing to educate those they are supposed to educate, often minorities. Instead of running schools, the state would send a voucher to each child, which the child's parents could use to pay for whatever education they think best. Vouchers are attractive in this situation (the failures are obvious), but they also create a Trojan horse that would probably be the opening wedge for abolishing public schools.

As is now happening at state universities, the real value of the voucher will gradually fall over time. Private tuition payments will have to be instituted to make up the financial gap, and what were public schools or publicly subsidized low-priced private schools will gradually become high-priced private schools. The link that was broken between parental income and educational opportunities in the nineteenth century is rejoined in the twenty-first century.

During the second half of the twentieth century, America's system of mass education was widely emulated. But the copiers (Japan and Europe) did not just copy, they improved. They upped the intensity. Into the 1950s the United States had the world's highest high school graduation rate—77 percent.[154] But by the 1990s that graduation rate had slipped to 72 percent, and improvements in other countries' graduation rates had reduced America's position to twenty-eighth of the twenty-nine developed nations in the world. The rest of the world also learned how to produce a much better educated high school graduate in the bottom half of the graduating class. The bottom 25 percent of the class in Japan and South Korea score above the American median.[155]

At the end of the twentieth century, America's elementary and secondary education is no longer world-class. As a result, too much of America's undergraduate university education has to be devoted to doing what others do in high school. When a country such as Singapore decided to benchmark itself against the world's best at each level of education, only America's graduate schools were targets for admiration and emulation.

The biggest skill gaps are found among those who graduate from high school but do not go on to complete a university degree program. Almost universally, foreign high school graduates add to the good skills they acquired in high school some form of high-quality postsecondary education such as the

German apprenticeship program. There is no equivalent in the United States.

But Americans don't have to look at the rest of the world to know that something is wrong. When scores on the SAT high school achievement tests are down 5 percent from their peaks, something is wrong. When 63 percent of American employers say that high school graduates have not learned the basic skills needed to succeed at work, something is wrong. Among these employers, only 4 percent say that graduates are good at writing and only 5 percent say they are good at math.[156] The ability to master instructions without having to be shown what to do gets more and more important. New production technologies such as statistical quality control and just-in-time inventories mean that average production workers have to master relatively sophisticated mathematical principles.

Those working in the educational system often respond that too much emphasis is being placed on the basics such as mathematics and they are not being given credit for teaching twenty-first century skills such as curiosity, the ability to work with others, computer literacy, and interest in lifelong learning. These skills don't substitute for mastering the basics, but when asked about these skills, an even higher percentage of American employers, 75 percent, say the school system is only fair to poor.

These are not anti-American comments by foreigners. They are the comments of those who hire or fire workers and raise or lower wages. Market wages are giving Americans the same message. Those who have taken the biggest reductions in wages in the last quarter of a century—male high school graduates—are precisely those who have to compete with better skilled workers in the rest of the world.

What we have is a gap in perceptions—a disconnect. While two-thirds of America's employers do not think high school students have the skills to succeed in the world of work, 90 percent of the teachers see the schools as doing a good to excellent job.[157]

Those who run the schools don't see the importance of skills in the same way as those who run the places where their graduates will work. In one sense this is not surprising. Because of low salaries, elementary and secondary teachers tend to come from the bottom of the educational distribution. Americans are asking people who were not themselves good students to teach others to place a high value on being a good student. It isn't going to happen. America is not going to get quality teachers without paying for them. Among the twenty-nine developed nations, only three pay high school teachers less, and four pay twice as much.[158] Yet it isn't sensible to pay top-quality wages to people who are not top-quality workers.

If the facts are clear and America doesn't act to change those facts, then the reasons for its inaction are the most interesting part of the situation. The inability to change lies at the heart of failure. The future will be different from the past, what was done in the past won't work in the future, yet the system won't change. The American school system has to change, yet it cannot.

Failures to adjust are never caused by ignorance about what should be done. Precisely the opposite. Everyone knows exactly what to do to improve the educational system. By far the world's shortest school year in terms of classroom hours of instruction in basic subjects has to be lengthened; Americans aren't going to learn twice as much per hour of classroom instruction. Teachers have to be paid enough to make it possible to recruit good college students into teaching. Some exit (graduation) standards have to be set; no serious producer of anything can work without a quality standard, and education is no exception.

It isn't surprising that those who work in the current system oppose change. It should be expected. Today's teachers don't want high academic standards set for themselves. Too many of them could not pass. They don't want an exit standard that would allow the quality of their teaching (the percentage of their students that passed the graduation examination) to be compared with the quality of others' results, where those who did not pass could not go to college, and where the parents of those who failed would hold them responsible. They don't want a normal-length working year. If they wanted longer hours of work and the money that goes with them, they would not have become teachers in the first place. Local school boards are made up of elected officials. How does one get elected and simultaneously flunk the children of the voters? How does one get elected and lengthen annual hours of instruction if this deprives local businesses of cheap after-hours high school laborers?

The opponents of change are well known. But there is no reason to believe that their opposition is particularly powerful politically. Their power comes not from the strength of their political position but from the political impotence of the forces advocating change. They care but not enough to overcome the vested interests.

America's lack of action stems from the fact that American education is neither good nor bad. It is both simultaneously. Where it is good, it is very, very good. This reality stops Americans from acting to change the system where it is bad.

Consider what happens to bright American high school graduates. At age eighteen they are behind their contemporaries in the rest of the world. Not even the smartest among them could pass the high school exit examinations set in any of the world's developed countries. But being bright, they will go to one of America's very good undergraduate universities. There they will work harder than their compatriots at European or Japanese universities, and by graduation 23 percent of American young people will have closed the skills gap with the best in the rest of the world. Many of these university graduates will then go on to graduate education, a form of education that barely exists in the rest of the world, and when they have completed it, 15 percent of the American population will be the best educated in the world.

The children of those advocating and understanding the

importance of change get very well educated in America. They will have the skills to play the economic game of the future even if those around them cannot. Since the global game has a team component as well as an individual component, they might do even better if their fellow Americans also had world-class skills, but they will do very well even if that local American team isn't world-class. They will simply join a global team where workers outside of America provide the skill sets that Americans lack.

As a result it isn't urgent that the parents of those who will ultimately be well educated devote their efforts to changing the skill acquisition system for other young people who will end up poorly educated. If their own children were going to be badly educated, they would quickly overwhelm the vested interests in the system that don't want change. But they don't need to blow up the existing system to get a good education for their children. The system gives them personally what they want.

Implicitly this is an enclave model of economic development. Part of the American workforce will have the skills necessary to take advantage of the new technology-intensive global economy. They'll march on to economic success, joining a global team and leaving the rest of the American workforce behind. The problem isn't that this model won't work. The problem is precisely that it will work.

The problems with the enclave model of economic development are not economic. It could work for skilled Americans just as it works for the software engineers in Bangalore, India. The problems aren't really even political. India shows that countries can coexist with great internal inequalities for long periods of time without blowing up politically. The problems are basically moral. Is one living in a good society if that society knowingly lets a major fraction of its citizens drop out of the first world and effectively become third world wage earners?

Despite the frequent reports calling for some system of apprenticeship education in America, the United States will never have a fully developed apprenticeship program such as those found in Germany. Such programs are built on traditions that America just does not have: respect for highly skilled craftsmen that came out of the medieval guilds in Europe. Nor are we going to have companies that make the investments in skills that those in Japan make. In their hard economic times during the 1980s, American firms cut back on their training expenditures. In their hard economic times during the 1990s, Japanese firms have expanded their training expenditures. Attitudes are different. Labor mobility is always going to be much higher in the United States than it is in Japan or Europe, and American companies aren't going to pay to train workers who will then go off to work for someone else.

Something different will have to be built that will work in the United States. America has a real shortage of midlevel skills and needs some system for retraining the millions of workers whose skills will become obsolete before they are ready to retire.

The basic problem in the United States is that every employer wants to free-ride the training system. "You train, I'll hire" is the American system. Whenever unemployment reaches even moderately low levels, there are complaints about the shortage of skilled workers by the very employers who themselves do no training. They know that they need a better trained workforce but think that someone else should take the responsibility for, and bear the cost of, creating it.

As we have seen earlier, without career ladders it is impossible for individuals to intelligently acquire the right skills on their own. Since they will be switching employers frequently, they don't know what skills they will need or how long those skills will be relevant to their earning opportunities. As a result they also, rationally, don't invest in skills.

When collectively it is clear that something must be done, but rational individuals and companies don't do it, society has to reorganize itself to make what is individually irrational into something that is individually rational. In the postsecondary skill training area there is a simple solution. Some countries such as France levy a 1 percent of sales refundable training tax. The purpose is not to collect taxes but to make it rational for every employer to train and not free-ride the system. Employers face a 1 percent tax, but their expenditures for training can be deducted from that tax. Thus if they spend 1 percent of their sales on training their workforce, they don't pay the tax. Since the money will be taken away from them if they don't train, training becomes a free good as far as the firm is concerned. No one tells them what skills to teach their employees, but they are effectively being told that they must teach some skills to their employees. Such a system aids everyone. It makes employers invest as if there were career ladders even when they have been abolished. If all employers have to invest, no one can be a free rider. If employers are making investments, employees can often make sensible complementary investments.

While the American economy could use a lot more investment in skills, education, and on-the-job training, it is important to note that skills by themselves do not lead to higher wages. With the data showing that wages are falling for males at all education and skill levels except the very highest, the supply of skills is already increasing faster than the demand for skills. To increase the supply of skills without an equivalent increase in the demand for skills would make wages fall even faster than they have been. Skill training has an important role to play in stopping wage differentials from rising, but only if services are restructured and monetary authorities permit faster growth.

Using a graphic metaphor developed by Professor Michael Sattinger, a professor of economics at the State University of New York at Albany, consider a group of dogs with a bunch of bones.[159] To get a more equal distribution of bones among the dogs, bone-hunting skills may have to be taught to those without them. But in the end the dogs can only find the distribution of bones that exists. If the economy generates a few big bones and lots of little bones, that's what the dogs will find, even if every dog has exactly equal bone-hunting skills. Since all of the new jobs in the American economy are service jobs, and since 20 percent of the jobs in the rest of the economy are being eliminated every decade, with these workers also needing to move into the service sector, a better distribution of jobs will require a different distribution of service jobs with better wages. Only if this is done can the American workforce find a more equal distribution of jobs after their skills have been augmented.

To change the distribution of jobs in the service sector, the policies that in the postwar period have converted services, and particularly retailing, into a low-wage sector full of part-time workers should be reversed. This process begins with laws requiring that the fringe benefit packages given to regular full-time workers must be given to part-timers, temporary workers, and contract workers. Per hour, this would raise the fringe benefit costs of part-time and contingent workers above those of regular full-time workers and quickly move services back to employing regular full-time workers. The ability to avoid paying for fringe benefits by employing other than regular full-time workers is what created the problem. Removing that ability would solve the problem.

If President Clinton's universal health reform package had passed in 1993, it would have pushed many service firms back toward more full-time employment. Under that proposal health care benefits had to be funded for everyone. Employer health care costs would have been much higher per hour for part-time workers than for full-time workers and firms would have moved away from part-time workers.

To raise productivity to cover the costs of higher wages, firms would have to provide more training or undertake more capital investment to cut the unit labor costs of the services they supply. Having to operate with a more skilled full-time workforce would make turnover more of a handicap (costlier), and firms would be forced to institute career ladders and other inducements (the opportunity for promotions and higher wages) to retain workers.

With a stable full-time workforce, a more egalitarian implicit social contract would emerge, forcing some additional wage equalization within the firm. It is much easier to treat those officially off the team harshly than it is to treat those officially on the team that way. Firms that have tried two-tiered wage structures for regular full-time employees (the airlines tried it with pilots a decade ago) quickly found that sociologically it did not work. An "attached" workforce has to be managed and paid differentially than an "unattached" one.

While it is true that low wages are a sign of low productivity and that low-productivity operations cannot pay high wages, cause and effect do not always run from low productivity to low wages. In this case they run in the other direction. Consider those years when measured productivity was falling in the service sector. There were many. How could that have happened? Technology was not disappearing or retrogressing. The answer is simple. If wages are falling, it is profitable for companies to move to lower cost, lower productivity, labor-intensive methods of production. When the automated fare-collecting machinery at the parking lot gate wears out and needs to be replaced, it is replaced with a cheaper human guard.

If service companies are forced to operate with higher wages, they have three choices: They can reorganize their production processes to justify those higher wages. They can pass on the new higher prices to their customers. Or they can go out of business.

The experience of continental Europe, where social legislation, social solidarity, and unions require service wages near those in manufacturing, indicates that companies do not go out of business. There are no services that are available in the United States but unavailable in Europe. Few firms raise their prices. Service prices relative to other prices are not in general higher in Europe than in the United States. Most firms find it profitable to make the investments necessary to move to more capital-intensive, skill-intensive, labor-saving, higher productivity forms of service production.

If the European wage structure were imposed on the American service sector, its productivity would quickly rise to European levels. What would happen would be very similar to what happened in manufacturing when Henry Ford dramatically raised the wages of his auto workers to $5 per day even though he had no shortage of people willing to work in his factories. He ended up with a better, more stable workforce and higher productivity.

Fringe benefit policies that reversed today's incentives to hire part-time and contingent workers and that narrowed the wage gap between services and manufacturing would, of course, cause an enormous reduction in service employment. This is necessary if the wage structure in services is to rise and become more egalitarian, and it's also good for the long-run health of the economy. With a higher rate of productivity growth in services, the noninflationary growth rate of the economy accelerates.

Democracies respond to public demands. Remedial policies to restructure services, institute an on-the-job refundable training tax, or reform America's secondary education system are not going to be implemented unless there is a public demand to stop a process that has for twenty-five years been leading to greater inequality. But there is no such demand. Instead, in every election the proportion of voters goes down, and those citizens who give up voting are precisely those workers whose incomes are falling. Voting percentages are twice as high at the top of the income distribution as at the bottom.[160] Those with stagnant or falling incomes may be a majority of the population, but they are not a majority of the voters.

There are many reasons for this. Voting is done on workdays, when getting to the polls is hard, rather than on Sunday, as in Europe, when finding time to get to polls is far easier. The importance of money to pay for TV spots in the American system makes many potential voters feel that what counts is money and not votes. Votes can be bought if you have enough money for enough advertisements. Those with the most money, usually incumbents, always win. In the 1998 elections, 99 percent of the incumbents in the House of Representatives won.[161] Realistically, if the seat in your district isn't empty (only 24 out of 435 were in 1998), it doesn't make sense to vote. The outcome is predetermined.

No one should blame politicians for not helping to solve the problems of those who do not bother to vote. Their job is to get elected and serve those who elect them. The blame has to go to a system that encourages not voting and a citizenry that doesn't care enough to vote even when they are hurting. Perhaps the median and below-median households have lost faith in democratic processes, believing that whoever is elected won't address their problems, but if those with falling incomes don't care enough to demand action, then no remediation will take place. The necessary changes will occur only if those who are now losing demand them. The top quintile of the workforce is not going to vote altruistically to help the bottom four quintiles.

The economy has, can, and will adapt quickly and easily to producing fewer goods and services for the bottom 80 percent of the population and more goods and services for the top 20 percent. If there are problems, they will be political ones. For how long in a democracy will a majority of the population read about the good things happening at the top of the wealth pyramid and remain happy about their diminishing prospects at the bottom? No one knows.

America—More Tools

One can debate the question of whether countries like Germany and Japan are investing too little in new tools. Maybe Singapore is investing too much. But there is no debate when it comes to America. Americans invest too little at this level of the pyramid. More tools are needed if sectors such as private services are to generate world-scale wages. Successful private builders also know that if they are to be successful, they must live in a society of builders. Good social infrastructure leads to successful private investments.

Americans have built a system that encourages personal consumption and discourages tool-building. One could easily rig the American system of incentives to persuade us to invest more and build more tools. It is simple to list the public policies that might correct the tendency of our society to underinvest. Many articles and books have already done so.[162]

Governments can increase investment by spending more of their own funds on infrastructure tool-building. They can run budget surpluses. The current $79 billion federal budget surplus provides more funds to the capital markets for private investment. A builder's vision could be constructed and sold to counteract all the private advertising favoring consumption. The man-on-the-moon program in the 1960s was such a vision. Those financial instruments (credit cards, home equity loans, low- or no-down-payment consumer loans) that make it easy for Americans to dis-save—spend more than they earn—could be restricted. The tax system could be shifted from an income/payroll-based system to a consumption-based one in which citizens are taxed only on what they take out of the system (consumption) and not on what they put into it (tools or work effort).

The problem is not figuring out what might be done to increase American tool-building activities, but getting ourselves organized to change the incentive structure embedded in the American system. The what-to-do is easy. The how-do-we-get-it-done is hard.

Americans won't do it until they persuade themselves that it is important to do it. Only those who see themselves as builders and who get pleasure from both building and admiring their building after it has been completed will deliberately adjust their systems to raise investment and lower consumption.

The World—Global Warming

At the environmental level of the pyramid, the issue is global warming. Even the ozone hole problem seems to be on its way to being solved.

A direct attack on global warming is not going to work. The goal must be to make better things happen—not to stop bad things from happening. Horror stories don't work as motivational devices. As a teenager in high school I was shown two sets of horror movies. Traffic safety officials showed us videos of horrible automobile wrecks full of mangled bodies. They did nothing to make us better drivers. We simply blocked out the horror stories. Accidents do happen, but not to us. Similarly, public health officials showed us movies of healthy pink lungs and cancerous lungs blackened from smoking. I noticed no diminution of smoking among my friends. Yes, cancer happens, but in the far distant future to some as yet unknown person. Some people smoke all their lives and don't get cancer. It could be me.

What has to be done is something similar to the process that has actually brought smoking under control. Over a twenty-five-year period, public education about the benefits accruing to nonsmokers from living in a smoke-free environment radically changed social attitudes about smoking. In the beginning polite nonsmokers could not ask a smoker not to smoke. Twenty-five years later a polite smoker could not smoke in the presence of nonsmokers without asking their permission. Over time social pressures slowly but surely changed habits and the definitions of what was acceptable. There was no debate about taking the freedom to smoke away from those who already smoked. It was not about being a big brother who knew what was best for someone else. It was about nonsmokers demanding a better environment.

When the process started, the entrenched position of smokers and tobacco companies seemed much too strong to be successfully confronted. But long-range goals were articulated, consistent pressure was applied, and the public was eventually persuaded that these goals could contribute to their standard of living. Restrictions were slowly imposed. Such changes in lifestyles and attitudes are not made easily or quickly. No one would have predicted at the beginning what has happened in the end.

The starting points for rethinking the issues of global warming are clear. The future generations that will have to cope with global warming are our children and our grandchildren. What inheritance do we wish to leave them? How much might we be willing to pay for an insurance policy to help them? Are we willing to buy them an option on a good environment?

If a journey of a thousand miles begins with the first step, there may be some very easy, cheap first steps that could be taken without a full commitment to the enormous costs of making the entire march. Mitigation is not prevention, but it is worth doing. Each step taken opens up an easy next step that might then be taken. About one-third of the carbon dioxide discharged into the air is now produced by motor vehicles.[163] Given the progress that has already been made on making fuel cells economically competitive with conventional internal combustion engines, a few billion dollars in extra R&D spending might have a good payoff.

To say that a problem cannot be solved given current technologies, thought processes, attitudes, and social institutions is not to say that it won't be solved.

Conclusion

As the world enters the economy of the twenty-first century, one building block will not be in place in the wealth pyramid. A global economy is emerging to replace national economies, but a global government is not emerging to replace national governments. As seen in the transition from local to national economies a century ago, a wide variety of unexpected and previously nonexistent problems arose. The same should be expected in the shift from national economies to a global economy. One of those problems is already visible. Nationally controlled international agencies that have to work through national governments have been largely ineffective in turning the Asian meltdown around and stopping it from spreading to Latin America. Some effective global financial regulations and an effective lender of last resort are needed. But neither is going to exist.

In normal times financial markets can be seen as black boxes that dampen the amplitude of the fluctuations in information that reach them. Fluctuating information arrives and fluctuating prices filter out, but the fluctuations in prices leaving the black box are smaller than the fluctuations in information entering the black box. Without a stable global economic system, the black box essentially reverses itself, and the fluctuations in prices leaving the box are much greater than the fluctuations in information entering the box.

Think of the fluctuations in the rate of exchange between the yen and the dollar since the Japanese meltdown began. Since 1990 the swings in information about the relative performance of the American and Japanese economies have been very small. Yet the yen went up from 160 to 80 yen per dollar between 1990 and 1995, down to almost 150 yen per dollar in 1998, and back up to 110 in early 1999. Industries cannot live comfortably with such swings.[164] Intelligent investing becomes impossible. If the world's first and third biggest economies are destabilized by big swings in their currency values, the global economy can only be destabilized with them.

But this is a problem the world is not going to solve. The global wealth pyramid is going to exist without a fundamental set of building blocks. There will be no manager of the system responsible for maintaining it or fine-tuning its performance.

The national governments that used to worry about the management and maintenance activities necessary to keep the economic system going are slowly being pushed out of business. Swings in global financial flows overwhelm all but the largest governments. Governments have lost much of their influence over flows of information and capital. They cannot control who crosses their borders either physically or culturally. They still have their armies, but they are afraid to use them when wars are fought in real time on the TV set.

At the same time, the powers of global corporations are rising. With their ability to move around the globe to whatever they consider the most advantageous locations and to play off one country against another in the bidding for attractive investment projects, their power, or perhaps we should say their freedom from government supervision, grows.

Global corporations expand; national governments shrink.

The same forces that are decreasing the powers of national governments are increasing economic inequalities—among countries, firms, and individuals. Governments, which have themselves been put in play by the global economy, will not be able to control these rising inequalities.

All geographic areas are on the globe, but many will not be in the global economy. Without skills and infrastructure, no country can play the global game. Those countries that don't play will fall behind those that do.

Firms will be global players or niche players. The midsized national firm is a species in danger of extinction.

The returns to capital are up and the returns to labor are down. On a global basis labor is more abundant relative to capital than it is in the developed world. As a consequence the earnings of capitalists grow, and the earnings of labor fall. Similarly the returns to skills are up and the returns to raw unskilled labor are down. On a global basis the supply of unskilled workers far exceeds that of skilled workers. At the same time, technology is raising the demand for skilled workers and lowering the demand for unskilled workers. Supply and demand matter.

Within America wage inequalities are sharply rising. Manufacturing is a sector with high and relatively egalitarian wages. Services is a sector with low and very unequal wages. The shift from manufacturing to services widens wage inequalities.

Historically, inequality rose in the first industrial revolution, fell in the second industrial revolution, and is now rising in the third industrial revolution. The first industrial revolution destroyed a stable rural society; the second industrial revolution built a stable industrial middle class; the third industrial revolution is now shaking the economic foundations of that stable industrial middle class and creating a two-tiered economy.

President Roosevelt took a direct interest in placing the pyramid on the back of the dollar bill as a symbol of durable wealth. The pyramid is one of the most durable structures that humans can build. But without management and organization it does not get built.

Epilogue:
A Salute to the Builders

American young people are often asked, "What do you want to be when you grow up?" For adults the equivalent question is "How would you like to be remembered?"

None of the current generation of world leaders, with the exception of the recent chancellor of Germany, Helmut Kohl, could answer that question for themselves or their countries. Chancellor Kohl wanted to go down in history as the man who reunified Germany and led the way to a united Europe. Without his consistent leadership, the common European currency, the EURO, would not have come into existence. Probably alone among the world's post–Cold War leaders at the end of the twentieth century, he will be in the history books a hundred years from now. But even he will probably be seen as a leader who was given his task by the Cold War and will be in the chapter along with other leaders such as President Truman who shaped the Cold War era and helped lead to the eventual demise of communism. Those who will be remembered for unifying Western Europe are the leaders right after World War II who wanted to use economic unification as a vehicle for stopping future wars between Germany and France.

In contrast, if you were to ask President Clinton where he wants to put his footprints in the sands of history, he could not tell you. As a result he is apt to leave no footprints in the sands of history. What he does will quickly be blown away by the winds of time and he will be forgotten, as are most American presidents. Nineteenth century presidents between Jackson and Lincoln (Van Buren, Harrison, Tyler, Polk, Taylor, Fillmore, Pierce, and Buchanan) lie unremembered and unmourned, as do the presidents between Grant and Teddy Roosevelt (Hayes, Garfield, Arthur, Cleveland, Harrison, Cleveland, and McKinley). It is too early to say which twentieth century figures will be forgotten, but it is safe to say that many American presidents of the twentieth century will be no better remembered when the twenty-second century rolls around.

If they have not left behind a vision that carries society forward and allows it to build, presidents are not worth remembering after they are gone.

History books remember societies that were empire builders— the Egyptians, the Greeks, the Romans, the Mayans, the Incas, the Spanish, the English—as well the individuals who built the empires—Alexander the Great, Caesar, Peter the Great, Napoleon. But the history books are also populated with people who built great ideas—Aristotle, Archimedes, Marcus Aurelius, Saint Augustine, Shakespeare, Goethe, Newton, Einstein.

Today building geographic empires has become irrelevant. With land and natural resources much less important to building a wealth pyramid, geographic empires don't create the wealth they used to create. They cost more to build than anyone gains from having them. That's why in the last half-century the French, the British, and the Russians have all given up their empires. But it is equally certain that as knowledge rises in importance to the construction of a modern wealth pyramid, those that create the big breakthroughs in technology will be remembered as the empire builders of our times. They redefine humanity's future.

Suppose that a historian in the year 3000, a thousand years from now, is sitting down to write a history book about people alive in the year 2000—us. What do you think that historian will say about us? What have we done that's important enough to be remembered a thousand years from now?

What do we say today about people who lived in the year 1000? Who can remember anything done between 950 and 1050? No one! That century of human beings is remembered as not worth remembering. Perhaps those in the year 3000 will say the same about us.

But I suspect not. What that distant historian will say is that this was the era that perfected biotechnology, and for the first time in human history plants, animals, and human beings were partly man-made. Efforts first focused on eliminating life-threatening genetic defects, moved on to address genetic weaknesses, and went on to make better, smarter, more beautiful human beings. In the late 1990s the taller man was already possible.[165] New biological terrain that changed the very nature of human beings was being explored and opened up, just as Columbus opened up the New World to European settlement. These explorations changed the basics of human existence—how humans think about themselves, what they imagine they can be, how they look, how they feel.

As tourists we go to visit the legacies of the great builders—the pyramids, the Parthenon, imperial Rome, the Mayan city-states, Machu Picchu, the Gothic cathedrals, the Great Wall, the Taj Mahal, Angkor Wat. What will the tourists a thousand years from now visit? Who will have built something that has lasted and is worth seeing? What of today's infrastructure will be seen as a historic heritage—something to marvel at? Perhaps nothing will be seen in that light. It is a basic rule that if you don't build in the present, there won't be anything worth visiting in the future.

History is clear. Those individuals and societies that are remembered were builders. Sometimes the building is physical; sometimes the building is intellectual. But those who are remembered are always builders.

Consumers—the defining characteristic of our era—are never

remembered. To understand why this is so, one need only think of how humans are different from other animal species. What has given us dominance on the surface of the earth is not the characteristics (strength, speed, killing abilities) that make the lion the king of the beasts. It is not the desire for consumption. Every animal species wants to be well fed, sheltered, and safe from predators. What makes humankind different is that by nature we are builders.

We build partly to make life easier for ourselves, but this alone does not make us unique. Beavers build dams to make life easier for themselves. Where humans differ is that we are interested in building tools that allow us to do new things that are not necessary if one is interested only in not starving, not freezing, and not being eaten by predators. We build tools that allow us to be adventurous explorers and better builders.

It is our tools that allow us to undertake new explorations and new adventures. From sailing ships to rockets to the moon, tools have allowed us to go where no human has gone before. From electron microscopes to space telescopes, tools have allowed us to see what no human has seen before. From lasers to computers, tools have allowed us to do what no human has done before. From the video camera to the TV set, tools have allowed us to enjoy what no human has enjoyed before.

Usually our interest in tool-building and exploration requires social support. Columbus was supported by Spanish taxpayers in the fifteenth century just as the space program was supported by American taxpayers in the twentieth century. Exploration and building upon that exploration are seldom individual activities and seldom cheap. Just as brilliant architects need someone to pay for their great buildings, creative thinkers and entrepreneurs need a social system to finance breakthrough activities.

Risks and uncertainties are what make it all fun. The highest mountains on the globe must be climbed even though everyone knows that nothing of value to the consumer will be found at the top. Space must be explored even though it is highly unlikely that anything of value to the consumer will ever be found there. Other animal species don't do things that don't have any payoffs in food, warmth, or safety.

Humans have a sense of coming from somewhere and going to somewhere. Their future is not determined by the stars. It is under their control. They can make investments that create a future different from what it otherwise would have been. Humans can leave their footprints in the sands of time. Few will do this in the sense that their names are remembered, but many can do it in the sense that they participate in efforts that are remembered far into the future. Their part of the journey was a step forward.

Great companies compete against themselves. They may be the best but they are never good enough, they can always become better. In the business world there is an easy way to define *better*. Better means more profitable. The best firms are those with the best profits and the highest market capitalization. The goal of becoming better is equally valid for humankind, but the definition of *better* is much more complex and difficult to determine.

In the last half-century America's goal was containing communism. America won. The contest is over. President Bush tried to replace the goal of containing communism with the goal of policing the world. The rest of the world probably doesn't want American policemen, but their wants aren't germane since Americans don't want the job. Americans decided against that option when they voted for President Clinton in 1992.

In the nineteenth century, when Americans also had no threatening military enemies, they talked about "manifest destiny" and being a "City Set on a Hill"—it was America's role to be an example of what could be. At that time democracy was very uncommon, and America was the model for rapid economic development. Here again the contest has been won. Most of the world's countries are now democracies, and even those that aren't put on the facade of democracy (periodic elections, parliaments). Today few areas of the globe place the preservation of traditional societies ahead of economic development.

President Johnson talked about the "Great Society," but it was a much too limited vision, since it ended up meaning only a society that had abolished poverty. Doing so is undoubtedly a good thing to do, but it is not something that involves everyone. In any case it has in fact been accomplished by many other societies— Scandinavia, Germany, Japan. Doing so would not make America a leader or a model. America would simply be catching up with the most advanced countries in the world. Americans have poverty because they don't want to do the things that would eliminate poverty.

In a similar manner Europeans talk about reducing unemployment as if that could be their ultimate goal. Here again it doesn't directly concern most of the population and has already been accomplished in America. Europeans have high unemployment rates because they don't want to do the things that would eliminate high unemployment rates.

Lowering unemployment and eliminating poverty are not visions. They are the economic equivalents of sweeping the streets and cleaning up the litter after a successful parade.

Historically, dynamic human societies, stagnant human societies, human societies in decline, and human societies that have become extinct can all be found. The dynamic living ones are those that have a vision, build upon that vision, and manage to keep the tensions of wealth creation in balance.

As builders construct wealth pyramids, they understand that each level of the pyramid is essential to the existence of the next. A social system that accepts, fosters, and is willing to pay for creativity lies at the center of twenty-first century success. The entrepreneurial vision of what might be built using new technologies pushes the pyramid upward. Tools and skills add building blocks. Environmental pollution does not slowly destroy the stones. The end result of the building is not the glittering market wealth at the top of the pyramid or even the high productivity growth rate within the pyramid. The real result is that a great pyramid has been built.

We end where we began. Mankind's first great achievements were the pyramids. Everyone understands that the Egyptian monuments were not built by the pharaohs, even if they were built for the pharaohs. They were built by the citizens of Egypt. And that is what we marvel about when we look at them.

We marvel at them because they embody social organization (immense labor supplies had to be organized) and individual genius (the master architect and builder). They stretched man's knowledge—the technology of the time—to its limits (how could they move stones of such size?). We puzzle about their skills (how did they cut stones of this size so perfectly?), wonder about their acquisition of natural resources (where did the great stones come from in a sandy desert environment?), are perplexed by their tools (what were their stone-cutting and stone-moving tools?) and are mystified about how they accumulated the wealth to complete them (the finances to feed the labor that cut the stones and laid them in place). It is the mysteries of their construction that attract us—and not the fact that they were the tombs of ancient pharaohs. A thousand years before Moses saw them, they existed. Thousands of years after we are gone, they will still exist.

Like real pyramids, wealth pyramids have to be built. The wealth pyramid differs from a real pyramid in that it is not fixed and static. The outside, the inside, and the modes of construction are continually in flux. If humans were to return to building real pyramids, they would not build as the Egyptians or Mayans did. They would build with very different technologies. Using our technologies we would pile up pyramid wealth—more and bigger pyramids—much faster than those ancient civilizations. Egypt had to mobilize its entire population to build pyramids during the six months when the Nile was in flood and farming was impossible. We would build machines to move stones. The economics, sociology, and technology of pyramid-building would be very different.

As we complete the third industrial revolution in the early twenty-first century, the art of building a wealth pyramid will be just as different from that in the twentieth century as today's real pyramid-building would be from that thousands of years ago.

But the same human motivation lies behind the desire to build a modern wealth pyramid. Can we build something requiring the best social organization and the highest level of individual genius, using the most advanced knowledge with the best entrepreneurs, requiring the highest level of skills and the purest natural and environmental resources, involving the most complex tools and the mobilization of all of our financial genius? Can we build, and leave for the rest of time, something that will become a marvel to be remembered?

That is the test for those who would be the world's great builders.

Endnotes

1. http://www.centercoin.com/currency information/FAQ/one dollar bill.htm.

2. "Emerging Market Indicators," *Economist*, June 1997–April 1998.

3. Council of Economic Advisers, *Economic Report of the President* (Washington, D.C.: Government Printing Office, 1999), p. 328.

4. John Plender, "Unbearable Lightness of Being," *Financial Times*, Dec. 8, 1998, p. 15.

5. *Financial Times* survey, Jan. 28, 1999, p. FT500 23.

6. "Overworked and Overpaid: The American Manager," *Economist*, Jan. 30, 1999, p. 58.

7. Seth Schiesel, "At Last, A New Strategy for AT&T," *New York Times*, Jan. 17, 1999, sec. 3, p. 1.

8. Ian Fisher and Norimitsu Onishi, "Congo's Struggle May Unleash Broad Strife to Redraw Africa," *New York Times*, Jan. 12, 1999, p. 1.

9. "Good Fences," *Economist*, Dec. 19, 1998, p. 19.

10. Peter Martin, "Gorging on Mergers," *Financial Times*, Dec. 22, 1998, p. 15.

11. "After the Deal," *Economist*, Jan. 9, 1999, p. 21; "Next Stop: Western Europe," *USA Today*, Dec. 24, 1998, p. 3B.

12. Martin, "Gorging on Mergers," p. 15.

13. "Business This Week—A Core Change," *Economist*, p. 5.

14. Robert H. Frank, *Luxury Fever* (New York: Free Press, 1998), p. 115.

15. "A Jury of the Presidency," *Boston Globe*, Jan. 7, 1999, p. 1.

16. "Forbes 400 Richest Include 189 Billionaires," *Boston Globe*, Sept. 28, 1998, p. A10.

17. "Wretched Excess," *Fortune*, Sept. 7, 1998, p. 124.

18. Frank, *Luxury Fever*, p. 115.

19. Nicholas Crafts, "Forging Ahead and Falling Behind," *The Journal of Economic Perspectives*, Spring 1998, p. 200.

20. Deborah Hargreaves, "Blueprint for Arresting Economic Decline," *Financial Times*, Dec. 17, 1998, p. 12.

21. "How America Stacks Up," *Fortune*, Dec. 21, 1998, p. 151.

22. McKinsey Global Institute, "Why is Labor Productivity in the United Kingdom So Low?" *The McKinsey Quarterly* #4, 1998, p. 44.

23. Stanley Cohen, "Dream On," *Boston Globe*, Aug. 2, 1998, pp. C1, C5.

24. Fortune 500, 1960–1998. http://www.pathfinder.com/Fortune /Fortune500/search.html.

25. "Online Sales," *Economist*, Dec. 19, 1998, p. 149.

26. Matthew Brelis, "Beyond Lonely: Life as a Telecommuter," *Boston Globe*, Focus, p. C1.

27. Serge Schemann, "Not Taking Losses Is One Thing: Winning Is Another," *New York Times*, Jan. 1, 1999, sec. 4, p. 1.

28. Samuel Brittan, "No 'Silver Bullet' Exists," *Financial Times*, Oct. 23, 1997, p. 16.

29. Stephen S. Roach, "The Boom for Whom: Revisiting America's Technological Paradox," Morgan Stanley Dean Witter, Economic Research, Special Economic Study, Jan. 9, 1998, p. 6.

30. "How America Stacks Up," p. 151.

31. Mishel, Bernstein, Schmitt, *The State of Working America*, (Cornell University Press, 1998), pp. 9, 23.

32. *Ibid*, p. 45.

33. *Ibid*, pp. 85, 157.

34. *Ibid*, p. 61.

35. Bernstein and Mishel, "Wages Gain Ground," *EPI Issue Brief* 129, Feb. 2, 1999.

36. Mishel, Bernstein, Schmitt, *The State of Working America*, p. 3.

37. Irwin Steizer, "Are CEOs Overpaid?" *The Public Interest* #126, Winter 1997, p. 33.

38. Adam Bryant, "American Pay Rattles Foreign Partners," *New York Times*, Jan. 17, 1999, sec. 4, p. 1.

39. Barry Bostworth, "Prospects for Savings and Investment in Industrial Countries," *Brookings Discussion Paper* #113, May 1995, pp. 12, 14.

40. Dertouzos, Lester, Solow, *Made in America: Regaining the Productive Edge* (MIT Press, 1989).

41. Lester Thurow, *Head to Head: The Coming Economic Battle Among Japan, Europe and America* (New York: Morrow, 1991).

42. Charles Kindleberger, *Manias, Panics, and Bubbles* (New York: Basic Books, 1978).

43. John Plender, "Unbearable Lightness of Being," p. 15.

44. *Financial Times* survey, Jan. 28, 1999, p. FT500 23.

45. "40.65 of Smaller Companies Hit by Losses," *The Nikkei Weekly*, Dec. 21, 1998, p. 2.

46. "Chinese Statistics Through a Glass Darkly," *Economist*, Jan. 9, 1999, p. 68.

47. Lucas & Harding, "Confidence in China Suffers as Full Gitic Debt Revealed," *Financial Times*, Jan. 11, 1999, p. 1.

48. Nancy Dunne, "US Steel Demands Quota Protection," *Financial Times*, Jan. 11, 1999, p. 4.

49. "Economic Woes Beset Asian Steelmakers," *Financial Times*, Jan. 22, 1999, Companies & Finance International, p. 3.

50. Mark Huband, "Egypt May Convert Dollar Reserves," *Financial Times*, Jan. 8, 1999, p. 2.

51. Masato Ishizawa, "Big Investors Shift Sights to Euro," *Nikkei Weekly*, Jan. 11, 1999, p. 1.

52. Graham Bowley, "The Hard Road to Bavaria From Birmingham," *Financial Times*, Nov. 18, 1998, p. 16.

53. Council of Economic Advisers, *Economic Report of the President 1999*, p. 370.

54. "US Seeks Input on New Rules for IMF," *New York Times*, Oct. 12, 1998, sec. A, p. 10; "As Economies Fail the IMF Is Rife with Recriminations," *New York Times*, Oct. 2, 1998, sec. A, p. 3.

55. Jane Chisholm and Anne Millard, *Early Civilization* (Tulsa, Okla: Osborne Press); *Encyclopedia Britannica*, vol. 8, p. 42, vol. 19, p. 204; John Romer, *Ancient Lives: Daily Life in Egypt of the Pharaohs* (New York: Henry Holt & Co., 1984); M. I. Finley, *Economy and Society in Ancient Greece* (Chatto and Windus, 1981).

56. Michael Calabrese, "Should Europe Adopt the American Economic Model?" Center for National Policy, *Policywire*, p. 1.

57. Stephen S. Roach, "Global Restructuring: Lessons, Myths, and Challenges," Morgan Stanley Dean Witter, Economic Research, *Special Economic Study*, June 12, 1998, p. 5.

58. "Japanese Semiconductors," *Economist*, Jan. 23, 1999, p. 64.

59. David S. Landes, *The Wealth and Poverty of Nations* (New York: Norton, 1998), pp. 13, 31, 53, 93; Alain Peyrefitte, *The Immobile Empire* (New York: Knopf, 1992), p. 420; Braudel, *History of Civilization*, p. 168.

60. Gerald Holton, "Einstein and the Cultural Roots of Modern Science," *Daedalus*, American Academy of Arts and Sciences, Winter 1998, vol. 127, p. 1.

61. Lorraine Daston, "Fear and Loathing of the Imagination of Science," *Daedalus*, American Academy of Arts and Sciences, Winter 1998, vol. 127, p. 73.

62. "The Road from Imitation to Innovation," *Economist*, May 18, 1996, p. 80.

63. Massachusetts Technology Collaborative, *Analysis of the Impact of Federal R&D Investment Scenarios on Economic Growth*, July 1998, p. 8.

64. Warren E. Leary, "Clinton Seeks $170 Billion for Research in Budget," *New York Times*, Feb. 3, 1998.

65. Reier, Rehak, Sullivan, "The World's Biggest Spenders on Research and Development," *International Herald Tribune*, July 4–5, 1998, p. 15.

66. *Ibid.*

67. "Spending on Information Technology," *Economist*, Nov. 14, 1998, p. 114.

68. Nathan Rosenbert, "Uncertainty and Technological Change," Federal Reserve Bank of Boston, *Technology and Growth*, June 1996, p. 93.

69. Wolfgang Keller, "Trade and the Transmission of Technology," National Bureau of Economic Research, *Working Paper*, series #6113, July 1997.

70. Adam B. Jaffe, "Patent Citations and the Dynamics of Technological Change," *NBER Reporter*, Summer 1998, p. 9.

71. Martin Neil Baily, "Panel Discussion: Trends in Productivity Growth," Federal Reserve Bank of Boston, *Technology and Growth*, June 1996, p. 274.

72. Jones and Williams, "Measuring the Social Return to R&D," *The Quarterly Journal of Economics* #4, Nov. 1998, p. 1129.

73. Martin Neil Baily, "Panel Discussion: Trends in Productivity Growth," p. 273.

74. Lester C. Thurow, "Needed: A New System of Intellectual Property Rights," *Harvard Business Review*, Sept./Oct. 1997, p. 95.

75. William J. Broad, "Study Finds Public Science Is Pillar of Industry," *New York Times*, May 13, 1997, pp. C1, C10.

76. Peter Passel, "The Wealth of Nations: A 'Greener' Approach Turns List Upside Down," *New York Times*, Sept. 19, 1995, p. C12.

77. Mishel, Bernstein, Schmitt, *The State of Working America*, p. 161.

78. Nina Munk, "Finished at Forty," *Fortune*, Feb. 1, 1999, p. 50.

79. Mishel, Bernstein, Schmitt, *The State of Working America*, p. 157.

80. Charles Murray, *Income Inequality and IQ* (The AEI Press, 1998), pp. 3, 7.

81. Ethan Bronner, "Other Nations Edge Past the US on High School Graduation Rates," *International Herald Tribune*, Nov. 25, 1998, p. 2.

82. "Layoffs and Silver Linings," *New York Times*, Oct. 21, 1998, p. 3.

83. Mishel, Bernstein, Schmitt, *The State of Working America*, pp. 228, 230.

84. Lester C. Thurow, "Wage Dispersion: 'Who Done It?'," *Journal of Post Keynesian Economics*, Fall 1998, p. 25.

85. David McMurray, "Japan's Universities Score Low on Creativity," *Nikkei Weekly*, Aug. 31, 1998, p. 19.

86. U.S. Department of Commerce, "Fixed Reproducible Tangible Wealth in the United States, 1925–1997," *Survey of Current Business*, vol. 78, Sept. 1998, p. 36.

87. *Ibid.*

88. Dean Baker, "The Public Investment Deficit," Economic Policy Institute, *Briefing Paper*, 1998.

89. Mishel, Bernstein, Schmitt, *The State of Working America*, p. 275.

90. *Statistical Abstract of the United States*, 1998, p. 555.

91. Kenneth S. Courtis, Deutsche Bank Asia Pacific Global Strategy Research.

92. "Saving," *Economist*, Jan. 30, 1999, p. 109.

93. "Savings Rate Turns Negative," *Boston Globe*, Nov. 3, 1998, p. D-1.

94. "A Better Way to Fly," *Economist*, Feb. 21, 1998, p. 21.

95. *Ibid.*

96. Alicia H. Munnell, "Is There a Shortfall in Public Capital Investment?" Federal Reserve Bank of Boston, June 1990, p. 9.

97. *Ibid.*

98. *Statistical Abstract of the United States*, 1998, p. 555.

99. http://cgi.pathfinder.com/cgibin/Fortune/Fortune500/f500 rank.cgi.

100. Sach, Loske, Linz, "Greening the North: A Post-Industrial Blueprint for Ecology and Equity," *New Perspectives Quarterly*, Spring 1998, p. 48.

101. Rush Limbaugh, "See, I Told You So," 1993, http://members. aol.com/jimn469897/ruh.htm.

102. Brown and Shogren, "Economics of the Endangered Specie Act," *The Journal of Economic Perspectives*, Summer 1998, p. 3.

103. "Different Places, Different Paces," *New York Times*, Oct. 22, 1998, p. 21.

104. William K. Stevens, "Expectations Aside, Water Use in US Is Showing Decline," *New York Times*, Nov. 4, 1998, p. 1.

105. "Reforestation Primal Dream," *Economist*, Jan. 9, 1999, p. 75.

106. Bill McKibben, "The Future of Population, A Special Moment in History," *Atlantic Monthly*, May 1998, p. 55.

107. Clifford W. Cobb, "The Roads Aren't Free: Estimating the Full Social Cost of Driving and the Effects of Accurate Pricing," *Redefining Progress*, working papers series on environmental tax shifting #3, July 1998, p. 17.

108. "Fuel Cells Intel on Wheels," *Economist*, Oct. 31, 1998, p. 69.

109. "In 2 Years Wolves Reshape Yellowstone," *New York Times*, Dec. 30, 1997, sec. F, p. 1; "Yellowstone Wolves and Diversity," *New York Times*, Jan. 4, 1998, sec. 4, p. 10.

110. "A Survey: The Deep Green Sea," *Economist*, May 23, 1998.

111. Scott Allen, "A Top NE Fishing Ground Collapses," *Boston Globe*, Dec. 4, 1998, p. 1.

112. Schmalensee, Joskow, Ellerman, Montero, Bailey, "An Interim Evalution of Sulfur Dioxide Emissions Trading," and Robert N. Stavins, "What Can We Learn from the Grand Policy Experiment? Lessons from SO2 Trading," in *The Journal of Economic Perspectives*, Summer 1998, pp. 53, 69.

113. Myers and Kent, "Perverse Subsidies Tax $s Undercutting Our Economies and Environments Alike," International Institute for Sustainable Development, 1998.

114. David Roodman, *The Natural Wealth of Nations* (New York: Norton, 1998), p. 26.

115. "Symposium Endangered Species Act," *The Journal of Economic Perspectives*, Summer 1998, pp. 3–53.

116. "In a Year of Heat Records, October Falls Just Short," *New York Times*, Nov. 17, 1998, p. D3.

117. Bill McKibben, "The Future of Population, A Special Moment in History," p 55.

118. William K. Stevens, "How Warm Was It? A Record-Book Year," *International Herald Tribune*, Dec. 20, 1998, p. 7.

119. "A Survey: The Deep Green Sea," p. 15.

120. David Ham, "Elucidations of Scientific Misconception about Global Climate Change," *The Nucleus*, Summer 1998, p. 28.

121. *Ibid.*

122. *Ibid.*

123. William K. Stevens, "As the Climate Shifts, Trees Can Take Flight," *New York Times*, Mar. 10, 1998, p. C1.

124. Edward N. Wolff, "Recent Trends in the Size Distribution of Household Wealth," *The Journal of Economic Perspectives*, Summer 1998, p. 131.

125. Ladd and Bowman, *Attitudes Toward Economic Inequality* (American Enterprise Institute, 1998), p. 14.

126. Federal Reserve Board, "1995 Survey of Consumer Finances," July 1997.

127. *Ibid.*

128. *Financial Times* survey, Jan. 28, 1999, p. FT500 23.

129. Mishel, Bernstein, Schmitt, *The State of Working America*, p. 259.

130. *Statistical Abstract of the United States 1998*, p. 555.

131. Mishel, Bernstein, Schmitt, *The State of Working America*, p. 257.

132. Nancy Ammon Jianakopolos, "A Comparison of Income and Wealth Mobility in the United States," *Journal of Income Distribution* #2, vol. 5, (1995); pp. 216, 217.

133. Edward N. Wolff, "Recent Trends in the Size Distribution of Household Wealth," *The Journal of Economic Perspectives*, Summer 1998, p. 131.

134. Ladd and Bowman, *Attitudes Toward Economic Inequality*, p. 110.

135. *Ibid.*, p. 18.

136. *Ibid.*, p. 52.

137. *Ibid.*, p. 115.

138. D. Quinn Mills, *The IBM Lesson* (New York: New York Times Books, 1988); and *Broken Promises: An Unconventional View of What Went Wrong at IBM* (Harvard Business School Press, 1996).

139. David Alan Aschauer, "Why Is Infrastructure Important?" *Is There a Shortfall in Public Capital Investment?*, Federal Reserve Bank of Boston, June 1990, p. 31.

140. Lester Thurow, *Towards a High-Wage High-Productivity Service Sector* (Economic Policy Institute, 1989).

141. U.S. Department of Commerce, *Business Statistics of the United States*, 1977, p. 70.

142. http://www.independent.org/tii/content/briefs/ b_antitru.html.

143. Eric Schlosser, "The Prison-Industrial Complex," *The Atlantic Monthly*, Dec. 1998, p. 51.

144. Statistical Bureau Management and Coordination Agency, *Japan Statistical Yearbook*.

145. Bryant, "American Pay Rattles Foreign Partners," p. 1.

146. "Spreading the Wealth," *New York Times*, Oct. 26, 1998, p. A10.

147. http://silk.nih.gov/public/cbz2zoz@www.trends97.rigic-dact.fy97.dsncc.

148. Over phone from American History Association.

149. "The Chaebol That Ate Korea," *Economist*, Nov. 14, 1998, p. 67.

150. Lazonick and O'Sullivan, "Investment in Innovation," Jerome Levy Economics Institute, Public Policy Brief #137, 1997, p. 12.

151. "From Lab Coats to Suits," *Economist*, Dec. 19, 1998, p. 85.

152. Detailed footnotes for this section found in Lester C. Thurow, "Needed: A New System of Intellectual Property Rights," *Harvard Business Review*, Sept./Oct. 1997, p. 95.

153. William Kingston, "Compulsory Licensing with Capital Payments as an Alternative to Grants of Monopoly in Intellectual Property," Research Policy #23, North Holland, p. 661.

154. Ethan Bronner, "Other Nations Edge Past the US on High School Graduation Rates," p. 2.

155. *Ibid*.

156. Johnson, Farkas, Duffett, McHugh, "Some Gains, But No Guarantees," New York City Partnership and Chamber of Commerce Research Report, July 1998.

157. Richard Morin, "Some Public Schools Don't Make the Grade," *Washington Post National Weekly Edition*, Jan. 18, 1999, p. 34.

158. Ethan Bronner, "Other Nations Edge Past the US on High School Graduation Rates," p. 2.

159. Michael Sattinger, "Assignment Models of the Distribution of Earnings," *Journal of Economic Literature*, June 1993, p. 833.

160. U.S. Census Bureau, Current Population Reports, P20–504, p. 1.

161. "After Newt," *Economist*, Nov. 14, 1998, p. 27.

162. Lester C. Thurow, *Zero Sum Solution* (New York: Simon and Schuster, 1985), p. 207.

163. Schmalensee, Stoker, Judson, "World Carbon Dioxide Emissions: 1950–2050," *The Review of Economies and Statistics*, Feb. 1998, p. 15.

164. Abrahams and Nakamoto, "World Status Begins at Home," *Financial Times*, Jan. 11, 1999, p. 13.

165. Barnaby J. Feder, "Getting Biotechnology Set to Hatch," *New York Times*, May 2, 1998, p. B1.

Index

LESTER C. THUROW is the Lemelson Professor of Management and Economics at the Massachusetts Institute of Technology, where he has taught since 1968. From 1987 to 1993 he was dean of MIT's Sloan School of Management. His previous books include *The Zero-Sum Society*, *Head to Head*, and *The Future of Capitalism*—all New York Times bestsellers.